£3

RESTRICTED ENTRY

RESTRICTED
ENTRY
CENSORSHIP ON TRIAL

Janine Fuller &
Stuart Blackley

EDITED BY NANCY POLLAK

PRESS GANG PUBLISHERS / VANCOUVER

Copyright © 1995 Janine Fuller and Stuart Blackley

1   2   3   4   5   98   97   96   95

First Edition 1995
All rights reserved. This book may not be reproduced in part or in whole by any
means without written permission from the Publisher, except for the use of short
passages for review purposes. All correspondence should be addressed to Press Gang
Publishers.

The Publisher acknowledges financial assistance from the Canada Council, the
Book Publishing Industry Development Program of the Department of Canadian
Heritage, and the Cultural Services Branch of the Province of British Columbia.

CANADIAN CATALOGUING IN PUBLICATION DATA

Fuller, Janine, 1958–
  Restricted entry

  ISBN 0-88974-053-4

  1. Little Sister's Book & Art Emporium—Trials, litigation, etc.
2. Gays' writings—Censorship—Canada. 3. Censorship—Canada.
4. Freedom of the press—Canada. I. Blackley, Stuart, 1955– II. Title.
Z658.C2F84 1995   363.3'1   C95-910524-7

Edited by Nancy Pollak
Designed by Val Speidel
Proofread by Robin Van Heck
Typeset in Berkeley Oldstyle and Frutiger Light
Printed and bound in Canada by Best Book Manufacturers
Printed on acid-free paper

Press Gang Publishers
#101-225 East 17th Avenue
Vancouver, B.C. V5V 1A6 Canada
ph: 604 876-7787
fax: 604 876-7892

To the memory of our mothers,
Anne Blackley and Ernestine Fuller,
and to Julie and Tim

Contents

□

□

Foreword
by Jane Rule

THE Little Sister's bookstore trial, described in this book in its full history, is only one of many conflicts between the various levels of the Canadian Government and the gay and lesbian community. Until recently it has been the Government who laid charges against such publications as *Body Politic,* Canada's first national gay newspaper, for sending obscenities through the mail, charges of which *Body Politic* was acquitted repeatedly in Canadian courts. The Government, aware that it couldn't win its case, was content to appeal each ruling with the hope of bankrupting the paper instead. Since the establishing of Canada's *Charter of Rights and Freedoms,* however, citizens have been able to charge the Government for maintaining laws not in keeping with the *Charter.*

The Federal Government has been promising for some years to include sexual orientation as a specific category for protection against discrimination. To date, it hasn't done so. Although Canadian courts have established that sexual orientation is already an implied category in the *Charter,* the Government has fought each case on such issues as spousal rights and retirement benefits for gay and lesbian couples to the Supreme Court of Canada. Our politicians are, therefore, not only stalling on their responsibility to pass clear legislation against discrimination, but actually spending taxpayers' dollars to perpetuate discrimination against gays and lesbians.

The courts, charged with upholding the law, often find themselves instead having to challenge a reluctant Government for maintaining laws in contravention of the *Charter,* stating over and over again that it is legislators and not judges who should be (re)writing the laws. Government, fearful of the moral conservatives among its ranks, has refused to take responsibility for reform of laws around age-old issues like prostitution, abortion and gay rights, and has only been forced into action at the insistence of the courts.

The legal process of forcing the Government to act is very expensive, beyond the reach of most ordinary citizens. When the law itself causes great financial hardship, as it has in the case of Little Sister's bookstore, with Canada Customs detaining and often destroying large shipments of books and magazines, the process of challenging the Government is all the more daunting, for with its all but inexhaustible resources the Government can see to it that legal costs skyrocket through endless delays and appeals. If the store can't be put out of business by the seizing of merchandise, it can eventually be bankrupted instead.

What the Government hasn't counted on is the growing anger and power of the gay and lesbian community as well as the sympathy of the majority of people, who, through such court actions as this, are learning that one of the chief enemies of the gay and lesbian community is the Government itself. Funds for this trial have been raised in the lesbian and gay community, but money and support have also come from publishers, booksellers' associations, associations of writers, and members of the general public whose sense of justice is outraged.

Although the Government so far has had more than its share of legal delays and victories, and even without them, financial victories, every case has served to educate not only the gay and lesbian community but large numbers of citizens. The media, in the past willing to turn a blind eye to persecutions of the gay community unless physical violence or murder were involved, are becoming more aware that issues of censorship are crucial to their own ability to do their jobs. The Little Sister's trial has been followed not only in the Canadian and international gay press but in regular newspapers, and on radio and television.

It is in the media where the change of attitude is most easily tracked. In the past, Gay Pride Days have gone unreported or underestimated in the numbers of participants, and have been pictured, if at all, only by our most flamboyant drag queens—to shock the public. In 1995 in Toronto, after the largest turnout ever, the papers published pictures to show the size of the crowd, to show Svend Robinson, one of two federal politicians who have come out, riding in a place of honour.

Most politicians seem to lag behind the voters in acceptance of a variety of sexual orientations. Many pay lip service to our needs while campaigning in ridings with large gay and lesbian populations but are either unwilling or unable to represent us fairly in the legislature. There, voices are still confidently raised against any accommodation of our rights. The Reform Party is the only one whose stated policy is homophobic, but members of other parties who make homophobic statements in public go uncensured. We need strength at the ballot box as well as in the courts to gain and then defend our rights.

In these long battles, financial defeat is one of the great dangers. We can lose because we simply can't afford to go on defending ourselves through the endless delays and appeals. The inequality of the contest is often shockingly plain. There at the Little Sister's trial sat a battery of federal and provincial lawyers against the one lawyer pleading Little Sister's case. We have to be prepared to go on raising money to sustain the actions in which we are now involved and to provide funds for the cases still ahead of us.

Those people who have volunteered to be on the front lines are also in danger of burnout. In all the work of preparing for a trial and living through it, people still have to earn their livings, tend family members and friends, simply have a life of a sort that can nourish the courage it takes to stand up against the State determined to humiliate, criminalize and bankrupt those who challenge it. We have to learn to live, even in the moments of high drama, with respect for our own ordinary needs, or we won't last for all the necessary political work ahead of us.

My father, who took pleasure in building everything from a stereo set to a house, could not understand how anyone could take pleasure in cooking a meal, doing the laundry, cleaning a house. "If somebody sat down and ate a stereo set I'd made, I'd never make another. If they used it just to get it dirty and throw it in the laundry again, I'd think, 'What's the point?'" Too many of us think politics is like building a house people can then live in with only occasional attention to repairs. But politics is really much more like housekeeping, chores that need to be done over and over again with willing grace if people are to live together in comfort and nourishment. Good housekeepers pace themselves for the daily round and the long haul, expecting the repetitive necessity of the job.

Raising money for this trial, whose bills are far from paid, and for the trials ahead should be considered chores as common as feeding the dog or putting out the cat. Being a witness to educate judges and writing articles to inform the public are as necessary and ephemeral as preparing meals. Challenging the Government in every way we can for our rights is washing the country's dirty laundry in public for all to see.

I salute the courage, good humour and staying power of everyone involved in this trial, and call on those qualities in every reader to join us in a lifelong commitment to the housekeeping of politics in which Little Sister's bookstore has an ongoing and much appreciated role.

□

Preface

WHEN the owners of Little Sister's Book and Art Emporium organized their first rally to protest Canada Customs' seizures, they had no idea where their four-page flyer and hand-held banner would lead. Back in 1986, Jim Deva and Bruce Smyth simply wanted the Canadian public to know what was happening to their bookstore, and they needed help demanding the return of the novels, academic texts, sex magazines, short story collections and health manuals caught in Canada Customs' censorious trap. They were protesting because they couldn't bear the prospect of any more seizures—and they felt very much alone.

By the fall of 1994, Little Sister's was no longer protesting in isolation. The bookstore owners and their ally, the British Columbia Civil Liberties Association, were putting Canada Customs on trial, and their fight to bring gay and lesbian materials across the border had grown into a full-fledged media event. The Canadian government was now routinely scolded by national and international human rights and literary organizations. And at least some mainstream Canadians were finally grasping the fact that bureaucratic censorship wasn't just a problem for gays and lesbians, but one that raised the fundamental question of who tells us—all of us—what we can and cannot read.

This book is the story of Little Sister's historic days in court, October 11, 1994 to December 20, 1994. The trial brought together a remarkable cast of witnesses: award-winning authors from Canada and the United States, experts from fields as diverse as sociology, epidemiology and semiotics, vice squad detectives, cultural critics, booksellers, Customs officials, artists and pornographers. Depending on their expertise and loyalty, the witnesses contributed either to a celebration or to a condemnation of lesbian and gay culture. Many Little Sister's witnesses offered testimony that delved even further into the realms of sexuality and sexual representation, and the persistent traditions of censorship.

This book is also the story of our personal and professional connection to the trial: Janine, as Little Sister's manager and as emotional support to the witnesses who faced the ordeal of defending their lives and work in court; and Stuart, as a journalist committed to Little Sister's struggle, most recently covering the trial for Vancouver's *Xtra West* newspaper and *Z* magazine in the U.S. Our friendship goes back almost ten years to our Toronto days when we volunteered for *Rites,* the now defunct newsmagazine "for lesbian and gay liberation." We sat side by side for much of the Little Sister's trial, and then shaped and wrote this book together, with Janine also contributing her stories of daily life.

Besides our personal involvement in the case, we are both passionately interested in gay and lesbian literature, and passionately opposed to censorship—and *Restricted Entry* reflects those "biases." Nevertheless, we have attempted to give a rounded account of the many different voices heard in the Little Sister's trial. *Restricted Entry* is not a blow-by-blow record of the trial (nor does it claim to be a history of censorship in Canada). The forty days of courtroom drama, with hundreds of exhibits and thousands of hours of testimony, would probably fill a CD-ROM disc. To avoid overwhelming our readers, we decided against including the testimony of all Little Sister's witnesses (or the governments', for that matter). We hope that no one will feel slighted by our choices, just as we hope that we have done justice to the ideas of the many witnesses presented in the book. We also took some liberties with the chronology of the trial in order to present the arguments of the governments and Little Sister's more clearly.

Finally, *Restricted Entry* is the story of an issue that will not fade when the verdict is rendered. Regardless of what the British Columbia Supreme Court rules in the Little Sister's case, some form of harassment of alternative bookstores—feminist, leftist, lesbian and gay—is bound to continue. It is the nature of the state to try to silence dangerous voices.

Fortunately, it is also the nature of uppity writers, booksellers, artists, publishers, civil libertarians, and gay and lesbian communities to ardently defend "the freedom of thought, belief, opinion and expression" in this country.

Janine Fuller
Stuart Blackley
October 1995, Vancouver, B.C.

□

Acknowledgements

WE began writing *Restricted Entry* in the spring of 1995, a few months after the Little Sister's trial ended. We had attended almost every court session, but neither of us had even fantasized about writing a book on the subject. The idea came from Cindy Filipenko, the editor of *Xtra West,* the Vancouver gay and lesbian bi-weekly. Cindy had approached Press Gang Publishers with a book proposal, but she was forced to drop the project due to health reasons. The baton was passed to Janine, who asked Stuart to co-author. Although we started from scratch, we owe a special thanks to Cindy for the original inspiration.

This book, like the Little Sister's case, is about a lot of people making enormous personal efforts to tell the truth, set the record straight (so to speak) and fight on. Without their support, *Restricted Entry* would never have been written. We're grateful to everyone in the publishing, arts and writing communities who have been such strong supporters and invaluable allies in the struggle. We thank everyone at Little Sister's who worked extra shifts, put up with answering questions in Janine's absence, and held the store together so she could co-author the book: Carolyn, Barry, John, Denna, Allen, Richard, Barb, Rebecca, John S. and Mark. We especially want to thank Jim Deva and Bruce Smyth, who supported the project from the very beginning, answering all those late night phone calls, reading the early chapters and cooking Janine dinner.

Our gratitude goes to the women and men who testified for Little Sister's and who submitted written evidence. We are privileged to have heard and read your courageous words. The trial would not have happened without your willingness to speak out; similarly, this book is largely a record of your brilliance and strength.

Thank you to Jane Rule for unswerving support, fiery words and wisdom. We are honoured to have your Foreword in the book. A special mention goes to Kim Mistysyn from Glad Day Books in Toronto, who was, as always, a great help; thanks also to Glad Day's Jearld Moldenhauer, who first got the bright idea to import lesbian and gay titles into Canada. We are grateful for the support of Louise Hager of Women in Print bookstore, and friends Persimmon Blackbridge and Lorna Boschman. Anne Griepenburg at Inland Books was a great help in sorting out the messy minutia of some Customs seizures; thanks also to Sandra Hargreaves at Inland. Thanks go to Becki Ross and Margaret Denike for some high-flying theoretical talks, and to Aerlyn Weissman for her support as filmmaker and friend. We're also grateful for the contributions of the many photographers whose work is used in this book; thanks especially to Daniel Collins.

The folks at the B.C. Civil Liberties Association helped us hang on while writing the book; in particular, we're grateful to L'il and John Westwood for their assistance with many details.

It's hard to thank Little Sister's lawyers Joe Arvay and Irene Faulkner enough, as well as the other staff at Arvay/Finlay. Irene offered advice, information and useful feedback at many stages of the writing. The background materials she lent us—court transcripts and other documents—were indispensable (please see Notes on Sources). Ken Smith (no relation to the judge) and barbara findlay from the Vancouver law firm Smith and Hughes also helped with some of our legal questions.

Our thanks go to the women at Press Gang Publishers, who signed on this book when someone else was going to write it and then took a chance on our ideas: Barbara Kuhne, Val Speidel, Della McCreary, Emma Kivisild and Shamina Senaratne.

Our editor, Nancy Pollak, was great to work with and a pleasure to get to know. More than that, she assisted with all aspects of Restricted Entry: directing, researching, editing and, especially, rewriting our material into gold. The task of creating a book in eight months is awesome, and would not have been possible without our three-way collaboration. Thank you, Nancy.

JANINE: I would like to thank my friends for waiting endlessly to meet me, and for giving me other things to think and laugh about besides the book: Tim, Pat, Shirley, Bernard, Andy, Connie, Elaine, Jules, Lisa, Margot, Myrna, Dougall, Ruth Anne, Julie N., Aerlyn, Bruce, Gill, Paul, Lezlie, Paula, Denise, Lisa, Lori and Bonnie. Special thanks also to my family: Rod, Marina, Joel, Janice, Elisa and my father, Jack, who called me almost every week to see how I was doing.

I'd like to thank Stuart for saying "yes" even though I gave him time to think about it.

Most of all, I could never have done this without the support, love and watchful eye of my partner, Julie Stines, who has waited years for that elusive holiday, read every page of the manuscript over and over, done the laundry, remembered to feed the cat, and without whom I couldn't imagine writing even one page.

STUART: My thanks especially to Tim Timberg, my heart's highway, campground and ultimate destination. Appreciations to Aerlyn Weissman for my walk with Pierre and my chat with Pat, and to Margaret Denike for all her generosity. I'm grateful to all my friends for their patience, support and a convincing show of interest in our progress. Thanks for the support of my family in Toronto: Alexa, Laura and Susan; in London: Craig and Lorrie; and in Vancouver: Barbra, Paul, Fraser and Lawrie. In particular, thanks to Becki and Ingrid, and through every frying pan *and* iron in the fire, Francesca Scalzo.

And thanks to Janine for asking—and for your energy, strength and good humour.

RESTRICTED ENTRY

ONE

Shaking the Foundations

TUESDAY, a wet January evening in Vancouver, 1992. By 10 P.M. few customers are in evidence at Little Sister's upstairs shop. The bookstore's clientele are taking their usual positions in neighbouring bars, and only a slow but steady stream of cigarette purchases keeps Jack Roebuck and John Lucke awake for the last hour of their shift. Scattered throughout the fiction, theory, porn and lube aisles of the bookstore are about eight gay men and lesbians considering their next options.

John, a part-timer doing his once a week shift, remembers directing a guy towards the community notice board in the stairwell, to tack up an apartment-to-share ad. Normally, it's harder to find a space on the notice board than to find an apartment in Vancouver's high-density West End. But if Little Sister's narrow stairwell is a bottleneck, it's also a handy place to run into your next roommate. Tonight, however, no one seems to be hanging around.

Suddenly a huge blast shakes the building. A wave of smoke from the stairwell instantly fills every corner and lung in the bookstore. Jack knows what has happened, but he can't bring himself to move. In the stench of smoke and the ringing aftershock, John can only think of the guy in the stairwell. He rushes over to the sea of debris, the stairs blown apart, walls damaged from the impact, paper ankle deep. No one is there.

Some customers race down the back steps rather than wait around for another explosion. Others—stunned, brazen or curious—wade among the books and paraphernalia fallen from the store's shelves. By the time Jack phones the owners, they are already on their way. The blast had reverberated in their apartment, blocks away. They too are familiar with what that sound means.

Jim Deva and Bruce Smyth, suddenly wide awake after an evening's unwinding, arrive within minutes. In half an hour, the police, local reporters and the gay press, and other staff who have learned about the explosion are working their way through the sidewalk crowds. Inside the building, remains of the bomb are embedded in the notice board on the stairwell turn. Someone hurled it from street level. Assembled, the device would look like a harmless tennis-ball canister, but it was a Polish percussion grenade, military issue. Exactly the same brand of "simulator" that had exploded twice before at the same location, within months of each other, several years earlier. No one claimed responsibility, no one identified who threw it, and no one was ever questioned as a suspect for any of the three bombings. The next day, Little Sister's bookstore opened for business as usual.

The Coast is Queer

For Little Sister's, business as usual has always been a little out of the ordinary. The bookstore's founders—friends Deva and Smyth, and their lesbian pal Barb Thomas—were transplanted from the Prairies, where listening to the Village People twice in a row on the jukebox could get the shit kicked out of you. They started the bookstore "and Art Emporium" in 1983 as a labour of love during a period when they struggled with unemployment and shared a house. Like other major cities, Vancouver drew the disenfranchised from the rural hinterlands, but provided few resources when they got there. Practising and aspiring lesbians congregated at Queenie's, the Quadra or Ms. T's, and danced at community centre fundraisers for feminist groups. But then as now, they never had a permanent dyke bar all to themselves. The Vancouver Women's Bookstore and Ariel Books, both founded in the 1970s, carried feminist and lesbian titles; gay men had no equivalent, dedicated bookstore. Since the 1970s, a succession of funky, volunteer rags—like *The Pedestal, Kinesis* and *Diversity* for women, and *Gay Tide* and *Angles* for mixed readers—had provided energetic, albeit hard-to-find voices for cultural and political dialogues. For gay men, West End bars flourished as never before, and gay rights and social groups provided some space for activism and community spirit. But beyond the seedy hotel interiors of the bars, or the gay nights at the warehouse clubs, life for Vancouver's gay population was, largely, publicly "closeted."

Leaving Alberta, Jim Deva had promised himself never to return to teaching or to take any job where he would have to hide his gayness. Bruce Smyth, a towering 6'6", both gregarious and shy, never had the option of disguise. Barb Thomas was a lipstick lesbian before her time. The idea of creating a bookstore and art gallery together, like many of their ideas back then, arose during a night of partying. They searched for months along the respectable Robsonstrasse, a prime location. High rents soon led them back to Thurlow Street, just off the Davie Street strip notorious for its hookers, strippers—and the gays and lesbians they aimed to please.

Deva negotiated a small amount of capital against his share in the family farm and began retailing with gay abandon. The space was a second storey walk-up, not originally designated for retail. But a sisterly county clerk cast a blind eye to the trio's application and they began renovating the new living and working space. On April 28, 1983, Little Sister's Book and Art Emporium opened with so little cash there was next to nothing on its shelves. Paintings artfully covered the expanse of walls.

The store spread throughout a large rambling room; the non-supporting walls were eventually removed to accommodate shelf space. The second room, a tiny, closet-like area, became Deva and Smyth's home, giving Smyth barely enough space to contain the frame of his bed or body, never mind Deva's. Little Sister's interior decor never moved beyond a motif of imminent collapse, and it never looked better than on opening day. Entering the bookstore was like entering a carnival. Every aisle was a side-show displaying the trends and ideas of the times—with moods, depending on the aisle, that could be sexy, thoughtful, goofy or euphoric. Here was a place to connect with other men and women, to find books and magazines from around the world, and to listen to the Village People on a continuous loop without fear.

The monthly gallery openings were a huge popular success, alternating local gay and lesbian artists such as Joe Average and Persimmon Blackbridge. But art sales were slow. The bookstore began encroaching on the gallery space as fast as the owners could afford to stock more books or to build the shelves. Smyth, the retail brain and a heavy smoker, realized they would sink fast without a range of quick-sale products. Little Sister's soon installed a coffee bar, pinball and pop machines, and carried discount cigarettes, lubricant and poppers. Responding to their customers, the store supplied a few magazines, including a little porn, but no videos—it simply didn't occur to the owners they could sell them. Again, requests from customers and an improved cash flow made gay porn video sales a possibility within a few years.

In its infancy, Little Sister's carried about five hundred titles, a considerable portion of the lesbian and gay texts in print in the mid-1980s. As the lesbian and gay publishing industry grew, so did the store. In Vancouver, the feminist cooperative Press Gang had been producing lesbian fiction since the late 1970s, and British Columbian authors like Jane Rule, Anne Cameron and David Watmough had found publishers and audiences internationally. By the mid-1980s, the targeting of gay and lesbian markets by mainstream American publishers was underway, following the emergence of gay themes in the works of acclaimed authors like Adrienne Rich, James Baldwin, Gore Vidal, Rita Mae Brown, John Cheever, May Sarton, Truman Capote and Christopher Isherwood. The mainstream was finally catching up to the pioneering efforts of grassroots publishers like Alyson and Naiad, who had arisen from the vibrant gay and women's liberation movements. In the English-speaking world, small lesbian/feminist and gay presses were flourishing along with specialty bookstores and an arithmetically expanding generation of writers and readers.

By December 1986, Little Sister's was financially over-extended again, preparing for the holiday sales. Like most independent bookstores, they were gambling on the year's biggest sales month to pay their distributors for their massive purchase of stock. On order, or already on the shelves, was $15,000 worth of merchandise—"every nickel" they had, said Deva.

But they hadn't gambled on Canada Customs. David Goble, the store's customs broker, broke the news. He told Deva and Smyth about conversations with Customs border officers who had warned they "had better things to do than read this stuff all day." If Little Sister's continued to import materials these Customs officers called "disgusting," every shipment would be delayed, "stringently" examined—and if even a line in a poem seemed to refer to, say, buggery, the book would be deemed obscene, and detained.

The threat proved accurate. Every imported shipment to Little Sister's was suddenly stopped at the Canadian border in December 1986. The store, virtually overlooked by Canada Customs during their start-up years, was now in the border guards' sights.

Welcome to Canada Customs

The mandate of Canada Customs is to detain any illegal imported material at the Canadian border: from guns and drugs to mislabelled textiles, from endangered species to books and magazines. Border inspectors are trained to assess a whole range of imported goods. For example, they may check to see if the grade of steel in a load of building materials is the gauge it claims to be, and not a lower, cost-cutting fraud that cheats the buyer and endangers the user. They may also peruse a shipment of books to see if anything appears obscene. Customs employees detain and review suspect materials, prohibiting those materials judged to be illegal, and eventually releasing those judged to be "innocent." Importers are entitled to appeal a Customs detention or prohibition; there is a multi-tiered, internal review process that often takes up to a year—and plenty of brokerage fees—for a final determination, during which time the goods in question are withheld. If the importer is dissatisfied with Customs' final determination, they have the option of taking the matter to provincial court—and beyond.

Under a regulation called Tariff Code 9956, Canada Customs is specifically empowered to block the entry of any "books, printed paper, drawings, paintings, prints, photographs or representation of any kind" that are "obscene, hate propaganda, treasonous and seditious" or child pornography. Customs has had the power to seize printed materials since 1847, twenty years before the nation's Confederation; the power extends to all cross-border shipments, including private mail.

Canada Customs draws on a section of the Criminal Code of Canada for its understanding of obscenity. Section 163(8)—formerly section 159(8)—reads: ". . . any publication a dominant characteristic of which is the *undue exploitation of sex,* or of sex and any one or more of the following subjects, namely, crime, horror, cruelty and violence, shall be deemed obscene" (emphasis added). Armed with Tariff Code 9956 and its companion document, Memorandum D9-1-1 (see Appendix A), Customs officers exercise "prior restraint" of any book, magazine or picture they believe to be obscene. The onus is on the importer—whether a bookstore, a newsstand or an individual—to challenge a Customs detention or banning. Canada Customs is bound by few time constraints or precedents; they may release a book and detain it again, repeatedly, at the same or another border crossing.

Until relatively recently, Customs officials and Canadian police, the two key enforcers of obscenity laws, interpreted "undue exploitation" as anything involving the explicit depiction of genitalia. Since the 1960s, court rulings and changing social attitudes produced more relaxed interpretations. Mainstream heterosexual pornography is now widely available throughout the country, mostly imported from the United States. For Customs, however, depictions of homosexual sex—specifically anal penetration—remained firmly lodged in the illegal realm of "undue exploitation."

In December 1986, the detentions of first 369 books, then another 59, then another 120, as well as 77 magazines, were more than a rude awakening for the owners of Little Sister's: the seizures by Customs threatened the bookstore's survival. Up until then, Smyth and Deva had relied on the protection of a low profile. Little Sister's non-explicit name was an informal tactic shared by other gay bookstores, a means of avoiding hostile attention. (First and foremost, however, "Little Sister" was their pet cat's name, as well as a nickname they shared among themselves.) The owners approached a lawyer who dealt with Customs issues and the reality of their predicament sank in. If they were unable to "free" the books through Customs' internal appeal process and decided to pursue a court case, they could expect basic legal fees of $5,000 (retainer) and trial costs of at least $10,000. Deva and Smyth quickly recognized that legal action was not really a viable option.

Although they started appealing the individual Customs detentions, they instinctively knew this would not be enough. The only other strategy was to go public, despite the risk of completely blowing their cover. They knew Customs operated on name recognition of importers. But Deva and Smyth didn't feel they had a choice.

"We both agreed that it was extremely unhealthy, both physically and emotionally, not to fight," said Deva. "This was a declaration of war [by Canada Customs] so we decided to declare war, too . . . It came from our sense of self-preservation."

Deva and Smyth penned their first press release and, on December 17, 1986, they threw their first protest rally at Canada Place, the jewel of Vancouver's waterfront redevelopment scheme. Canada Place housed the office of Conservative Member of Parliament Pat Carney, then minister of

National Revenue and responsible for Customs. Outside Carney's office, the rowdy crowd of artists, civil libertarians and librarians, dykes and fags and a few other radicals were met by local TV and print media, but no minister. They demanded the immediate replacement of the Customs officer responsible for the recent detentions, and the return of those books that could be "easily and readily viewed as neither obscene nor pornographic." But their primary demand was the "re-evaluation of the present sweeping Customs regulations which make it possible for one Customs agent to apply his or her opinions and existing prejudices in making decisions regarding what is or is not pornographic." Little Sister's urged the demonstrators to take practical action by educating their communities about the issue, and to donate to the legal fund of Glad Day, the Toronto gay and lesbian bookstore taking action against Customs for the banning of *The Joy of Gay Sex* in 1986.

Although no official response came from Pat Carney or Customs, within days a few of the hundreds of detained books and magazines began trickling back to the store, including novels by Jean Genet (*Querelle*) and Anne Cameron (*Dzelarhons*), and porn magazines from the First Hand series, such as *Cum* and *Truck Stop*. After almost a year of individual appeals for each remaining title, Smyth simply asked Customs to return all the books found to be not obscene. (Even in his after-life, Oscar Wilde had to wait a year to win the highest level of Customs' appeal process, and the release of his novel *Teleny*.) Customs informed Smyth they couldn't locate the books any more. About a quarter of Little Sister's first major detention, after being deemed not obscene, had been classified as "abandoned to the Crown" and destroyed.

The media exposure around the December seizures caught the eye of the British Columbia Civil Liberties Association. The BCCLA had a successful track record of court challenges since its inception in 1963, from arguing against school prayer or restrictions on abortion services, to supporting critics of public officials. True to its civil libertarian bent, the BCCLA was eager to challenge the country's censorship laws. Their president, philosophy instructor John Dixon, approached Little Sister's with an offer of support, and he spoke at the December rally. Dixon's experience as a civil rights activist, coupled with the wicked suavity of his ad libs, made him a formidable ally in Little Sister's dealings with the media and the law. Soon after the rally, he committed the legal and financial support of BCCLA to help Little Sister's mount a legal challenge to Canada

Customs' powers. Together, they would argue for freedom of expression. .Dixon wanted to give Customs "the mauling it deserves."

Obscenity through the Ages

Despite the constitutional renovation of the *Canadian Charter of Rights and Freedoms* in 1982, which guaranteed "freedom of thought, belief, opinion and expression," the hope for a renewed commitment to freedom of expression had stalled under the Conservatives' Brian Mulroney.

When Little Sister's troubles began, Canada's obscenity legislation was still framed within century-old concepts designed to protect the largely illiterate Victorian-era populace, dominated by the ruling elite, from their own tendencies towards "sedition and sexual license." The law of the land, vis à vis obscenity, patched together such historical vestiges as the prohibition against publicly exhibiting "a disgusting object or an indecent show" (1892), and a concern about crime comics (1949).

Actually defining an "obscene item" was always regarded as a difficult legal problem, but moral concerns loomed large. In 1868, a ruling focused on "the tendency of the [obscene] matter . . . to deprave and corrupt those whose minds are open to such immoral influences . . ." (*R. v. Hicklin*). The concept of "undue exploitation of sex" appeared in the 1959 revision of the Criminal Code. A 1962 ruling defined a test for community tolerance, more or less outlining what "the average man" would tolerate his neighbour indulging in, pornographically speaking (*R. v. Brodie*).

In the mid-1980s, the Conservative government made two hamfisted attempts to rewrite the obscenity law. The proposed bills were roundly condemned by civil libertarians, feminists, librarians, the cultural community and even fundamentalist Christians—for differing reasons—and both bills died ignominiously. Then, in 1985, Canada Customs had a run-in with the young *Canadian Charter of Rights and Freedoms*. The section of the *Customs Tariff Act* prohibiting the importation of "immoral and indecent" goods was found by the Federal Court of Appeal to violate the right to freedom of expression. With the borders now wide open, the government quickly legislated Tariff Code 9956, which brought Customs in line with the Criminal Code's obscenity provisions. The legislation passed with the unanimous support of all political parties.

The Customs document entitled Memorandum D9-1-1 is the practical arm of Tariff Code 9956: concrete guidelines to help Customs officials make their determinations about obscenity at the border and in later appeal reviews. In theory, Customs officials use D9-1-1 to assess any suspicious item "in its entirety." When a book or magazine is seized at the border, Customs mails the importer a Notice of Detention/Determination, called a K 27, which names the seized book or magazine and the reason it is being held. The Customs official simply checks off one of the K 27 boxes: (a) Sex with violence; (b) Child sex; (c) Incest; (d) Bestiality; (e) Necrophilia; (f) Hate propaganda; (g) Anal penetration; or (h) Other. The most popular K 27 check-off for Little Sister's was box (g), despite the fact that anal penetration had never been specified in any version of Canada's obscenity laws.

Hard Years for Glad Day

Little Sister's wasn't alone in attracting Canada Customs' negative attention. Glad Day Books, the country's original gay and lesbian bookstore, was launched in Toronto by an American, Jearld Moldenhauer, in 1974. After enduring a raft of Customs seizures in 1985—due to the introduction of Memorandum D9-1-1—Moldenhauer decided to fight back. He initiated a case against Canada Customs in April 1986 for its banning of his shipment of *The Joy of Gay Sex,* a book that had been selling elsewhere in Canada for about ten years. The book was a tame, gay version of the popular heterosexual *The Joy of Sex,* and contained drawings of anal sex and other sexual practices performable by two men. (Interestingly, despite its depiction of anal sex, *The Joy of Sex* had never been detained anywhere, never mind banned.) Glad Day had been advised by their lawyers that selecting one representative item from the mass of materials detained due to anal penetration was their best strategy. They needed a focused, winnable, precedent-setting case that would open the borders for similar books and magazines. *The Joy of Gay Sex* was to be Moldenhauer's test case.

The case was heard relatively quickly. In May 1987, the Customs ban on *The Joy of Gay Sex* was overturned. Ontario Provincial Court Judge Bruce Hawkins stated that the book was not obscene, that it dealt "rationally and unsensationally with the sexual practices of a substantial segment of the male population. However repugnant the concept of anal sex may be to the heterosexual observer, it is, I find, the central sexual act of homosexual practice." Hawkins rose to unusually poetic heights in his legal judgement on the act, declaring, "to write about homosexual practices without dealing with anal intercourse would be equivalent to writing a history of music and omitting Mozart."

But Hawkins' judgement did not provide the precedent-setting relief that Moldenhauer had sought. Canada Customs appeared to treat the ruling as an isolated decision about an individual title, and continued to detain gay magazines and books without missing a beat, Mozartian or otherwise.

In May 1987, Little Sister's and the BCCLA launched their first legal action: a court challenge to Customs' ruling that two separate issues of the Los Angeles-based *The Advocate* magazine were obscene because of suggestive advertisements. A trial date was set for May 1988. Little Sister's carried the few available gay political newspapers and magazines, like the *New York Native* and *The Advocate,* and Canada Customs was regularly detaining them—but only in shipments to Little Sister's and Glad Day. Other Canadian newsstands and bookstores imported the same materials with impunity. (Customs' diligent detention of undue sexual content destined to the two stores meant that the safe sex information that dominated these journals since the discovery of AIDS was not available to many gay readers.)

In April 1988, a few weeks before the trial and over two years since *The Advocate* had first been seized, Little Sister's walked into court only to hear the government concede "their error" in detaining the magazines. Case closed. Deva and Smyth were amazed. For years, the government had strenuously resisted releasing their books and magazines, and detentions had continued unabated. Deva and Smyth realized, like Moldenhauer before them, that Canada Customs had emerged unscathed and unrepentant. At most, Glad Day had won the right to import a book that was by now out of print (*The Joy of Gay Sex* was later re-issued) and Little Sister's had won the right to sell magazines that were thirty-odd issues out of date. In fact, they hadn't even won that: Canada Customs had incinerated the entire shipment.

"We Were 'Out' and We Went For It . . ."

The 1986 seizures had brought Little Sister's a tremendous amount of publicity, good and bad. Along with the threatening phone calls— Deva and Smyth didn't take them seriously at first—business picked up. "To be quite honest, it was the first major Customs seizure that did it," said Deva. "After that, we were 'out' and we went for it. There has been nothing but hassles from Customs since, but the support from the community balanced it off."

Finally, there was the hope of a profit after years of living out of the till. But the strain of the early lean years had already brought major changes in the store's focus. The widening gulf between gallery and bookstore revenues had led to Barb Thomas' departure in 1986 and a painful rift between the co-founders that took years to heal. Thomas went on to pursue her art ventures, and the bookstore's ambience of "culture," long since eroded by the owners' desperate will to survive, was now gone. In place of the gallery, a kind of energetic marketplace and community centre had taken root.

For Smyth and Deva, the determination not to be intimidated or bankrupted had also taken root. They now became advocates of precisely the explicit lesbian and gay sexual material the state found most offensive and their customers found so hard to find. (The owners, however, drew their own, very strict line by refusing to stock child pornography of any sort, as well as materials depicting violence against women.) Deva and Smyth had finally located gay porn magazine publishers who would deal with them, provided the Customs risk was assumed by the store. They ordered whatever was available. Living so close to the financial and legal brink, Deva and Smyth decided to protect their small, heady profit. With two friends, they opened a restaurant located on the street level of their building. They gave it a generic name: Thurlow's.

In December 1987, the first bomb was thrown into the empty stairwell of the bookstore. Two months later, while Deva and co-owner Gaston Nadeau were dining downstairs at Thurlow's on a busy Saturday night, a second bomb was tossed in through the back door. It exploded three feet away from their table. Thurlow's was packed. Pieces of glass crashed down on the patrons but miraculously, after the smoke cleared, no one had a mark on them. If the bomb had rolled under a table, the police said, it would have killed someone.

Expressing one's disapproval of retail goods by bombing the offending store is relatively rare behaviour in Canada. (Although not unprecedented in Vancouver: In 1983, the anti-porn Wimmin's Fire Brigade torched three Red Hot Video stores with Molotov cocktails.) The devices thrown into Little Sister's building can hurt and kill, but they are not designed to do so; their main effect is to simulate the effects of warfare during army manoeuvres. It certainly felt like war to the bookstore's owners. Smyth and Deva had tried to keep their involvement with Thurlow's quiet, but Deva was certain the terrorist assumed "the whole building is full of faggots, let's blow them up from the bottom this time." A lone customer showed up for dinner at Thurlow's the next evening, saying he had recently moved to Vancouver from Beirut and got off on the energy. Soon after, the restaurant quickly closed for good. Within two months of the second bombing, all but one of the original staff of the bookstore had left.

Enter Mr. Joseph Arvay

Deva and Smyth confronted their problems with Customs with a new fervour. The BCCLA's John Dixon had approached one of the province's most impressive young lawyers, Joseph Arvay. Deva was dubious about whether a lawyer existed who could do justice to their cause and to the controversial material involved, particularly a heterosexual lawyer. Their previous counsel had dealt well with the relatively mild gay depictions in *The Advocate,* but he wasn't prepared to handle the defence of gay and lesbian S/M materials—and these were clearly a major irritant to Canada Customs. Deva asked Joe Arvay point blank where he stood. Arvay replied that he had no problem and, as Deva said, "you could just tell to look at him that he really had no problem. Then he started asking questions about why I thought S/M was important. Immediately we knew this was the guy to handle the case."

Joe Arvay's involvement with the Little Sister's case in the coming years would overlap with his work tackling some of province's most highly charged political cases, including the prosecutions of two former premiers (and counting). In his mid-forties, dangerously unaffected in his charm, Arvay's relaxed courtroom style masks a daunting intellectual capacity, and he riffs legal theory like a jazz musician, inspired by the elegance of exact case law. Arvay was immediately attracted to the epic scope of the Little Sister's case and the passion of the people involved.

In their early meetings, Arvay, the bookstore owners and the BCCLA worked out a basic strategy. After the debacle over *The Advocate,* Deva and Smyth wanted to avoid any trial based on a legality defined so narrowly that it might win its legal point without producing the justice they sought in the real world. They all wanted to tackle Canada Customs head-on, challenging the constitutional basis of its powers. In essence, Little Sister's would pose an embarrassing question: How can a supposedly modern democracy allow government bureaucrats to detain/ban books and magazines in an arbitrary, inconsistent and almost invisible manner? Little Sister's was going on the offensive, after years of constant harassment and discrimination.

Little Sister's and the BCCLA decided to challenge the *Customs Act* and the *Customs Tariff* under the *Charter of Rights and Freedoms'* section 2(b), the right to freedom of expression (see Appendix B). And they would go a step further. The targeting of gay and lesbian bookstores by an apparently homophobic Customs would also be confronted. Little Sister's would argue that Deva's and Smyth's personal right to equal treatment under the law, guaranteed in section 15 of the *Charter,* was being violated. (The *Charter* does not offer explicit protection on the basis of sexual orientation, but the equality provision of section 15 has been interpreted to cover gays and lesbians.)

The precise focus of the case, however, would be a challenge to prior restraint: Canada Customs' power to seize a book at the border and force the would-be importer to prove the publication's innocence. This was at the core of Little Sister's near-daily frustration with Customs. The courts might ultimately decide that prior restraint was a "justifiable limit" on personal freedom—that is, a limit the government would allow under section 1 of the *Charter*—but that Customs' use of prior restraint violated free speech seemed beyond dispute.

On June 7, 1990, the bookstore, the BCCLA, Jim Deva and Bruce Smyth filed their ambitious Statement of Claim in B.C. Supreme Court, launching one of the most dramatic attacks on state censorship in Canadian history (see Appendix C). The trial date was set for September 1991. In the meantime, Little Sister's and the BCCLA would be footing the enormous legal costs of preparing the case. The tasks of dealing with the media, mobilizing the community (both grassroots and professional) and fundraising threatened to balloon into a full-time job and more. Deva and Smyth still had a bookstore to run, a community to serve—and now a court case to fund. Clearly, another warm body was needed, someone with good communication skills . . . maybe a writer, with bookstore experience, an outgoing personality . . . maybe some theatre background, good with people, someone with political savvy . . . willing to work like a Clydesdale . . . They might as well have run a Help Wanted notice saying: "Only Janine Fuller need apply."

It's the fall of 1989 and I'm sitting in the Choo-Choo bar having a final drink with friends before my lover, Julie Stines, and I board one of the last VIA Rail trains to ride from Toronto to Vancouver. We take last-minute photos in the dollar booth, trying to pack everyone in. The pictures are neither focused nor a very good likeness, but they're still in my wallet. The seductive female VIA Rail announcer purrs "final boarding" as our friend Paul runs towards us with a cooler jammed with beer—"You can't get Red Baron out West," he cries—and hoists the bag up to me.

JANINE

Julie and I rattle down the train aisles, bottles jingling, our knapsacks bouncing from one passenger's head to the next. We have our own berth, which seems entirely decadent except for the half-price ticket sale. This is where our adventure began . . .

With no real plans and no real destination, we headed for Vancouver with high hopes to keep on going 'round the world. Unannounced, we crashed on a friend's pull-out couch for the first week. Realizing his hospitality was being tested, Julie and I moved to one of Vancouver's livelier, cheaper hotels. As if that wasn't enough, we then both had to get root canals.

Broke and grounded in Vancouver, we found our own apartment. It soon became obvious that jobs were inevitable. Julie found work as a tree pruner (no experience, but lots of enthusiasm). After firing off résumés to bookstores without luck, I decided to apply in person at this place called Little Sister's. My résumé was a hand-scrawled couple of pages recounting a rather eclectic work history. I did, however, have a few years' experience at the Toronto Women's Bookstore and at Bookcity. The bulk of my résumé listed years of theatre experience, some video work and performance art, and my last job, as theatre director at a student theatre company.

After a quick once-over, the Little Sister's guys called me into their back room for a more thorough interview. I sat cross-legged, trying to sound intelligent about some of the more exaggerated claims on my application. In the blink of an eye, I was hired.

I'd left Toronto to find a nice calming atmosphere and Little Sister's seemed just the ticket. What could be more soothing than selling books to the gay and lesbian community, reading passages of your favourite author on quiet nights at the till, or talking with customers about the latest exciting novel? Other than believing in the tooth fairy, this was the most gullible I've been in my life.

Within the first few months of the summer of 1990, we were revving up for something called the Gay Games and screaming about detentions by Canada Customs. I had no idea what these Games were: maybe croquet tournaments near a local beach or an afternoon of tennis at the Stanley Park public courts. Well, the Gay Games were much bigger than anything I had imagined. Thousands of lesbians and gay men arriving from around the globe, competing in countless sports and, yes, even croquet. Little Sister's, like the city, was teeming.

My real introduction to the store, and to the politics of Little Sister's, came with overseeing our book table at the Gay Games writers conference. I sold books and passed out information about the store's upcoming legal battle with Customs. I was very comfortable selling books; I was amply embarrassed using a cell-phone to communicate with the bookstore; and I was just beginning to grasp the magnitude of the court challenge Little Sister's had launched.

I'd lived in Toronto, performed in many fundraising benefits, protested at anti-censorship rallies in support of Glad Day Books, but this was all still very new to me. During the conference, I saw how Customs meddled with the arrival of works by authors who were scheduled to read. My eyes began to open; Customs' interference was like an Exit sign assaulting the pupils, blasting bright red light into a darkened room.

At the conference I was too busy with book table duties to attend many workshops. I made displays, piling the books like dominos and straightening them again after the enthusiastic crowds had left. Little Sister's table was organized to perfection, ready for any author's inspection at any moment (I was in awe of the authors). I was also suffering from a dismal stomach flu, which I muffled with vast amounts of aspirin and an addictive supply of Rolaids. My condition didn't lend itself to social chit-chat. But while I passed the hours marvelling at the panellists—John Preston, Sarah Schulman and Dorothy Allison, to name a few—I grew more and more aware of the importance of linking communities and struggles. The censoring of a Vancouver bookstore had parallels with what many of the authors spoke and wrote about. I also learned that, however bad you feel, vast quantities of Rolaids are a mistake.

Vancouver was never the same after the Gay Games. Their spectacle and size fuelled the gay community for years. The Games was where I took my first tentative steps, soon to become hulking strides, in publicizing Little Sister's battle with Canada Customs. Eventually, we found the grassroots support that ignited the very heart of the case. From artists and booksellers, individuals and groups, the support started to build. By the time the trial finally began in 1994, Little Sister's had raised thousands of dollars from our many communities.

Creativity was the common ingredient in most fundraising efforts. In Toronto, the Women's Bookstore, Pages and Glad Day bookstores held a benefit party at the Bamboo Club on trendy Queen Street West. Artists donated their work to raffles, and artist-run centres like Vancouver's Video In threw video night benefits.

During the trial, local gay-owned bed & breakfasts offered free accommodation to the Little Sister's witnesses—a month's worth. Simon Fraser University sponsored a public lecture series that dovetailed with the trial—and paid for witnesses' airfare; some faculty members at the Universities of British Columbia and Victoria offered similar support. Individuals gave what they could, from spare change in penny jars to the $10,000 from a New York woman, who donated at the urging of a Canadian friend in the publishing industry. (At first I thought a friend was trying to put one past me, but when the handwritten cheque arrived days later, I sat down and stared at it in disbelief.)

Over the years, people would use their considerable creative talents to design flyers, buttons, T-shirts and even a 'zine, all to raise funds and awareness around the court case. Publishers and booksellers gave money at trade shows or donated a percentage of sales on designated Days of Resistance against Canada Customs. Periodicals offered pages of free advertising space and published articles chronicling the struggle. What started quietly in 1990 now had an almost folkloric reputation because of the endless trial delays.

With the delays, Joe Arvay's strategy was constantly deepening and expanding, which meant more witnesses and more costs. In 1994, I flew to New York and Toronto, then drove across Canada on a summer fundraising tour before the trial. Accompanied by Julie, and identical twin lesbian sisters Pat and Shirley (plus a few pals along the way), we handed out more flyers than we travelled miles. We dropped them in bars, bookstores, coffee shops; we handed them out at art openings, concerts, rallies and Pride Days. My lover and friends have been to more benefits over the past few years than any other social activity. The drive across Canada, in a van brimming with flyers, camping equipment, sisters and lover, was the supreme test of friendship and, personally, my greatest trial . . . probably theirs, too.

Going on the Offensive

Little Sister's was putting the federal government on trial. The defendants—the Minister of Justice, the Attorney General of Canada, and the Minister of National Revenue (responsible for Canada Customs), collectively known as "the Crown"—would now have to constitutionally justify Customs' powers and practices in a court of law.

Evidently, they weren't in any hurry to do so. After Little Sister's filed the claim in 1990, the case stalled while a series of Crown lawyers made yearly court appearances, often reiterating the same argument: instead of a *constitutional* trial, a "statutory review" of Canada Customs would suffice. The Crown argued this would be an "equally effective avenue" for addressing Little Sister's concerns. Yet even this review, involving rational concepts of administrative law, in contrast to the messy rage that Customs ignited in Little Sister's, never happened. Instead, skirmishes would crop up as the Crown attempted to delay or dismiss Little Sister's claim.

In September 1993, when the government requested another postponement, Arvay's and Little Sister's patience was wearing thin. The annual crop of Crown lawyers pleaded for more time; one wept and there were a number of emotional outbursts. As Arvay said, "The Crown's characterization of the case as unprepared, out of control and in a shambles certainly appears to be the case—for the defence." Arvay was ready for trial, but he was becoming distressed. The yearly adjournments were eroding his case. Two of Little Sister's witnesses had already died of AIDS—Toronto writer Jay Scott, one of the country's leading film critics, and David Goble, the bookstore's customs broker—and two others were living with AIDS or cancer.

The judge set a new trial date for the spring of 1994, and that date was eventually shifted to October 11, 1994. What had begun as a ten-day trial in 1991 was now scheduled for forty days—fully two months of high courtroom drama.

TWO

O SCanada

The Advocate ▴ The Joy of Gay Sex ▴ The Joy of Lesbian Sex ▴ Men with
the Pink Triangle ▴ Querelle ▴ Dancing on My Grave ▴ Erotic Poems from
the Greek Anthology ▴ Harold Norse: Love Poems 1940–1985 ▴ Rushes ▴
Slashed to Ribbons in Defense of Love ▴ Death Trick ▴ Black Looks: Race
and Representation ▴ Teleny ▴ In the Tent ▴ Straight Heart's Delight ▴
Dzelharons ▴ Prick Up Your Ears ▴ Coming to Power ▴ Leading Edge ▴ Bad
Attitude ▴ The Story of O ▴ Raging Peace ▴ Macho Sluts ▴ The Throne
Council ▴ Caught Looking ▴ Woman Hating ▴ The Young in One Another's
Arms ▴ Herotica ▴ Oriental Guys #3, 4 , 5 and 6 ▴ The Wings of the
Phoenix ▴ Lion Warriors ▴ Gay Roots: Twenty Years of Gay Sunshine ▴
Hothead Paisan #7 ▴ My Deep Dark Pain Is Love ▴ Flesh and the Word ▴
Out of Bounds ▴ Outrage ▴ This Universe of Men ▴ 1993 Australian Gay
and Lesbian Short Story Anthology ▴ Parisian Lives ▴ Quim #4 ▴ Passport
#78 ▴ Love and Rockets Sketchbook 2 ▴ Tom of Finland Retrospective ▴ The
Satanic Verses ▴ Restless Rednecks: Gay Tales of a Changing South ▴ The
Smile of Eros ▴ Street Lavender ▴ Surprising Myself ▴ Drummer #152 ▴
Meatmen ▴ Muscle Bound Roman Conquests ▴ Warriors for Love ▴ RFD
#73 ▴ Frisk ▴ Bedrooms Have Windows ▴ Tear-drops on My Drum ▴ Urban
Aboriginals ▴ Shadow of Love ▴ Uncertainty of Strangers ▴ Outlook ▴
Safestud ▴ Best Guide to Amsterdam ▴ Body Piercing ▴ Coming Along Fine
▴ Cut/Uncut ▴ On Our Backs ▴ Belinda's Bouquet ▴ Three Literary

Friendships ▲ *Doc and Fluff* ▲ *Empire of the Senseless* ▲ *Introducing Amanda Valentine* ▲ *The Naked Civil Servant* ▲

—SOME BOOKS AND MAGAZINES DETAINED
OR BANNED BY CANADA CUSTOMS

THE cameras crowd around the monumental glass doors of the British Columbia Provincial Court. The courthouse is an architectural marvel, adorning postcards in every downtown hotel lobby. Its soaring glass structure looks more like a giant solarium than the province's highest court. On the steps, a scrum of reporters, photographers and camera operators often attracts passers-by, who strain for a view of what will appear on the six o'clock news.

This day is historic if only because a Little Sister's trial is actually beginning as scheduled. No more delays, no more press releases about delays, just the key people from the B.C. Civil Liberties Association and Little Sister's standing on the steps. At the centre of competing photo ops are Janine Fuller, handling questions for the bookstore, John Dixon, fielding for the BCCLA, and Svend Robinson, Canada's first openly gay member of Parliament, lending his presence to the cause. The spectacle is unfolding on national Coming Out Day, an irony the mainstream press neglects to capture.

Dixon, an impressive debater, is clearly on his oatmeal today. He's waited a long time for this trial and savours every pronouncement. Fuller pops in and out of the cluster, readying her responses. Jim Deva shuffles about in the dress pants and fancy shoes he seldom, if ever, has occasion to wear. He and Bruce Smyth take the last drags of their cigarettes. Irene Faulkner, the articling student assisting Joe Arvay, pays off the cab and carefully counts up the precious boxes of court documents. Behind the cameras, almost unnoticed, a troop of Lesbian Avengers are called into action to ferry the documents into the building. Hoisting four and a half years of accumulated evidence, they make trip after trip with boxes piled onto wobbly carts, bungy cords straining. Arvay, who walks with crutches, suddenly realizes he's forgotten the ceremonial lawyer's shirt that is customary in Canadian court proceedings. Irene Faulkner sets off to track down a shirt, struggling against the clock, while Arvay reviews the last details of his opening address to the judge.

Jim Deva will testify first. Janine Fuller's testimony is being withheld until further down the line, so she can address any unanswered questions that may arise during the lengthy trial. The courtroom is standing room only as press and supporters jockey for position. After the first week, the case will move to the much larger Courtroom 65 to accommodate the crowds, but during the opening days, Deva is forced to sit on the courtroom floor. The judge's remark that "Mr. Deva be offered a seat" is one of very few pleasantries observed during the extremely tense first week of the Little Sister's trial.

At Long Last

After four and a half years, three postponements and a dramatic change to Canada Custom's Memorandum D9-1-1 just days before, the trial had begun. The Honourable Mr. Justice Kenneth Smith, the relatively new B.C. Supreme Court judge assigned to the trial, had tried only ten previous cases and was seen as a largely unknown element. But Mr. Justice Smith's experience in both civil and criminal law offered some hope that he would be less squeamish about the more controversial materials than, say, a judge with a background in maritime law.

Arvay had scheduled Little Sister's witnesses (see Appendix D) into thematic groups, based on the legal points he hoped to score. The first week brought together booksellers, book distributors and librarians to describe the economic, practical and psychological burdens that Canada Customs imposed on the industry. In particular, these witnesses would expose the homophobic targeting of lesbian and gay publications and booksellers.

The next witnesses would help Arvay illustrate how it was virtually impossible, as well as inappropriate, to expect Customs officials to interpret whether a work was obscene. Artists, authors and cultural critics would be called to deconstruct gay and lesbian culture. Their testimony would reveal the fluid, subjective and historically complex nature of sexual images and text. In a way, Arvay would demonstrate how an obscenity trial really works; by extension, he would show how absurd it is to expect Customs bureaucrats to make correct judgements about boxes of books.

Another task for Little Sister's was to explore the meaning of lesbian and gay communities, and the significance of queer literature and culture to those communities. Social scientists, writers and historians would examine how Canada Customs fit into a long tradition of state repression of sexuality, and of homosexuality in particular. They would also speak about the conventions and etiquette of gay and lesbian s/m, a strong trigger for Customs.

Finally, Arvay would tackle the nightmarish quality of Customs' internal procedures: the lack of accountability, the excesses and inconsistencies, the unsalvageable and essentially unconstitutional nature of their systems.

Arvay and Irene Faulkner faced an impressive cast of legal opponents. The Crown's team, headed by Johannes (Hans) Van Iperen, a well-seasoned lawyer with an undramatic style, also included Neena Sharma and Daniel Kiselbach. There was another antagonist, too. The Attorney General of British Columbia had been granted intervenor status and was represented in court by an aggressive duo, lawyers Frank Falzon and Angela Westmacott. (Ironically, Falzon and Westmacott had previously worked under Arvay when he had been associated with the AG's office.) The province was concerned that an erosion of Canada Customs' powers —in particular, the power of prior restraint—would impact on film classification regulations in the Motion Picture Act. Clearly, Little Sister's assault on censorship was worrying the state on many levels.

Throwing the Book Back at Customs

The question underlying the trial—should Canada Customs have the right to decide what Canadians read?—has very concrete significance. The vast majority of books and magazines consumed by Canadians are imported, an oft-times lamentable side effect of living beside a neighbour with ten times the population. Ninety percent of the books and magazines sold at Little Sister's, and almost all the material at issue in the case, is produced in the United States (although not necessarily *by* Americans). Canadian publishers are taking bigger steps towards marketing queer fiction, theory and history, but the trend is relatively recent. As a result, many of the lesbian and gay materials that Canadians may want to read, including works by Canadian writers published abroad, are subject to Customs' scrutiny.

Arvay's strategy with the booksellers was to demonstrate the truth of the two key elements in Little Sister's Statement of Claim: (1) that Canada Customs regulations are applied in a discriminatory, homophobic fashion to Little Sister's and to other gay and feminist bookstores (and overwhelmingly to their gay and lesbian materials); and (2) that Customs places an unfair onus on the person whose material has been seized or detained to get their books released.

For Jim Deva, taking the stand brought a kind of fulfilment. "It felt very therapeutic, almost confessional, like getting out everything I totally wanted to say," said Deva after his lengthy testimony about Little Sister's early history and ongoing harassment. "There was nothing I needed to discuss further, it was all said. Joe Arvay was like a choreographer." Much of Deva's testimony reflected his desire, as a bookseller, for free access to literature.

"We will always keep our doors open despite Canada Customs," Deva said. "What I am here for is because the books mean a great, great deal to me."

The testimony of Jearld Moldenhauer, the former owner of Glad Day Books in Toronto, was electrifying. (Fed up with Canadian censorship, he had sold Glad Day in 1991, returning to Boston where he owns another bookstore of the same name.) Moldenhauer had helped lay the groundwork for Toronto's gay liberation movement, not only opening the first gay bookstore—Glad Day Books grew out of a backpack from which Moldenhauer had hocked books at early gay meetings—but also co-founding Canada's first national gay newsmagazine, the *Body Politic,* both in the mid-1970s. Moldenhauer appears remarkably youthful although his two decades of fighting in some of Canada's hardest censorship battles have taken their toll.

Growing up in the United States, Moldenhauer had made a profound connection between the U.S. Bill of Rights' First Amendment—the right to freedom of speech—and his growing sense of gay pride. "It is not my role to play censor of any kind," Moldenhauer testified. "In fact, it was largely because of an internalized dimension of censorship, the suppression of ideas, that I had cast myself into the role of bookseller to begin with."

The Crown was intent on discrediting both Moldenhauer and Deva for carrying obscene materials. Little Sister's had already sampled the government's strategy in two earlier court appearances, in the falls of 1992 and 1993, when their case was delayed. On both occasions, former Crown lawyer Mary Humphries had reiterated that the Little Sister's case sought nothing less than "to create an enclave of homosexual pornography, the parameters of which were unknowable, a significant portion of which is child pornography." The fact that Little Sister's refused to carry anything they considered child pornography would in no way deter the Crown from tarring them with that brush.

But Moldenhauer took a strict civil libertarian stand and opposed any such self-censorship, making himself an easy target for the Crown. By his second day of testimony, he had already choked up during an account of Glad Day's relentless harassment by police and Customs, and the most explosive issue was set to ignite.

Senior Crown lawyer Hans Van Iperen immediately asked Moldenhauer if he would censor the NAMBLA bulletin, the newsletter of the North American Man-Boy Love Association that advocates intergenerational sex. Moldenhauer had already acknowledged that he carried the bulletin.

"Well, I mean, I suppose you might want to censor Greek literature because it's all full of man-boy love," Moldenhauer answered. ". . . I would not censor that, no."

". . . Do paedophiles buy NAMBLA?" asked Van Iperen.

"I would assume so," Moldenhauer said.

"I understand you're against all censorship?" asked Van Iperen.

"Yes."

"But in your view, can anything ever be obscene?" Van Iperen asked.

"Probably not. I don't find human expression obscene," said Moldenhauer. "I don't know. It's just a political word . . . There's plenty of bad taste out there."

Angela Westmacott, counsel for the B.C. Attorney General, was less circumspect than the Crown in her cross-examination, as was Moldenhauer by the end of his ordeal in the witness box.

"Mr. Moldenhauer," Westmacott said, "Mr. Deva testified . . . that [Little Sister's] has guidelines in place that they won't order books that are patently misogynist or depict violence against women or anything to do with paedophilia. I take it from your testimony that you had no such guidelines . . . ?"

"No, no I don't," said Moldenhauer. "I just don't believe in that. As I said, I think if people need to know what other people think—even if it's hateful—it's important that ideas are not swept under the rug, one way or another. I mean, plenty of people hate gay people. I want to know about that so I can deal with it . . ."

". . . Would it be fair to say there are no restrictions or limitations at all on the type of material you would order for your bookstores?" Westmacott asked.

"Yeah, if it came out of the gay or lesbian culture," Moldenhauer replied, ". . . [then] we wished to offer it to our community."

"Mr. Deva also testified on behalf of Little Sister's that the bookstore would remove books from the shelf that their customers found disturbing," said Westmacott. "I take it as well that you wouldn't follow this practice."

"I find that totally loathsome," said Moldenhauer. "I mean, you just create an incredible web of censorship; everyone is acting as censor. Everyone doesn't like something, so suddenly your shelves are empty."

Moldenhauer's fiery responses during cross-examination had probably labelled him as an extremist, yet it had just as clearly revealed him as principled and sincere. That he was a maverick, even in gay circles, was no secret, and his emotional responses had moved like a dangerous force through the velvet-box atmosphere of the tiny courtroom. Moldenhauer's early appearance in the Little Sister's trial made it very clear that some gays and lesbians were totally unwilling to conform to conventional, heterosexist "community standards," even if it meant suffering the consequences.

Misadventures in the Book Trade

Other booksellers had no trouble substantiating Customs' fixation on lesbian and gay titles. Louise Hager had owned one of Vancouver's most respected bookstores in upscale Kerrisdale for fifteen years without even being aware of Customs' interest in imported books. But before her new bookstore, Women In Print, opened its doors in early 1994, she testified, an advance shipment of lesbian-themed books was seized by Customs. (The books, including the feminist anthology *Against Sadomasochism*, had still not been returned in September 1995.)

Later in the trial, Arvay was able to corroborate from high-level Customs officials that, with the exception of a handful of feminist, leftist and comic bookstores, such as Spartacus in Vancouver and Bold Print in Winnipeg, the country's thousands of bookstores never had detentions, delays or communication with Canada Customs. Glad Day Books and Little Sister's, in contrast, had been subjected to delays and detentions every month, often weekly, for years.

Michael Foster of Crosstown Traffic Comics, an Ottawa store, testified about receiving K 27 notices of detention that informed him the offending comics had already been destroyed. His frustration at pursuing Customs' complex, confusing appeal process was echoed by Sandra Haar, a writer and worker at the Toronto Women's Bookstore. Haar described the bookstore's first detention—the outrageous lesbian comic *Hothead Paisan*—

and the litany of incorrect notifications and conflicting advice she received from the different Customs agents she contacted. The store's distributor for alternative comics, the San Francisco-based The Last Gasp, was now demanding prepayment to offset the risks of exporting to Canada. Haar's testimony made it clear that Customs' actions put small independent bookstores, with their chronic cash flow problems, in a serious bind about importing any gay and lesbian materials.

Dennis Mahoney described the seizures and detentions from the perspective of an American book distributor. Mahoney worked as customer services manager at Inland Book Company in East Haven, Connecticut. With yearly sales of U.S.$15 million, Mahoney testified, Inland handled about 25,000 books annually for around 6,000 publishers, and shipped to almost 40 other countries and 350 Canadian stores. Inland was one of the largest wholesalers and distributors of American small presses— publishers who individually lack the clout of the large mass media conglomerates. Small presses depend on distributors like Inland to reach their audiences, and Inland was Canada's significant link to foreign English-language writing beyond the mainstream. About 15 percent of their titles had gay or lesbian themes.

In 1993, Mahoney testified, an estimated 73 percent of their shipments to Canada were detained. (Canada and Japan were the only foreign countries whose border practices ever posed problems for Inland; Japanese officials had once stopped a shipment of their books.) In May 1993, the largest detention in Canada Customs' history seriously jeopardized Inland's relationship to all its Canadian customers. Half a ton of books, close to $10,000 in merchandise destined for thirty-six bookstores, was seized and held for weeks at the Fort Erie, Ontario point of entry. University, religious and other respectable bookstores felt Customs' sting for the first time.

If the massive detention was intended as a display of Customs' power, it backfired badly. Media reaction was swift. Editorials, including one in the neo-conservative Globe and Mail, denounced Customs' practices. Customs also earned condemnation from the 60th congress of PEN (the international writers and human rights organization) taking place in Santiago de Compostela, Spain.

Mahoney described the background to the May 1993 detention. Since the introduction of the Goods and Services Tax (GST) in Canada in the early 1990s, Inland had observed a pattern of escalating detentions and increased damage to books (Customs was not known for its gentleness). Why the domestic GST would create such problems wasn't clear, but Inland had sought protection. They hired a consolidator to assemble all titles destined to Canadian stores into a single large shipment. At the border, the shipment would be cleared and brokered—the administrative process of passing through Customs—and then divided into individual packages for each store. In effect, Customs could no longer distinguish between Inland's shipments to naughty and nice bookstores. When Inland's consolidated package arrived in May 1993, Customs officials "stripped the shipment" whole of every suspect title. Many of the suspicious titles were, in fact, destined for all thirty-six stores.

Inland now believed it was a target of Canada Customs. They set out to create a system that would tell Customs officers which titles had been denied entry in the past, and which books had been detained, reviewed and cleared. (Customs keeps some records, but they have no reliable system of tracking a title's history of detention, prohibition or release.) Inland requested a list of prohibited titles to alert both its customers and Customs of the problematic material, and offered to submit new titles to Customs' pre-clearance procedure.

"We felt we had made every effort to work with Customs to make this an efficient and expeditious process," Mahoney testified. "We knew we were going to have books detained and, as much as we didn't like that, we were willing to live with it."

"Why didn't you like the pre-clearance procedure?" Arvay asked.

"Because we were practising self-censorship," Mahoney replied simply.

Customs offers an advance review option to publishers who are concerned their books might not pass the Memorandum D9-1-1 test. In a 1993 letter, Customs informed Inland just how unreliable that option was: "Please understand that the advance review [pre-clearance] will by no means eliminate any possible detention of shipments at the time of importations, as opinions rendered by Prohibited Importations, or by commodity specialists, are not binding, and regardless of an opinion, Customs officials reserve the right to scrutinize invoices and shipments."

As a contingency plan, Inland created a computer flag and invoice notation called "SCanada," which they announced on an Inland Special Gay and Lesbian Title Promotion: "Please note SCanada indicates that a title has been seized by Canadian Customs. Order these at your own risk."

It was now up to the individual Canadian bookseller: Would she or he try to import a prohibited book? If the book was seized or if shipments arrived at the store with missing books, the store would be responsible for paying Inland, no matter what the outcome. This had become Inland's only acceptable terms for conducting business in Canada.

Although the fact was persistently denied by high-ranking Customs officials, Inland was the subject of a "hot indicator" at the border crossing at Fort Erie. (Little Sister's was the target of a "lookout" in Vancouver's post office Customs assessment division.) The hot-indicator would flag Inland's name on Customs' database and give details of any past "problems."

Cut Off at the Source

Inland wasn't entirely alone. The distributor Golden-Lee, based in Avon, Massachusetts, also found itself contending with Customs detentions. The common denominator seemed to be that both did business with Glad Day Books in Toronto.

Kim Mistysyn, who testified as the manager of Glad Day, described the situation with Golden-Lee. In July 1994, Customs had detained, then banned, a shipment of *Bizarre Dreams,* a collection of gay erotica. (An irony: the book's co-editor, Caro Soles, lived in Toronto.)

In early September 1994, Mistysyn received the following letter:

> Dear Kim,
> Please understand that as of September 1, 1994, Golden-Lee will no longer ship books to you. I wish we could be more supportive of your struggle against the Canadian laws banning the erotic material which we distribute in the United States. However, we are in the business of selling books (erotic and otherwise) and not in the business of tracing shipments and arguing with customs.
> As I am sure you are aware every shipment we send to you, whether containing questionable material or not, is detained for months at a time. When shipments are returned to us they are always missing books. Further, the books returned to us are so damaged that we have to write them off as unsalable.
> We understand that you are a small business and are being severely damaged by the practices of customs but unfortunately we are a small business too. The time we have to spend tracing and

sorting out orders does not pay. I hope you can understand our position.

> Sincerely,
> Laurel Miller
> Sales Manager

This was an unsettling blow. Glad Day and Little Sister's depended on distributors like Golden-Lee to bring small press books into Canada. Yet to avoid financial ruin, these distributors were being forced by Customs to play the role of censor. If other distributors followed suit and discontinued their support of gay and lesbian publishers and booksellers, Canada's queer communities would face a severe cultural drought.

Meanwhile, other bookstores and distributors were not harassed when they traded in the same books as Glad Day and Inland. For example, the California-based distributor Bookpeople was shipping the prohibited *Bizarre Dreams* into Canada without a hitch. As Janine Fuller discovered at book conventions in Canada and the U.S., some distributors were incredulous to learn of seizures of books they also carried—like David Leavitt's *A Place I've Never Been,* Sarah Schulman's *Girls, Visions and Everything,* David Wojnarowicz's *Memories That Smell Like Gasoline* and many other titles stocked in mainstream bookstores.

Celia Duthie, owner of the fleet of Duthie bookstores in Vancouver, testified about the "fairly substantial section of porn or erotica" in her stores that appealed to "all sorts of sexualities." Duthie Books, she said, never experienced Customs detentions. She also described a remarkable incident, which became one of the more popular trial tidbits reported by the media.

In August 1994, the Crown asked Arvay for copies of several banned books that Little Sister's would be using as evidence. Arvay needed six copies of each title, which included John Preston's *In Search of a Master* and *Once I Had a Master,* and two lesbian fiction anthologies edited by Karen Barber, *Bushfires* and *Afterglow,* all published by Alyson Publications. The Catch-22, Janine Fuller realized, was that importing the books through Little Sister's would probably be impossible—an irony that seemed to have utterly escaped the Crown. She approached Celia Duthie, who agreed to import them through her own broker and shipper. In solidarity, Alyson Publications agreed to donate the books. When the shipment arrived at Customs, the invoice was briefly examined by a Commodity Specialist who then waved the box through, untouched. Duthie had successfully imported banned books. Little Sister's couldn't have dreamed up a more dramatic example of Canada Customs' discriminatory practices.

Different Strokes for Different Strokes

Although Customs seemed focused on gay and lesbian publications, a few books intended for mainstream audiences did catch the bureaucracy's eye. These included Bret Easton Ellis' novel *American Psycho,* about a serial killer and his grisly, misogynist murders, and, at the other end of the literary spectrum, Salman Rushdie's *The Satanic Verses,* an irreverent and profound comedy on the nature of Islam that earned Rushdie a death threat from some fundamentalist Muslims. Both books were backed by big publishers and their releases were huge media events. In Ottawa, communications at the highest levels of government would take place, though not fast enough to avoid international embarrassment.

American Psycho was detained by Customs, examined and declared to be of sufficient literary merit to enter the country, despite the fact that Ellis' original publisher, Simon & Schuster, dropped the book due to the brutality of its sexual violence. When *The Satanic Verses* was briefly detained by Customs in 1989 as possible hate literature, at the instigation of one complainant, Canada became the only Western nation to give some credence to Rushdie's persecutors. Even the prime minister, Brian Mulroney, was moved to publicly condemn Customs' actions.

But it was Madonna's 1992 blockbuster book, *Sex,* that received the most extraordinary attention from Customs—extraordinarily kind, that is. Provocatively encased in a metal cover, *Sex* presented Madonna's sexual fantasies in text and photos, fantasies that often veered towards S/M and kiddie porn. Canadian advance sales were brisk, and the waiting list at the Vancouver Public Library numbered in the several hundreds.

Madonna's book was as anticipated by Customs and the federal government as it was by her fans. Publisher Time/Warner was concerned that *Sex* might hit a bump at the border, so they hired the prestigious Toronto law firm of Osler, Hoskin & Harcourt to run interference at Customs' top level. When *Sex* finally reached the border, its admissibility had already been secured through the economic and political clout of both the author and publisher. Later in the trial, Joe Arvay would thoroughly question Customs bureaucrats about *Sex*'s kid-glove treatment. (See Chapter 7.)

On the second day of the 1993 American Booksellers Association convention in Miami Beach, Florida, I head for the autograph area to hound, cajole and beg some big-name writers to lend their support to our

JANINE upcoming trial. It's my impossible dream, as I line up for hours to spend just three seconds with Anne Rice, or hastily hand a flyer to Maya Angelou as she crosses the convention hall. In 1992, at the Anaheim convention, I'd lunged like a linebacker when Stephen King tried to get off an escalator, blurting out something incomprehensible about admiring his article in *Gauntlet* magazine and his commitment to free speech, then handing him a flyer with such determination that, if he'd had a bodyguard, there would have been consequences. Such are the humiliating moments that desperation and determination bring.

Each year before the ABA, Joe Arvay and I would make a wish list of who I should ask to testify. Each year, I'd return home with calluses from folding flyers and a few victories to report. At the 1993 ABA, John Preston, distinguished author of many books banned in Canada, agreed to testify for us. Deacon MacCubbin, the owner of Lambda Rising—a kind of gay and lesbian literary "conglomerate"—agreed to put forward a motion in support of Little Sister's legal struggles at the May 1994 annual general meeting. We strategized with the ABA executives—including an ex-Canadian who'd left the country disgusted by Canada's prudish censorship laws—and they confirmed that 1994 would be a good time for the motion to come from the floor.

Deacon worked on the wording while Jim Deva and I encouraged him. When the motion was introduced, Deva gave a quick synopsis of Little Sister's past decade and outlined our legal defence. The motion was seconded by the outgoing ABA president, Chuck Robinson, and passed unanimously. But even before this vote, the ABA had been keen supporters of the case through the American Booksellers For Freedom of Expression Foundation. With the B.C. Civil Liberties Association, the ABFFEF helped us get a U.S.$20,000 grant from the MacCarthur Foundation in 1992, a hugely important donation.

In June 1992 we passed a similar motion at the Canadian Booksellers Association AGM in Toronto. It was a sweaty meeting, a near-miss for our cause. Jearld Moldenhauer, Stuart Blackley and I waited for Bruce Walsh to make his short presentation on censorship. Bruce had spearheaded Censorstop, a volunteer group promoting anti-censorship advocacy in Canada, and he and Stuart had worked all week on his speech. Suddenly, a CBA board member suggested that, because the meeting was running late, Bruce's presentation would have to be dropped.

Jearld looked at me in outraged disbelief. This was exactly what he had grown to expect from Canadians around censorship, and it was happening again, right on cue. We all shouted from the floor that Bruce's story must be heard, and he was allowed to proceed. With the final minutes of the meeting ticking down, I brought forward the motion we had collectively hammered out, choking on the words as though on the verge of puberty. The motion passed overwhelmingly and I looked over at Jearld with a "see, Canadians *can* get behind this" grin.

Disappointingly, the CBA resolution didn't rate a peep in any major news media. But a bridge had been built. East and West had finally met, Glad Day and Little Sister's had joined together for the first time for an invaluable sharing of history and struggle. At the end of the day I was on Toronto Island, calling Jim Deva from a pay phone at the ferry dock, the CBA conference hall miles of water away.

It was a hot, unbearable Toronto summer day, and Stuart and I were relieved to have finally found this island oasis. A sickening feeling about how the meeting could have gone still overpowered any sense of triumph, but we now were in paradise—and about to witness a lesbian marriage. What more appropriate ending to the day than a celebration of our lives, our loves? We didn't know it at the time, but the friend getting married would also end up testifying at the trial in 1994. Back then she was simply Becki, not Professor or Dr. Ross, and she was marrying Ingrid and everything else seemed thankfully far, far away.

Over the years, other organizations would adopt strong positions against the Canadian government and Customs' practices. We were becoming an international story. PEN U.S.A., PEN Canada and PEN International all adopted resolutions against censorship in Canada. The Canadian Book and Periodical Council's Freedom of Expression Committee was a tremendous supporter of our case. Individual writers and artists gave benefit readings, performances and screenings of their work: Pat Califia in San Francisco, Michael Ondaatje in Guelph, Timothy Findley in Vancouver. Aerlyn Weissman and Lynne Fernie's documentary film about Jane Rule, *Fiction and Other Truths,* and John Greyson's feature film on AIDS, *Zero Patience,* both had western premieres to sell-out benefit audiences in Vancouver.

Without the support of these comrades, Little Sister's would have felt like a tree falling in the forest, unseen and unheard.

PREVIOUS PAGE: *(l. to r.) Bruce Smyth, Jim Deva and Janine Fuller, October 1994.* DANIEL COLLINS

ABOVE (LEFT TO RIGHT): *Kim Mistysyn, manager of Glad Day Books in Toronto; the storefront; Jearld Moldenhauer, founder and former owner.* CYNTHIA REDMAN, KIM MISTYSYN, DEREK NORMAN

BELOW: *John Dixon of the British Columbia Civil Liberties Association speaks at Little Sister's first protest rally, December 17, 1986 in Vancouver* LITTLE SISTER'S ARCHIVES

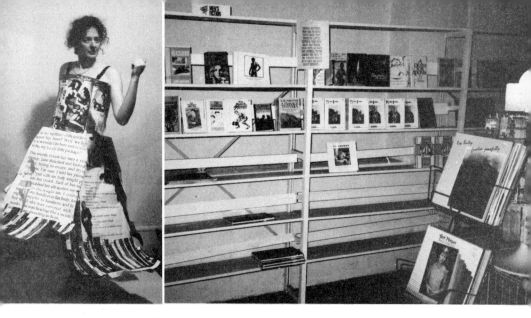

ABOVE LEFT: *Lisa Lowe, performance artist and one-time Little Sister's employee, performs her solo piece, "Seized Materials," at one of the many fundraising benefits for the bookstore. Costume by MaryLou Trinkwon.* MARYLOU TRINKWON

ABOVE RIGHT: *Little Sister's empty shelves, courtesy of Canada Customs' seizures, 1988.* JOHN KOZACHENKO

BELOW: *Little Sister's float and parade contingent, Vancouver Gay Pride 1991. (l. to r.) Jack Roebuck, Lisa Lowe, Julie Stines, Bruce Smyth, Janine Fuller, Roger Legace, Gaston Nadeau and Jim Deva.* LITTLE SISTER'S ARCHIVES

ABOVE: *Protesting the third bombing of Little Sister's in early January 1992.* JOHN KOZACHENKO

BELOW: *In the summer of 1994, Janine hit the road with (l. to r.) Pat, Shirley and Julie, to raise awareness and support for the upcoming trial.* JANINE FULLER

THREE

Strange Bedfellows

JOSEPH ARVAY: *Where are we today insofar as the development of feminist ideology [around pornography] is concerned . . . ?*

CAROLE VANCE: *. . . I think it would be fair to say that at the very early stages of the anti-pornography analysis, most feminists were quite taken with it. You know, it was novel and it was quite forceful. It made a number of interesting and important points. As you moved into the 80s, the force of that analysis just began to diminish because people began to question it and it became very clear that there was no unanimous opinion within feminism about this, about the nature of pornography, about the degree of sexism in it, about whether it constituted a special danger. Of course, some people clearly thought it did but other people clearly thought it didn't.*

And there remained also great disagreement about whether it was desirable in any shape or form to have states or governments in any way intervene . . . Some feminists concluded that if feminists themselves can't agree about this, it's a little foolish to be handing this [power] over to a state, which is usually not feminist-controlled . . .

SOON after Joe Arvay starting working with Little Sister's, he realized their case would be profoundly affected by another trial: that of Donald Butler, the retailer of mainly heterosexual porn whose Winnipeg video shop was raided in August 1987 by local police. Some of the seized tapes were found to be obscene and Butler fought his convictions all the way to the Supreme Court of Canada. At last, Canada's 1959 obscenity law would be facing a constitutional challenge.

Butler's lawyers argued that the law violated his right to freedom of expression under the 1982 *Charter of Rights and Freedoms*. His lawyers weren't the only ones arguing that line: Joe Arvay also appeared before the Supreme Court, representing the B.C. Civil Liberties Association. Arvay and the BCCLA had been busy preparing the Little Sister's trial, where they too had planned to tackle the obscenity law and its use by Canada Customs. But the Butler case had overtaken Little Sister's, so it was off to Ottawa as intervenors, in hopes of influencing the precedent-setting case.

When the historic *R. v. Butler* decision came on February 27, 1992, it wasn't BCCLA's arguments that carried the day. Instead, the Supreme Court embraced the views of another intervenor, the feminist Women's Legal Education and Action Fund (LEAF). The unanimous *Butler* ruling declared that the obscenity law was legitimate, even though it clearly violated freedom of expression. In the parlance of section 1 of the *Charter,* the law was a reasonable limit that could be "justified in a free and democratic society." Then the Supreme Court went further. It reinterpreted the old provisions to incorporate some supposedly modern, supposedly progressive beliefs about the effect of pornography on society—and on women in particular.

In essence, the Supreme Court accepted what the pro-censorship LEAF had argued: Pornography that is violent, degrading and/or dehumanizing violates women's right to equality, which is explicitly guaranteed in the *Charter of Rights and Freedoms'* section 15. (Unlike in the U.S., where attempts to enshrine an Equal Rights Amendment in the constitution were blocked by right-wing forces, Canadian feminists had successfully lobbied for the inclusion of sex equality in the *Charter.*) According to the *Butler* decision, ". . . if true equality between male and female is to be achieved, we cannot ignore the threat to equality resulting from exposure to . . . violent and degrading materials. Materials portraying women as a class worthy of sexual exploitation and abuse have a negative impact on the individual's sense of self-worth and acceptance."

Supporters of the *Butler* decision, notably LEAF and other pro-censorship feminists, claimed a revolution in obscenity law. No longer would the offence be based on antiquated notions of indecency and immorality, they said, but on *harm*. "The harms-based approach . . . in *Butler*," said

LEAF's Helena Orton at the time of the decision, "shows that the court has refocused its approach to obscenity. The court recognized that community standards in Canada will not tolerate harms to women . . ."

Butler divided pornography into three categories: (1) explicit sex with violence, real or implied—this would almost always be judged obscene; (2) explicit sex without violence, but which subjects people to treatment that is degrading and dehumanizing—this may be judged obscene, depending on the risk of harm; and (3) nonviolent, explicit sex that is neither degrading nor dehumanizing; according to *Butler,* "[this] is generally tolerated by society . . . unless it employs children in its production."

The *Butler* ruling also constructed a three-stage test for obscenity. First, the court would consider whether the material was harmful according to community standards. Despite some fiddling, *Butler* maintained the existing idea of "who" the community is: ". . . the arbiter [of obscenity] is the community as a whole. The courts must determine as best they can what the community would tolerate others being exposed to on the basis of the degree of harm that may flow from such exposure." Obviously, this wording leaves a judge enormous discretionary powers to apply, as *Butler* says, "a general instinctive sense of what is decent and what is indecent, of what is clean and what is dirty."

The second test considers whether the material "may be said to exploit sex in a degrading or dehumanizing manner." *Butler* considers such materials to harm women (and sometimes men) and to ". . . run against the principles of equality and dignity." Significantly, the terms "degrading" and "dehumanizing" are not defined.

The final test involves considering whether the material, though violent or degrading, is redeemed by a "wider artistic, literary, or other similar purpose." This test of "internal necessities" demands that the work be judged as a whole and that any sexual content be internally consistent with the work's larger purpose. Says *Butler,* "Artistic expression rests at the heart of freedom of expression values and any doubt in this regard must be resolved in favour of freedom of expression."

The Supreme Court also considered the issue of consent, addressing the feminist concern that some pornography promotes a rape myth: that women enjoy being sexually assaulted and abused. In a significant passage, *Butler* says, "In appreciation of whether material is degrading or dehumanizing, the appearance of consent is not necessarily determinative. Consent cannot save materials that otherwise contain degrading or dehumanizing scenes. Sometimes the very appearance of consent makes the depicted acts even more degrading or dehumanizing."

This idea of "fake consent" was destined to become the *carte blanche* by which some judges would find queer S/M materials to be obscene. In fact, *Butler* has so far proven to be a disaster for lesbians and gays. When Little Sister's finally entered the courtroom in October 1994, Joe Arvay could no longer argue against the obscenity law itself—*Butler* had settled that matter. But what he could argue for was *an interpretation* of *Butler* that respected gay and lesbian lives.

Dworkin, MacKinnon and LEAF

LEAF's persuasive arguments to the Supreme Court were drawn from the blueprint of feminist anti-pornography theory, most forcefully articulated by two Americans, Andrea Dworkin and Catharine A. MacKinnon. Indeed, MacKinnon helped write LEAF's brief in the *Butler* case, when she lived in Toronto in 1991 and taught at Osgoode Hall Law School.

MacKinnon and her followers see porn as causing actual harm—physical, mental, emotional—not only to the female porn model and actor, or to the woman confronted against her will by porn in daily life, but to women in general, living in a sexist culture dominated by an often misogynist view of their sexuality. The sexist packaging of women, pervasive in advertising and all modern media, has been under attack by feminists since the 1960s. For pro-censorship advocates, however, pornography is seen as especially degrading, and almost the root cause of women's oppression. As the principle of this concept, American author Robin Morgan famously declared in 1974: "Pornography is the theory, rape is the practice." (Morgan later moved away from such a literal expression of feminist concerns.)

Throughout the 1980s, Dworkin and MacKinnon attempted to get their harms-based framework legislated. But they didn't want to reform criminal obscenity laws. In fact, they vehemently opposed criminal law restraints on pornography, saying that such laws only empowered male-dominated courts and police, not women. Instead, they viewed porn as a civil rights issue, where women needed *power,* not protection. MacKinnon and Dworkin took a civil law tack, advocating municipal ordinances that would give women the right to sue pornographers—retailers, producers, consumers—for damages. Ordinances were introduced in Minneapolis and Indianapolis, but they failed, hitting the wall of the American constitution's protection of freedom of speech.

Catharine MacKinnon, opposed to criminal sanctions in her own country, was nevertheless happy to fashion a revised criminal law in Canada. LEAF and other feminists found MacKinnon's anti-porn theories attractive, and the opportunity to influence the obscenity law was irresistible. LEAF is a non-profit group founded in 1985 to fight for the rights of Canadian women under the equality guarantees of the 1982 *Charter*. Largely composed of volunteers—mainly lawyers, law teachers and students—LEAF does important test case litigation and research, and has intervened in issues as diverse as reproductive freedom, child support and the rights of sexual assault complainants. Like other professionally oriented feminist groups, LEAF has an uneasy relationship with the grassroots, and while the organization has a healthy share of lesbian members, it has never been closely identified with lesbian rights.

LEAF intervened in *Butler* to inject a feminist slant *à la* MacKinnon into the country's censorship apparatus. According to LEAF's Karen Busby, writing post-*Butler* in a Canadian law journal, the existing law had been riddled with a moralism "rooted in negative perceptions about sex, sexuality in its varied forms and women's bodies in general." LEAF rejected such moralism and wanted the law to reflect "a harms-based paradigm that was capable of recognizing the effect of pornography on women in society."

LEAF claimed to have moved the law away from morality and smut, towards equality and harm. The *Butler* decision would mean that mere sexual explicitness, in any combination of genitals and genders, was no longer a concern; the problem area became those scenarios that depicted the subordination or injury of women. Theoretically, this paradigm shift would provide radical relief for gay porn, since most gay obscenity charges (and Canada Customs seizures) featured depictions of male anal penetration—neither sexist nor violent, and presumably no longer "degrading." *Butler's* new focus on pornography's threat to women's equality seemed to spare lesbian and gay porn altogether.

The truth, of course, lay elsewhere. And LEAF was at least partially responsible. An infamous remark by Kathleen E. Mahoney, Calgary law professor and co-counsel in LEAF's *Butler* intervention, showed how LEAF had pandered, consciously or otherwise, to judicial homophobia. In the May/June 1992 issue of *Ms.* magazine, Mahoney told Canadian journalist Michele Landsberg how LEAF helped sway the Supreme Court: "How did we do it?" said Mahoney. "We showed them the porn—and among the seized videos were some horrifically violent and degrading gay movies.

We made the point that the abused men in the films were being treated like women—and the judges got it. Otherwise, men can't put themselves in our shoes."

Yet other feminists, on both sides of the border, could clearly see the dangers of giving the courts a pro-woman tool to do a policeman's job. As early as 1985, American feminist Carole Vance had warned of the anti-lesbian and anti-gay implications of MacKinnon and Dworkin's theories in an eerily prophetic passage in the landmark Canadian anthology, *Women Against Censorship*. With co-authors Nan Hunter and Lisa Duggan, Vance looked at how anti-porn municipal ordinances could be used: "Practically speaking, the ordinances could result in attempts to eliminate the images associated with homosexuality. Doubtless there are heterosexual women who believe that lesbianism is a 'degrading' form of 'subordination.' Since the ordinances allow for suits against materials in which men appear 'in place of women,' far-right anti-pornography crusaders could use these laws to suppress gay male pornography. Imagine a Jerry Falwell-style conservative filing a complaint against a gay male bookstore for selling sexually explicit materials showing men with other men in 'degrading' or 'submissive' or 'objectified' postures—all in the name of protecting women."

The Flow of Harm
Shortly after the 1992 *Butler* decision, Glad Day Books in Toronto found itself facing Vance's worst-case scenario in two obscenity trials of gay and lesbian periodicals. The first case—*Glad Day v. Canada,* also known as the Hayes decision—involved a motley collection of explicit gay literature, satirical comic books and soft-porn magazines seized by Canada Customs before *Butler.* The second case—*R. v. Scythes,* the Paris decision—concerned the police seizure of a lesbian sex magazine, *Bad Attitude,* published in the U.S. (To date, *R. v. Scythes* is one of few Canadian obscenity trials initiated and resolved post-*Butler.*) The decisions came down within months of each other, and both raised unsettling questions about how the new obscenity law could be applied in some very old, very homophobic ways.

Judge Frank Hayes' 1992 guilty verdict in the Customs seizures of Glad Day's porn was a bold leap into a perspective on homosexuality common to pulpits of another century. On trial were publications like *Advocate Men,* a pin-up style magazine; *Movie Star Confidential,* a trashy comic book; and *Humongous—True Gay Encounters,* short stories about explicit gay sex between strangers. In his ruling, Hayes liberally paraphrased the language and conceptual framework of *Butler.* But *Butler's* concern about "dehumanizing" sexual representations of women became Hayes' concern about "sub-human" sex—his basic evaluation of homosexual acts. Depictions of anal penetration were decried as not "positive, affectionate, or human." While *Butler* referred to the "flow of harm"—a somewhat simplistic notion of cause and effect between image and action—Hayes made the notion literal: "clearly harm would flow from the release" of *Harry Chess,* a comic detective parody. Hayes' assessment of the tame, consensual sex in the magazine *OG (Oriental Guys)* was that there was ". . . a strong inference of a risk of harm that might flow from the community being exposed to this material." As for *Wolfbiorin the Viking,* a cartoon illustration of four men having oral and anal sex, Hayes offered a skewed version of *Butler* when he wrote: "[this publication] is such that society would formally recognize it as being incomparable [sic] with its proper functioning." (*Butler* actually reads: "[materials that] predisposed persons to act in an antisocial manner as, for example, the physical mistreatment of women by men, . . . which society formally recognizes as incompatible with its proper functioning.")

A little later, John Scythes, the new owner of Glad Day, found himself facing the judicial wrath of Justice Claude Paris of the Ontario Provincial Court. Two months after the *Butler* ruling, Toronto police had charged Scythes with the possession and sale of *Bad Attitude,* a low-gloss quarterly from Cambridge, Massachusetts. When Justice Paris delivered his guilty verdict in early 1993, he had obviously convinced himself that depictions of lesbian s/m were indistinguishable from straight porn. *Bad Attitude* contained a story by Trish Thomas entitled "Wunna My Fantasies." Thomas' raunchy tale explored an s/m encounter between two strangers. Although explicitly a sexual fantasy, and explicitly lesbian, Paris declared the story in violation of women's equality. *Butler's* "community tolerance test is blind to sexual orientation or practices," Paris wrote, after commenting that he had "detected during this trial a concern that the Court will find relevant the sexual orientation of *Bad Attitude.*" It wasn't; Paris was confident that sexual orientation was irrelevant: "This material flashes every light and blows every whistle of obscenity. Enjoyable sex after subordination by bondage and physical abuse at the hands of a total stranger. If I replaced the aggressor in this article with a man there would be very few people in the community who would not recognize the potential for harm. The fact that the aggressor is a female is irrelevant because the potential for harm remains."

Adapting to What the *Butler* Saw

Needless to say, the Little Sister's case was in for a major rewrite after the 1992 *Butler* decision. Joe Arvay described their amended Statement of Claim in a letter to the B.C. Civil Liberties Association, explaining the bookstore would now "take into account the fact that the Supreme Court of Canada has decided *Butler.*" One of BCCLA's original attractions to the Little Sister's case was that it offered a means to argue against the existing obscenity law. *Butler* meant that game was over.

"It is critical," Arvay wrote, ". . . that we emphasize in the claim, more than we have to date, the difference between homosexual and heterosexual pornography. The emphasis and the focus of the case, however, remains on the evils of prior restraint."

Ironically, *Butler* could be viewed as actually bolstering Little Sister's position. As a ruling based on equality principles, *Butler* lent itself to supporting Jim Deva's and Bruce Smyth's claim that their right to equal treatment under the law was being violated. Further, Canada Customs' fixation on materials with anal penetration seemed no longer supportable.

But the reality of life post-*Butler* was anything but rosy. Little Sister's faced a censorious climate and harsh legal interpretations of "degradation" in lesbian and gay S/M material. Canada Customs behaved as though nothing had changed, seizing exactly the same materials as before. And freedom of expression was now juxtaposed against a slippery concept called "harm."

There are moments in everyone's life when someone asks you to do something, you breezily say "sure" and soon discover you've made a big mistake.

JANINE
Agreeing to be a panellist at the 1993 National Association of Women and the Law (NAWL) conference in Vancouver was just such a moment. I was caught off guard one fall morning, strolling around Vancouver's gorgeous sea wall, finishing the last few kilometres of the Walk for AIDS. Jane Farrow, another Toronto transplant, approached me. She was organizing a panel on censorship, at a feminist law conference, and did I have any suggestions for panel-

lists . . . ? She mentioned a woman she knew I wasn't crazy about, then Jane said, "I know you're really busy . . ." (lengthy pause, opening up like a crater) and I fell headlong.

"I'll do it, Jane, when is it?"

I gave the February conference little thought. But the closer it got, and as more people learned about my participation, I sensed the vibes. This wasn't going to be a church social. Maybe it was the way friends and acquaintances looked when they heard the news. Mostly a kind of "thank god it's you, not me" look. Or an "Oooohhhh Janine . . ." and then silence. Any NAWL event would be full of LEAF members and supporters, and this was their first post-*Butler* conference. For some observers, the panel had become a feminist version of *The Clash of the Titans* and I was no Titan.

I knew I was in deep trouble when Jane kept dodging me, probably anticipating I was on the verge of dropping out. I phoned the people I was still talking to and asked for advice. It became apparent that I couldn't give a political dissertation on the *Butler* decision or a feminist analysis of the censorship debates. I wasn't a lawyer or a theoretician. I was a bookseller and could only speak about how censorship impacted on me directly.

Mere days before the conference, I was hunched over the computer at Little Sister's, trying to pound out an interesting, snappy piece that I could just read out and be done with. But it was neither snappy nor interesting. I had to face facts: in trying to detail the daily doses of censorship, I had become long-winded. Frantically, on the day of the event, I arranged to have coffee with Persimmon Blackbridge, my friend from the Kiss & Tell artist trio. Persimmon has an incredible ability to cut through things, making it sound far less confusing than it really is; sometimes she even makes you believe you thought of something yourself. Persimmon is also very calming—and calm was what I needed. I left her and headed for the conference.

The butterflies had departed my stomach and were free-floating through my bloodstream when I reached the conference site, a downtown hotel. Jane gave me a couple of words of advice, a nod of encouragement, then sent me on my way. I was lugging a box full of books and magazines that had been stopped by Canada Customs over the years. I was determined to make one point, if only one: The books and magazines being stopped by Customs were not just gay male or S/M, but a real cross-section. They were as varied as the people in the room waiting for the panel to begin.

I took a seat on the platform, depositing the box on the table in front of me. To my left were the two other panellists: law professor (University of

Calgary) and LEAF rep Kathleen Mahoney, who had been LEAF's co-counsel on *Butler*; and Anne Derrick, the lawyer for *Pandora*, a feminist newspaper in Halifax. *Pandora* was busy fighting a human rights complaint from a man, who claimed the collective discriminated *against men* in their editorial policies. Whew.

Anne Derrick spoke first, then Kathleen Mahoney talked about LEAF's involvement in *Butler*, extolling the decision's merits. I was there to give the other side, the fallout for gay and lesbian bookstores and artists after *Butler*. My voice was about as forceful as flour is flavourful, and the words I had so diligently written were now completely illegible. The room was full; for me, mainly full of strangers. Whenever I lost my focus, I zoomed in on the small corner where Persimmon, the other Kiss & Tell girls and my co-worker, Lisa Lowe, were sitting. I brought out book after book, magazine after magazine, describing how each had been held by Customs. I tried to give a detailed account of what it meant to face these detainments, invasions, day after day. Kathleen Mahoney then defended LEAF's involvement in *Butler* and railed against pornography. There was hardly a word from Anne Derrick after her initial remarks.

The women from the floor soon got into the act, speaking for and against censorship—mostly for. I thought things were as heated as they could get, then a woman accused me of using emotional blackmail in my presentation. Hey, I *was* emotional. The room was emotional. The conference, and the fate of detained books, were emotional. I didn't really respond to her criticism. People expected me to, but I simply didn't know how to. Her accusation was something I would have expected at another conference altogether. I mean, this was a feminist conference, and hadn't women been fighting for years against being called "emotional," as a way of silencing us in the male world? I felt like I'd been punched in the gut.

The room started to boil. When Kathleen Mahoney described "felching" as something she thought was an obscene sexual act between two men, another women countered by saying that she didn't find it obscene at all. (I'm still not sure what felching is.) If anything was becoming clear, it was that nothing was clear, even for the women in this room. Near the end, a very handsome woman with an American accent took the floor. Her name was Ann Scales and she spoke about the need for the two sides to work together, to find some resolution. She was willing to help Little Sister's, but she was also steadfast in her defence of *Butler*. But Canada Customs, she said, should not be messing with gay and lesbian material.

The panel ended with the obligatory thank-yous and we stood up to depart. I piled the books back into the box and was starting to leave when a woman stopped me.

"Are you really serious about working with LEAF on this, because if you are, then maybe I could do something . . . ?" I followed her to the back of the room where Ann Scales stood talking. Ann was a visiting law instructor at the University of British Columbia; she made her home in New Mexico. She was immensely sympathetic to what I had just experienced and gave me her name and number. "Call if I can be of any help in the court case," Ann said.

Little Sister's lawyer Joe Arvay did eventually call Ann Scales and she testified at our trial. But that day, I was reminded how many bridges still needed to be built—and that nothing comes easy when it really matters.

The Vance Advance

Professor Carole S. Vance, anthropologist and epidemiologist at the Columbia School of Public Health in New York, presents herself as a surprisingly low-key warrior in the porn wars. An elegant woman, Vance wears her formidable reputation with a reserve that may be her best defence; after all, she has spent years as a field observer in the feminist trenches. The Little Sister's trial, however, demanded that she step up, front and centre, as an expert witness in a court of law. It was no small move.

In essays and lectures throughout the 1980s, Vance had charted the pornography-censorship controversies with an anthropologist's dispassionate rigour, though she personally held an undisguised bias against state regulation. She had organized the famous 1982 feminist conference on sexuality at Barnard College, New York, which had erupted into a take-no-prisoners scandal, cutting the first deep divisions among contemporary feminists on the issue of pornography. The range of the Barnard conference had been deliberately, provocatively wide, and the personal attacks unleashed on its organizers and participants by anti-porn advocates had been ferocious. Vance grew to be especially critical of the alignment of anti-porn feminists with the Religious Right over their shared concern for the "degradation of women"—and their shared faith in government intervention to solve the problem. Among other things, she had spent over three hundred hours observing the U.S. Attorney General's Commission on Pornography (the Meese Commission, 1985–86).

From the early days of formulating his strategy, Arvay had looked to

Vance's work to expand the feminist debate beyond narrow anti-porn arguments. He wanted to convince the court that not all feminists were pro-censorship and that LEAF represented only one stream of feminist thought. The obscenity law was a reality, but *Butler's* interpretation was still far from settled, and Arvay saw the Little Sister's case as an incomparable chance to steer Canada's obscenity law in the direction of freedom of expression. Vance's strong credentials as an anti-censorship feminist would help.

Like other Little Sister's witnesses, Vance had submitted a written version of her testimony to the Crown years before. She had made herself available as a witness, only to have the trial postponed; when October 1994 rolled around, she was tied up with other commitments and, regrettably, was dropped from the witness schedule. But at the last moment, Vance was parachuted in when Arvay sensed a dangerous weakening in the pro-porn, anti-censorship angle of the Little Sister's case.

The problem arose during the punishing cross-examination of Becki Ross, Little Sister's expert witness on lesbian representation. Ross' cross-examination was an ordeal, and Arvay feared that the reasonable face of anti-censorship feminism had been undermined. He urged Ross to call Vance from a pay phone in the courthouse during a lunch break. Ross not only got through to Vance, but quickly conveyed how imperative her appearance would be for Little Sister's. Within twenty-four hours, Vance had arrived in Vancouver, prepared for almost anything.

"The Underlying History of Sexuality"

With Carole Vance, the Crown and the provincial Attorney General pursued their most vigorous preventative measures against any would-be witness—save perhaps Ann Scales—and for good reason. As far as the government was concerned, *Butler* had signalled the end to the feminist porn debate. A victor had been declared and there was to be no rematch. For hours, the government lawyers and Arvay wrangled over Vance's presence. The Crown argued that they had neither sufficient notice of her sudden appearance nor time to prepare their cross-examination. Furthermore, they said, her evidence was irrelevant. Vance sat unobtrusively in the dock during an entire day of debate, waiting patiently for the judge to determine if, legally speaking, she would appear at all.

Justice Kenneth Smith pointed out the next day that Arvay's witness list was merely a courtesy to the defence, who were claiming they had been "lulled into a false sense of security" in thinking Vance wasn't going to testify in person. Then Smith decided that the only way he could judge the relevance of her evidence was by hearing it first. This became his established pattern: to admit almost all testimony, and then assess its weight.

Justice Smith's predisposition to hear Little Sister's evidence, rather than to allow the Crown to decide what would be helpful for him to hear, was tremendously encouraging to the bookstore's contingent. After the first week in the tiny courtroom, where the emotional testimony of Jearld Moldenhauer spilled messily over the legalistic boundaries, and the restless public seemed to threaten the proper management of his trial, Smith's remarks came as a relief. Little Sister's supporters had been alive to any signs of judicial displeasure towards Arvay's approach. But Smith showed an unwavering attention to all the witnesses and a talent for legal debate with both sides. He was loosening the reins, to the point of a rare smile or dry remark, and tensions in Courtroom 65 gradually eased.

When Vance was finally allowed to speak the next day, she began by explaining the basis of her expertise. She described how the contemporary study of epidemiology focuses on social behaviour, not simply on traditional ideas about the spread of disease. (Later, during cross-examination by the Crown, Vance offered a succinct picture of her work: "The focus . . . is to examine the underlying history of sexuality . . . Many scholars see certain common themes regarding the history of sexuality and the history of regulation, in which cultural factors [such as] sexuality, gender, the family, and others . . . influence the development of thinking about text, sexual text and imagery, and influence the history of regulation.")

Vance explained that in English-speaking countries, concern about the danger of sexual materials is very high, typically connected to "dangers of mortality, of death, of health risks, of moral dissolution, of individual dissolution, notions of social decay, notions of great danger of pollution to particular social classes or groups, notions of moral impurity, and notions almost, in some cases, of disintegration and degeneration of the government and the society."

Arvay wanted to establish the arbitrary nature of many assumptions about sex and morality. He asked Vance to clarify what she meant by the "special" treatment of sex, where "the normal rules that people use to think about things or evaluate things . . . are not the rules that are necessarily applied to sex."

"Well, for example," Vance said, "there is the idea that sexuality is an uncontrolled force in the way that other human desires or emotions are not thought to be . . . A contrasting example would be food preferences. Differences in preferences about sexual acts in no way can be compared to the way food preferences are thought about."

"Are we talking about . . . ?" asked Arvay.

"Someone likes broccoli, someone doesn't."

Vance, the expert lecturer and vivid storyteller, presented a time line of attitudinal changes towards sexuality and its representations. She described how the requirement that sex be linked to procreation and marriage gave way in the late Victorian era to interest in "whether [sex] gave the individuals participating in it pleasure, intimacy, connection . . ." This shift was accompanied by panic about the falling birth rate in white middle-class marriages, concerns about marital lust, and an obsession over the threat of prostitutes to the family. But towards the end of the 19th century, the importance of pleasure, consent and choice had entered the public discourse on sexuality.

The emerging scientific and psychological perspective on sexuality seemed to offer a rational retreat from the Christian-tinged moralism of the past, but Vance noted an interesting phenomenon.

"In many ways, this [new] biomedical discourse mapped over the [old] theological discourse," she said, "and it was not surprising that many of the acts that religious authorities thought were immoral were then described by the biomedical authorities as pathological."

Vance spoke with the tolerance and curiosity of an anthropologist, and her manner was almost serene, compared to the staccato-like confrontations that had characterized earlier testimony. Arvay allowed her to unfold the backdrop to the contemporary sex debates, and the courtroom became a temporary oasis, blossoming with the fascinating shapes of human sexuality.

These conflicting moral and scientific discourses never simply disappear, said Vance, but continue to co-exist and transmute. And they find expression—and reaction—in a range of cultural representations, from high art to pornography. The "special" nature of sex, said Vance, makes the evaluation of these depictions highly subjective. People have little opportunity to see different materials and are unaccustomed to frank talk about sexual images.

"People's reaction to [a sexual] image often evokes their opinion of the practices being shown," said Vance. "Do they themselves like it? Do they themselves do it? Do they find it disgusting, unnatural, repulsive, frightening? . . . I think there is a tendency for people to assume that the most [normative] acts are easily consented to and don't require a special inquiry about whether consent was obtained or not. Based on my interviews, I have also observed that the acts with which individuals are most unfamiliar are the ones in which they think consent has probably either not been obtained or [was] very problematic."

Vance discussed the troubling notion that "fantasy equals reality" in sexual images, especially with regard to photographs or film.

"Do we think [a sexual image] is a documentary? And if so, of what?" Vance asked, posing an essential question. She invited the court to consider how people interpret a fictionalized war film differently than they may interpret a porn image. "Because of assumptions we make about the conditions of [a war film's] production . . . we don't even think about it very much. We don't seriously leave [the theatre] and say, 'That was a good movie but it is really unfortunate that all of these people are now dead.' "

Throughout Vance's testimony, Arvay was constructing a body of historical evidence leading up to the feminist anti-pornography movement. Vance struggled to remain even-handed in her assessment. She described how the early anti-porn movement held educational events, publicly and privately, to expose the troubling aspects of pornography. But some feminist slide shows on pornography, for instance, began to take on predictable, even manipulative, features, such as focusing on s/m images, even though s/m represented a very small percentage of the porn market.

"s/m pornography became a very key example to [anti-porn feminists] of the harms of pornography," said Vance. "And embedded in s/m, to them, was non-consent, force, coercion, real activity as opposed to fantasy, and a whole set of activities that they believed women could not consent to."

As Vance's testimony progressed, the government lawyers became increasingly uncomfortable with her remarks on the Meese Commission, the U.S. government's investigation into pornography during President

Ronald Reagan's second term. An earlier American commission—the U.S. Commission on Obscenity and Pornography (1970)—had undertaken an extensive sociological probe into the relationship of pornography to violence against women, and had found no ascertainable link. But these findings were unacceptable to the Republicans of the mid-1980s, and the Meese Commission was specifically charged with determining new ways to control pornography. Meese essentially shifted the focus of inquiry from scientific verification to first-person accounts of harm from pornography.

Arvay knew that the Meese Commission's findings, which had virtually replaced the earlier commission's views in all U.S. government discussions of pornography, would be heavily relied on by the Crown during the Little Sister's trial. Indeed, Meese was cited in the *Butler* decision as part of that "substantial body of opinion" supporting a harms-based definition of obscenity.

After senior Crown lawyer Hans Van Iperen protested that Vance's testimony on Meese would not be "helpful" to his lordship, Justice Smith turned to Arvay.

"Mr. Van Iperen tells me he is not going to introduce any evidence with respect to the Meese Commission," said Smith.

"Except the [provincial Attorney General] isn't telling you that," replied Arvay. "In fact, the province is telling you it might."

Angela Westmacott, representing the province, admitted they had "not indicated one way or the other" whether they would cite Meese in their evidence, implicitly reserving the right to do so. Arvay argued for the relevance of Vance's testimony as an expert witness by suggesting that the Meese Commission was "the closest thing, for an ethnographer, to a laboratory" in her area of expertise: anthropological research into the regulation of sexual norms. Once again, Justice Smith elected to hear Vance's testimony.

"[The Meese Commission] spent a great deal of time devising a system to categorize pornographic material," Vance began, "and they came up with a system of four categories. They were: violent and degrading; non-violent and degrading; non-violent and non-degrading, and mere nudity."

"And was there any consensus as to the kinds of practices or representations of practices that would fit in any of those categories?" Arvay asked.

"Well, it turned out that there was not," Vance replied. "That is, a great deal of discussion went into determining these categories with, apparently, a fair amount of agreement about the meaning of the categories. At the end of the discussion, one Meese Commission member said, 'Wouldn't it be helpful to the American public if we, in our report, could simply provide examples of what we mean by these different kinds of pornographic categories?'

"And, thus, the Chair invited members to provide examples of what they thought should belong in each category and . . . a great disagreement ensued between Commissioners about what to put in each category. Disagreements about what was degrading, disagreements about what was violent, ranging from, 'Is homosexuality degrading? Is oral sex degrading? Is s/m violent? Is nudity of a certain kind possibly degrading?' It was a very elaborate discussion and they, in fact, could not reach an agreement."

Vance's testimony made it clear that disagreements about what was pornographic or obscene, even among government appointees who felt themselves most qualified, had reached absurd levels. In effect, Arvay was suggesting, "What, then, could we possibly expect of a Customs officer, armed only with Memorandum D9-1-1?"

By the end of her testimony, Vance had presented a credible history of the shifting, emotionally charged attitudes towards sex and its representation. She had unmasked the biases behind societal "norms" and exposed the subjective, almost paranoiac, mindset behind a community standard of obscenity. Whether Vance had counterbalanced the weight of *Butler's* recent interpretations in Justice Smith's mind remained to be seen. But she had successfully laid the groundwork for many Little Sister's witnesses to come.

□ FOUR □

Name Your Pleasure

JOSEPH ARVAY: *To what extent does sexual arousal play a role in your motivation in writing a book such as* Macho Sluts?

PAT CALIFIA: *Well, because the work is sexually explicit, it would be ridiculous for me to claim that arousal is not one of the effects that I intended to have upon some readers. But it is by no means the only response that I expect readers to have from the work.*

I use sexuality in the fiction partly as a way to intrigue the reader and engage their attention. I also attempt, as a writer, to disturb. There are also parts of the writing that I would expect to cause a reaction of anger and grief and, in that process of getting the reader very deeply emotionally engaged with the fiction, I hope to encourage them to think about some of the ideas in these pieces.

THE capacity crowd that awaited Pat Califia, the hottest S/M writer on the lesbian scene, was suitably shocked at her appearance. Known for her controversial look—mass of peroxide-blond hair, aviator sunglasses, body swathed from head to toe in black leather—Califia rose from the courtroom's public gallery where she had been quietly sitting all along, her face displaying a kind of thoughtful vulnerability. She wore a calf-length skirt topped by a boxy, beige corduroy jacket that almost anyone's dad could have lent her. It was the fashion equivalent of the simple black dress that defence lawyers traditionally require of their scandalous female clients. But Arvay had specifically ruled out black. Califia was in camouflage, to legitimize herself and to disarm the Canadian judge who was about to hear her unflinching account of lesbian S/M.

Califia has a long history of moving straight into the centre of controversy. From office work in the early 1970s at the Daughters of Bilitis, the first lesbian organization in the U.S., to best-selling author of fiction, essays and sex manuals in the 1980s, she had chosen to risk more and more of herself personally and politically. Califia's writing came relatively late, after years of activism first as a feminist, then as a lesbian and finally as an openly S/M dyke. From "Jessie," her first published short story, to the best-selling fiction collection *Macho Sluts* and the collected essays of *Public Sex,* Califia has been admired and attacked for her lesbian-centred approach to S/M, as well as for her exposé of the whole S/M subculture. Her "masterly" depiction of that world seemed to dare her increasingly heterosexual readership *not* to be turned on sexually and conceptually by desire's relationship to power and pain. In an era when unequal power dynamics were usually criticized, Califia laid bare those dynamics—and celebrated and practised them openly.

Arvay tendered Califia as one of a few witnesses summoned to talk about their own creative work. *Macho Sluts* had the distinction of being Little Sister's most frequently banned book. In fact, it had rarely been out of Canada Customs' internal appeal process since its release in 1989 by Alyson Publications. The stories in *Macho Sluts* don't simply experiment with established S/M motifs—the Victorian incest triangle, encounters with cops, group sex, leatherman with leatherman—they seem to defiantly cross every taboo. Customs appeared hell bent on detaining every individual copy of the book, both before and after the *Butler* decision. *Macho Sluts* went through the entire Customs appeal process, to the highest level in Ottawa, five times in as many years, and was found to be admissible each time. Yet earlier determinations had no apparent impact on later seizures.

Nothing seemed to bother Customs as much as gay and lesbian S/M. In court, Arvay's task was to deal rationally and sympathetically with the most misunderstood, demonized material the bookstore could be accused of distributing. On the stand, Pat Califia's task was to defuse the

S/M myths and prejudices, particularly those created by anti-S/M feminists. As Carole Vance had testified, S/M porn historically has been "the epicentre of harm" for the feminist anti-porn movement. It seemed the clearest reflection of men's infliction of physical pain and mental cruelty on women. What to make, then, of lesbian S/M imagery and fiction, or of gay men's, or, for that matter, of the dominatrix in heterosexual porn?

Arvay began by asking Califia her motivation as editor of the frequently detained *The Lesbian S/M Safety Manual,* a 1988 sexual health guide.

"The purpose was to educate women who do S/M with other women," Califia said, "about ways to fulfil fantasies about dominance and submission in ways that are physically and emotionally safe, provided that both partners are consenting adults and both of them find these types of fantasies mutually pleasurable . . .

"While I don't think that mainstream mass-market pornography should be banned, a lot of it is not very accurate from a sex education standpoint. A lot of it describes people doing things that, in fact, could be damaging or could be dangerous to their health. I was very concerned, especially for people who were isolated, who did not have the opportunity to be educated by more experienced members of the community, that injury or even death might result if people took that mass-market pornography as their model."

Califia's intentions as a writer were especially important to Arvay. The characterization of S/M as the mere infliction of pain for sexual pleasure was central to the Crown's case, which made no distinction between the pain and degradation of a sexual assault and S/M's rituals of pain/pleasure and submission. As *Butler* had stated: "Sometimes the very appearance of consent makes the depicted acts even more degrading or dehumanizing." But it was *the reality* of consent, rather than its appearance, that was fundamental to the mainstream's horror of S/M. The very fact that people *do* consent, with fervour and full knowledge, was what made S/M so disturbing to the traditional legal and anti-porn feminist ideas of consent.

Califia began by telling the court how the desire to express herself sexually was interwoven with the desire to write. She described her process with "Jessie," a short story that first appeared in the 1981 anthology *Coming to Power: Writings and Graphics on Lesbian S/M.*

"I wrote 'Jessie' long before I ever actually did any S/M," Califia testified. "It was during a period of my life when I was suffering from [extreme] writer's block. I would begin a piece of fiction and I wouldn't be able to complete it and I would destroy it. So I decided to write something that was not necessarily for publication. I would write something that was about my own sexual truth, even though I'd never seen a piece like that written by a lesbian. Certainly not by a woman who thought of herself as a feminist . . . [But] I would just tell a piece of what was true for me.

"That short story was a breakthrough for me as a writer. I was able to complete it. I was eventually able to share it with others and it became more than a work of fiction. It became an organizing tool. It became a way to signal to other women who might be interested in the sexual practices that there was someone else . . . who was available to discuss those things with them. And it gave other women permission, whether they were writers or not, to start to think about and make that sexuality more public."

Califia's account of her emergence as a writer would be echoed by other queer writers appearing for Little Sister's, both novelists and theoreticians. Arvay wanted to show the court that, for lesbians and gays, "freedom of expression" meant being able to honestly depict their sexual realities. Yet honest depictions of lesbian and gay lives have traditionally been equated with, and condemned as, pornography. Legal and philosophical debates about freedom of expression often split over the relative value of different "speech" and whether to protect the more controversial forms. Pornography has been demoted by many to speech without meaning because its appeal seems to lie less in intellectual than in physical stimulation. Arvay wanted to make clear the relationship between pornographic writings and "high value" speech, like philosophy, politics and culture.

He asked Califia to explain the role of sexual explicitness in her work.

"It's partly because I think that if you cannot find any fiction that describes people who are like you," Califia began, "people who have the kind of relationships you would like to have, people who have the kind of sexuality you would like to have, then you begin to feel as if you're crazy. You don't exist. You're marginal, you're not important, and this creates a great deal of self-hatred and self-doubt. It also creates, I think, a lot of repression and just plain human misery. So partly the fiction is written in an attempt to make it easier for others . . .

"It is my belief that fiction can sometimes be even more useful as an educational tool than non-fiction. It's easier to absorb. It's more entertaining. It's often more accessible."

Arvay also wanted Califia, like Carole Vance, to counterbalance the strong, pro-censorship accent of feminism, especially in the light of *Butler.*

"You have many times . . . said that you are a feminist," said Arvay, "and I would like you to address the question whether there's any contradiction between you as a feminist and your work?"

"Well, I think that feminism is a very large category that covers a wide variety of political opinions and strategies," said Califia. "I certainly support the majority of the mainstream feminist agenda for equal work, better education for work, protection from domestic violence or sexual violence of any kind.

"I think where I part company with some members of the women's movement is on the specific issue of censorship. I don't feel that it would improve the status of women in our society for the state to have broader powers of censorship. And I also feel that one of the central pillars of the repression of women is the social control and limitation, or repression, of our sexuality, and that part of my work is about attempting to restore more autonomy to women and more choices."

By the conclusion of Califia's testimony, the gentle, scrubbed face of s/m seemed to have carried the day. A brief pleasantry was exchanged between the Crown's lawyer and Califia on her mispronunciation of a Dutch town, where she had lectured; Hans Van Iperen was, "given his background," in a position to know. But there was no cross-examination.

In fact, the Crown and the Attorney General (AG) treated the writers and artists as essentially irrelevant to their case, saving their most vigorous cross-examination for the expert witnesses—the sociologists, the law professor, the anthropologist. They were definitely interested in science, but seemed really not to care, legally or otherwise, about the cultural significance of lesbian and gay lives.

It was a drizzly Thursday morning, nothing unusual for Vancouver in October, but the glass ceiling of the courthouse felt oppressively close. The exterior dampness seemed to slither through the panes

JANINE separating us from the cold greyness, and the interior air felt completely sterile. Julie and I had just picked up an impeccably dressed Pat Califia and J.C., her imported moral support from Seattle, at their bed & breakfast. Today was Pat's day to take the stand and she had certainly risen to the wardrobe challenge.

During our countless phone conversations about testifying, a constant topic had been clothes and appearance. We were both growing our hair for the trial and carefully shopping for just the right outfit. Black leather wouldn't do and T-shirts were out, so the options were pretty grim. Pat finally decided on a jacket-and-skirt combo. I picked a conservative black overcoat, silk pants and tasteful white shirt. I looked like I'd come straight from the convent. I had lots of conversations with lots of witnesses about what to wear—as though we were all going to the prom from hell. The greatest fear for many of us, besides the utter terror of being on the stand, was that our wardrobes wouldn't survive our testimony.

Although I dutifully complimented Pat on her stunning court get-up, it was her outfit for the Little Sister's benefit later that night that I longed to see. The benefit was also the Canadian launch of Pat's 1994 book of essays, *Public Sex: The Culture of Radical Sex,* from Cleis Press.

Of course, launching *Public Sex* inevitably meant importing it. Weeks earlier, Felice Newman at Cleis had phoned Little Sister's to say the books had left their California warehouse. Jim, Bruce and I took up an anxious wait for the fifty copies to clear the border and arrive safely at the bookstore. If there was an author whose name might catch Customs' eye, it was Pat Califia.

The shipment from Cleis arrived on an uneventful Friday afternoon. In the back office of Little Sister's, the three of us checked out the box the way NASA prepares for a space launch. There was no evidence of inspection, no stamps saying it had cleared Canada Customs, none of the ugly orange tape used by Customs when they search, pillage and then re-seal a shipment. I slid an X-acto knife across the top of the box and ripped open the protective paper inside. There lay *Public Sex,* all fifty copies, untouched. It was as though we'd won the lottery twice: we had Pat Califia *and* we had her books.

After testifying, Pat and J.C. returned to their B & B to unwind. Pat did an interview with filmmaker Aerlyn Weissman, another with Stuart Blackley. Then she retired for a short nap. We agreed to meet each other at the benefit; Denna, one of Pat's greatest local fans and a truck owner, volunteered to pick them up.

I arrived an hour early to work the door and set up the book display. The venue was out of the West End, across the Granville Street bridge at Flygirl, a moving women's dance club that pretty much happens at the same spot every other Saturday night. The bar was up and running, the stage and microphone were all set. And the joint was packed, thank god. Whenever I organize an event, I have two fears. The first is that the audience won't show up, the second is that the performer won't. So far I was batting one for one. But as the hour clicked by, my second fear escalated. Had I given Pat clear directions? Had I said when the doors opened, when she would start the reading? The room was packed and all eyes where focused on the empty spotlight in the middle of the stage. I phoned the B & B. No answer. Denna arrived. She couldn't find Pat anywhere. Maybe she was caught up in some wild sexual romp that she couldn't extricate herself from . . .

Just when I was about to completely lose it, the door swung open and Pat sauntered in. She was not wearing corduroy. She was in leather and quickly set to work giving the audience what they'd come to expect: a rousing talk on sex and writing and censorship and fighting back. This was Pat Califia at her best, even though she was fighting a cold and staving off collapse. At the end, she signed books, not hastily scribbling her name, but thoughtfully taking time and talking with each woman. As the book line-up began to wane, another cluster of women would join at the back. After the last book was signed, Pat slipped out the front door, exhausted. The Little Sister's defence fund was $800 richer, the box of books was twenty pounds lighter and we were all walking on the moon.

"What was Pat Califia really like?" women asked me later.

She was nice. Really, really nice.

Articulate and Dangerous

Ann Scales is exactly the sort of radical pro-censorship feminist whom Pat Califia opposes. She's a self-declared member of the "MacKinnon-Dworkin camp" and the equal of Califia and Carole Vance in the super-charged rhetoric of the porn debates—but on the anti-side. Joe Arvay first encountered Scales at a 1993 lecture she gave while a visiting instructor at the University of British Columbia. As an out lesbian and professor of law at the University of New Mexico, Scales has carved a unique and significant perspective within the feminist anti-porn movement.

Arvay aimed to present Scales as an expert witness on three matters: (1) the nature of lesbian porn in the U.S.; (2) the evidence of whether lesbian porn creates a substantial risk of harm; and (3) the political worth of porn, particularly certain works by Pat Califia. Like Vance, her theoretical opposite, Scales sat through hours of preliminary sabre-rattling while the Crown and the provincial AG challenged her credentials and sought to limit the scope of her testimony. Her expertise in American law, rather than Canadian, was seen as damning; even the quality of her Harvard degree was questioned. As with all witnesses asked to comment on the nature of pornography, the Crown wanted to know if Scales had conducted experiments "utilizing accepted scientific methodology." (The Crown had a very strict sense of which social science experiments— those with stringent controls—they would accept as expert opinion.) Scales answered patiently, her head cocked to one side, exuding an air of polite attentiveness towards her interrogators that they might not necessarily have deserved. Her poise throughout was remarkable, not only for the authority it lent her testimony, but for creating an atmosphere of respectful legal exchange among all parties.

Arvay's daring gambit was to bring Scales in as a key witness for Little Sister's, despite her adamant opposition to the porn trade, her belief in the harm it can cause women and her support for *Butler*. Few people outside Little Sister's inner circle, certainly neither the Crown nor the AG, had any idea how well she could articulate a persuasive case *against* the bookstore, if she so desired. Arvay planned to carefully contain the range of Scale's expert opinion, enabling her to defend the unique nature of lesbian erotica while preventing any inquiry into the harmfulness of heterosexual or homosexual porn in general. He stage-managed her testimony with superb agility and finesse, even during the rough and tumble of cross-examination.

"Now, Professor Scales," asked Arvay, "can you tell me without telling me what your opinion is—be very careful about this, I don't want to know what your opinion is—but can you tell me how you would have gone about acquiring information respecting whether or not lesbian pornography causes harm."

Arvay had embarked on an extremely delicate operation: to confine the question of harm to lesbian porn only. He was happily aided by Frank Falzon, counsel for the AG. Falzon had no objection to Scales' qualifications to speak on the nature or politics of lesbian porn. He did, however, take issue with her credentials on "whether there is any evidence that lesbian pornography creates a substantial risk of harm."

"As your lordship will know from having read the *Butler* decision," said Falzon, "the whole issue of obscenity is now inextricably bound up with . . . whether the material in question creates a risk of harm. It is that very question, my lord, that has occupied thousands and thousands of pages of study by social scientists . . . Professor Scales has advised your lordship that she has neither the training to conduct those studies or to examine them from the point of view of their methodology."

Falzon spoke further, then Arvay interrupted.

"I might be able to shorten things," he said.

Justice Smith turned to Arvay and asked if he was prepared to make a concession. Arvay formed his words with apparent reluctance.

"Yes . . . We do not anticipate Professor Scales to say that she could prove that there was no harm caused by this material," said Arvay. " All she would have told you is that she, in her research, could find no studies which made the connection between lesbian pornography and harm. I'm prepared, though, my lord, to withdraw my request that Professor Scales be advanced as an expert on expressing an opinion on the issue of pornography and harm."

"All right," concluded Smith. "Well, then, Mr. Falzon, I guess I don't have to hear from you."

"Much to your pleasure I'm sure, my lord," Falzon playfully replied, unaware that Arvay had much more to lose than he did if Scales had been allowed to freely express herself on the subject of pornography and harm.

Strolling through the Lesbian Porn Industry

After a day of preliminaries, Arvay was finally allowed to lead Scales through her testimony. He asked her to describe the "lesbian pornography industry" in the U.S. (The commercial availability of erotic representations by, for and about lesbians is historically recent, as are the concerns of pro-censorship feminists about s/m porn. Scales is a pioneer of feminist jurisprudence vis à vis lesbian s/m porn.) She told the court her research revealed that, compared to the approximately 1,600 mainstream—read: legal, male-produced and heterosexual—porn videos produced annually in the U.S., there have been a few more than a dozen lesbian-produced sex videos, in total, in the last seven years.

"There are . . . only eight [lesbian] magazines published worldwide that I have ever been able to locate that always or ever have sexually explicit materials," said Scales. "Also, with the exception of a magazine entitled *On Our Backs,* which has begun to turn a profit, I'm given to understand, these are essentially not-for-profit enterprises. The publisher of *Bad Attitude,* . . . a lesbian erotic magazine, . . . describes that operation as a labour of love and a political commitment. That, in my opinion, is a fair description of the entire 'industry.' "

Arvay brought Scales around to Pat Califia's work, the hot spot of lesbian sex writing. He inquired about the possible value of *The Lesbian S/M Safety Manual*.

"I think it clearly advances the political purpose of increased visibility of sexual minorities," said Scales. "I would not distinguish sharply between the political and the health purposes. I mentioned earlier the concept of 'sexual repossession,' a very important concept in terms of women's sexual health, which is a political issue."

Scales went on to define her concept of repossession.

"The history of [women's] subjugation is replete with taking away from women both control over their reproductive lives and information about sexuality. So to have women producing material, intended for women, about women's sexual health is, in my opinion, a valiant and important political act."

Califia's novel, *Doc and Fluff: A Dystopian Novel of a Girl and Her Bike,* has been frequently detained by Canada Customs, and it became the focus of hectic, confused cross-examination by Crown lawyer Neena Sharma and, later, the AG's Frank Falzon. *Doc and Fluff* concerns a butch biker named Doc who rescues another woman, Fluff, from a brutal male biker gang. The male bikers retaliate by raping a woman, and Doc sets out for revenge. In testimony, Scales summarized the novel's intention: "The . . . mythological construct of this book is a sort of cathartic reversal of roles, where the women seek retribution against the violent men. A cathartic reversal, for example, as in the movie *Thelma and Louise* . . . A kind of apocalyptic revenge of women for sexual violence."

During cross-examination, Sharma clearly believed that *Doc and Fluff* provided an unassailable example of the harmful effects of lesbian s/M materials.

"I take it that one aspect of feminism, particularly anti-pornography feminism, is that . . . violent pornography serves to validate some people's views about violence against women. Is that right?" asked Sharma.

"That is a hypothesis which in each case would have to be informed by the depictions at issue," said Scales. "That is one of the major concerns, you are quite correct."

"In terms of that criticism directed at pornography and the [rape] scene in *Doc and Fluff*, would you agree with me that it is problematic because it may serve to validate someone's views [that] violence against women is okay?" asked Sharma.

"No."

"Well, . . . would you agree that *Doc and Fluff* . . . is available to the general audience? That's reasonable, isn't it?"

"Yes," said Scales.

"Would you agree with me [that] in the general audience there may be someone who has views that violence against women is okay in a general population?" asked Sharma.

"Yes."

"So my question is, from a feminist anti-pornography perspective, it's reasonable that that one scene may be problematic?"

"I cannot answer that question simply," said Scales, "because even within members of the community that identify themselves as radical anti-pornography feminists, there are disputes about the appropriateness of such depictions, even in context . . . I personally find neither the depiction in *Doc and Fluff,* nor the gang rape scene in the movie *The Accused,* to be risky or dangerous or problematic in any significant way."

In cross-examination by the AG's counsel, Scales managed to convey some theory—the "ethics of lesbian sex" perspective—on that most contentious of issues: consent.

"The *Butler* decision," said Scales, ". . . says that the *appearance* of consent may in fact render the depiction more degrading. That idea comes from radical feminist anti-pornography work that focuses more on the mainstream pornography. In lesbian . . . S/M materials, the [proponents] of this concept of ethics have tried, as I understand their work, to get beyond a legalistic idea of consent to establishing rules for actual equality between the participants."

"Are you aware," said Falzon with exasperation, "that the very same description that you just gave with respect to lesbian S/M is made in defence of heterosexual S/M?"

"I don't believe that's true," said Scales. ". . . In the lesbian materials, there is a deeper interrogation. Consent is not the end of the matter [and there is] an ongoing interrogation of the actual quality, comfort and well-being of the parties involved . . . Part of what I have called the ethics of [a lesbian S/M] encounter includes the [script], the authorship of the encounter by the participants, and the ongoing negotiation about what is going to happen next and how far [they] can go together and making sure that the participants have the ability and equal authority to bring that activity to a halt. In mainstream pornography, the script is not authored, ordinarily, by the participants."

The province seemed to gradually realize that Scales might be a very useful witness to their own case. Regardless of the nuances of her own beliefs, Scales could skilfully articulate the radical feminist view that porn, whether lesbian, gay or straight, was potentially harmful. Falzon's original demand that Scales not be allowed to give expert opinion on the potential for harm in lesbian pornography came back to haunt him.

"You would have the court . . . appreciate that, even within the feminist lesbian community, there is a very strong debate ongoing concerning whether the depictions of these scenes is in fact harmful to women?" suggested Falzon.

"Well, if Mr. Falzon is going to . . ." Arvay interrupted. Falzon made another attempt to get Scales to answer, but Justice Smith stopped him.

"Mr. Falzon," Arvay hammered the irony, "wanted to stress at the outset that this witness was not qualified to express an opinion on that, my lord." Falzon had prepared the ground for his own legal out-manoeuvring and Justice Smith had no alternative but to stop his line of questioning.

Scales weathered the cross-examination with ease, answering questions with an unnerving precision and freshness that made her seem as unpredictable a witness for Little Sister's as she proved to be for the government. (As Arvay had said earlier outside the courtroom, *à la* Bette Davis, "fasten your seat belts, it's going to be a bumpy ride.") With the weight of Scales' authority finally tipped in the bookstore's favour, Arvay's gambit had clearly paid off. The government's best shot had been scored against themselves.

How Special! But *How* Special?

The question of the special nature of gay and lesbian pornography had stirred up controversy long before Little Sister's walked into the courtroom, to the point of threatening the case altogether.

As Ann Scales pointed out, lesbian porn bore practically no resemblance in its creation or production to mainstream pornography; nor could gay male porn appropriately be called an industry, though it mimicked the heterosexual business quite successfully on a smaller scale. Yet a disproportionate number of obscenity cases and Customs detentions involved this tiny corner of the porn trade; it was gay and lesbian porn that ended up on the legal testing ground of *Butler*, a law with a nominally heterosexual orientation. Little Sister's believed gay and lesbian porn couldn't, and shouldn't, be judged by heterosexual standards.

Ironically, the idea that queer porn had a special nature presented a problem for both the B.C. Civil Liberties Association, co-plaintiffs with Little Sister's, and for LEAF, the influential feminist intervenor in the *Butler* decision. Although worlds apart in their beliefs about the legal regulation of porn (BCCLA was strictly anti-censorship; LEAF was pro-censorship), neither could comfortably deal with gay and lesbian pornography as a distinct category.

For LEAF, the problem was that queer porn, especially in the S/M vein, complicated and challenged their conception of pornography, which was rooted in a heterosexual model. LEAF's leadership embraced the basic anti-porn, pro-censorship position of Dworkin, MacKinnon and Scales, albeit adapted to the equality environment of the *Canadian Charter of Rights and Freedoms*. They had been stonily silent on the subject of Customs detentions and obscenity charges post-*Butler*, despite harsh criticisms from the lesbian and gay targets.

But not all LEAF members were comfortable with that silence. West Coast LEAF, the Vancouver-based affiliate, had considerably more sensitivity to the impact of Little Sister's struggles. At their initiative, a meeting was set up with Janine Fuller almost a year after the 1993 National Association of Women and the Law conference. (In Toronto in June 1993, LEAF also finally met with anti-censorship feminists concerned about homophobic fallout from *Butler*.)

During this period, both *Butler* and Canada Customs were getting plenty of bad press. The targeting of gays and lesbians in obscenity trials and at the Canadian border finally piqued the curiosity of mainstream media, including the *Globe and Mail* and the CBC in Canada, and the *New Yorker* and *Playboy* in the U.S. The commentators disparaged LEAF, Catharine MacKinnon and Andrea Dworkin, who responded with dismay and defensiveness, agreeing that *Butler* was being misapplied, but accepting no responsibility.

West Coast LEAF decided the best way to support Little Sister's was to send the minister of National Revenue, David Anderson, a polished critique of Customs' harassment of gay and lesbian materials, and of Customs' misapplication of *Butler*. Their letter, eventually endorsed by the national LEAF office and then virtually ignored by the federal government, supported Little Sister's claim of discrimination by Canada Customs and called for a cessation of the targeting. LEAF, however, couldn't bring themselves to demand an end to Customs' power of prior restraint.

In drafting their position, LEAF had grappled with how to distinguish themselves from the civil libertarian perspective. They decided to focus their arguments on the equality aspects of Little Sister's case: the discrimination against the store on the basis of sexual orientation. LEAF saw a need to "retain legitimacy in the arena of fighting for equality for lesbians."

In a section of an earlier position paper, called "Things to stay away from," LEAF named exactly what BCCLA most dreaded in the court case with Little Sister's: "seeming like we're arguing our [lesbian and gay] porn is better than your [heterosexual] porn." But unlike the BCCLA, LEAF was challenged by how to defend lesbian S/M porn (as their draft said: "*Bad Attitude*—can we just ignore this stuff?"). Their reliance on "equality" as the *raison d'être* for censorship—simply stated, some porn should be censored because it is an agent of women's inequality—immobilized LEAF in the face of sexual images that celebrated raw power dynamics. Yes, they could use "equality" to argue for gay and lesbian rights, but as LEAF's Karen Busby later wrote: ". . . lesbians need to talk about S/M in more detail, including whether and how to make equality arguments specific to S/M and sexual minorities. LEAF will not take a firmer position on lesbian S/M in litigation until a much clearer, systemic equality analysis emerges from lesbian communities across Canada."

For very different reasons, the BCCLA had also been troubled about distinctions being drawn between heterosexual and gay porn in the post-*Butler* era. Arvay himself had no qualms about embracing the distinction, but members of the BCCLA were hesitant about steering the Little Sister's case away from a pure, civil libertarian focus on freedom of expression, regardless of content.

In the fall of 1993, the federal government made a mild overture to the bookstore; there had been a change of government in Ottawa (the Tories were gone, the Liberals were in) and perhaps an out-of-court settlement was possible. Little Sister's, Joe Arvay and BCCLA hammered out a proposal. The co-plaintiffs would withdraw their action against Customs if the government agreed to "repeal and amend Customs Memorandum D9-1-1 so as to allow entry into Canada of all books and magazines respecting gay and lesbian issues or relationships and intended for a gay and lesbian readership." Their letter observed that this proposal "leaves intact Customs' ability to detain and prohibit entry of mainstream pornography which is misogynist [and is covered by *Butler*]" and, further, "It involves a recognition . . . that gay and lesbian pornography is sufficiently different and complex from mainstream heterosexual pornography . . ."

Although members of BCCLA helped write the proposal, other members later balked at the implications of saving only gay porn from Canada Customs' clutches, rather than challenging the whole prior restraint apparatus. On April 11, 1994, member Phil Bryden presented a resolution to the BCCLA board that the association withdraw as co-plaintiff from the case "to give Little Sister's the freedom to instruct counsel and to take such steps . . . as Little Sister's deems to be in their best interests without binding BCCLA to approaches to the case that we may consider to be inconsistent with our goals." Bryden made it clear that he wasn't suggesting the BCCLA drop its commitment to the bookstore, but that it re-assess its role. An internal debate ensued among the civil libertarians, some of whom were concerned that such an abandonment would badly hurt the BCCLA's reputation among gay and other community groups. In the end, the resolution was dropped and the BCCLA continued to hold firm. The government, in the meantime, rejected the settlement proposal outright.

Getting, and Not Getting, the Picture

Despite all the talk about lesbian porn during the Little Sister's trial, actual images were sorely lacking in Courtroom 65. That is, until one of the few lesbian pornographers "worldwide" made a surprise, unscheduled appearance at the tail end of one day. Robin Hand is an intense, fresh-faced young woman, twenty-odd years old, a relative newcomer to Vancouver. Hand was a member of the Hey Grrrrlz collective that published *Lezzie Smut,* Canada's sole entry into the international world of lesbian porn periodicals.

Lezzie Smut is a post-punk 'zine, one of the many cheap, self-produced magazines that have sprouted since the mid-1980s. *LS* is entirely devoted to lesbian porn and politics, and open to any woman who wants to make sexually explicit material for other women in a collaborative mélange of models, editors and desk-top designers.

Hand testified about how she got involved with both *Lezzie Smut* and

Little Sister's. Upon moving to Vancouver, she had roomed with her friend Paula Wellings.

"Paula was working at Little Sister's bookstore," said Hand, "and there was a paucity of sexually explicit material for women, specifically pictorial material. And one day somebody came into the store and asked her where the 'lezzie smut' was, and there was none or it was very limited, and she had to explain that it didn't get through Customs and there was very little of it anyway.

"I believe she complained to her co-worker and he told her to write to her MP. Instead, she asked me if I would be interested in doing a sex 'zine with her, specifically for lesbians. And of course, I said 'Right on, that would be really cool.' "

The sense of empowerment that Hand felt in creating lesbian porn had been hard won in Canada. For over a decade, lesbian feminists had struggled over sexual self-representation and censorship. Perhaps no group of artists in Canada had put themselves more on the line in the feminist porn debates than Susan Stewart, Lizard Jones and Persimmon Blackbridge, known collectively as Kiss & Tell. Through performance, video and photographic installations since the late 1980s, the Vancouver group had used their bodies and words to express the paradoxical strength and vulnerability of sexual subjectivity. Kiss & Tell's work had been exhibited across Canada, the U.S., England, Australia and the Netherlands. And their work had been seized—in three different media, in three separate incidents—by Canada Customs.

Persimmon Blackbridge, with Lizard Jones, had modelled for the sex photographs in the interactive show "Drawing the Line," their first collaboration. She has a heroic, Amazonian presence, especially striking in the repressed atmosphere of a courtroom, with her hair both dark and waist-length, and short and blond, neatly split down the middle—an uncanny photographic subject and witness. As with Hand, Blackbridge's testimony allowed Arvay to humanize the dry legal and theoretical discussions of sexual imagery.

"All three of us in Kiss & Tell were involved in the feminist anti-pornography movement at one time or another," Blackbridge told Arvay. "But in the process of looking at and discussing imagery with other feminists, we realized that we had more questions than answers."

Blackbridge described Drawing the Line: "The photos are arranged on the gallery walls, starting with relatively non-controversial photographs with no nudity or explicit sex, and ending with photos which are deliberately constructed to cover a range of problematic and controversial issues. Viewers are invited to express their opinion of the various photographs, to 'draw the line' as regards their personal limits. Women viewers write their reactions directly on the walls around the photographs . . .

"The gallery walls are soon scrawled over with writing. The pictures float in a sea of text, no longer functioning as separate sexual images, but set literally within the context of debates, discussions, and disagreements about sexual representation."

Blackbridge tried to do justice to the complexity of their creative tasks.

"Sometimes, as women, we are acknowledged only as victims, or only as self-affirming subjects," said Blackbridge. "Neither position reflects our actual lives. Our sexuality is far more complex. We respond to sexual images in very individual and sometimes conflicted ways. And it's not because we've learned our sexuality from pornography. We learned it from cartoons, commercials and comic books. We learn it from our friends and families. We aren't pure, we're complex mixtures of rebellion, analysis and internalized sexism. We have to look at what we really are in order to think about where we want to go and how to get there."

The international success of Drawing the Line led to its run-ins with Canada Customs. Kiss & Tell's work began to regularly criss-cross the border, destined for exhibits or magazine reviewers. The first detention involved the U.S.-based *Libido* magazine, which ran a feature article on their show; Customs also detained the photographic print sent to the magazine for layout when it was mailed home. *Deneuve,* a glossy lesbian cultural magazine that reviewed the show and reprinted a photo, was seized on its way to Little Sister's. Then the book *Drawing the Line,* published in Canada but distributed by Inland in the U.S., was stopped on a return trip to Canada, en route to Edmonton.

Blackridge believed they could have won an appeal through Customs.

"But we didn't pursue that possibility," said Blackbridge. "We had never dealt with Canada Customs before. We had no understanding of the process, we didn't know how or where to begin, what would happen and how much it would cost. And besides our ignorance and lack of money, we also found the prospect of an appeal frightening.

"We were scared . . . that we would have to stand up and defend sexual pictures of ourselves, face to face with men who had already decided that those pictures of our bodies were obscene. We weren't willing to go through that. Getting back a $200 photograph and some magazines didn't seem worth it, so we let them go. I'm here now because this case is worth it."

As veterans of cross-border skirmishes, Kiss & Tell were clearly not intimidated by Canada Customs.

"We'll continue to explore sexual representations, as women and as lesbians, despite the actions of Canada Customs," said Blackbridge. "We will continue to show our art internationally despite the fear of losing our work. And we will continue to be at risk whenever our work leaves the country, whenever we send photos to foreign reviewers, whenever our work appears in foreign publications, until Customs' policies are changed."

FIVE

Churning Out the Sex Tracts

Crown lawyer Hans Van Iperen asked the witness to turn to a page of illustrations in Gay Ideas, *by Richard D. Mohr.*

PIERRE BERTON: *I know the picture.*

HANS VAN IPEREN: *Could you describe the picture in your own words very briefly?*

BERTON: *Yes. It's a depiction of anal sex by three men, two of which are supplying the sex and the third is receiving it.*

VAN IPEREN: *Okay. And it is fair to say that the penetration is by two men? And there is [another] photograph there by Robert Mapplethorpe?*

BERTON: *Yes.*

VAN IPEREN: *What does that picture show?*

BERTON: *It depicts a man shoving his wrist up a man's anus.*

VAN IPEREN: *Sir, the evidence will be that the [Customs] officer at the bor-*

der . . . referred the book to Ottawa for an opinion and, of course, the opinion was to release it. Do you think it is totally unreasonable for a person to have some concerns about these pictures although, and I fully agree with you, the text itself should offend no one?

BERTON: *The pictures are essential to the text. [Mohr] goes into the text based upon those pictures and uses them as examples, as everybody does who writes books which require illustration.*

VAN IPEREN: *But my question was . . . that the person making this first examination, when they look at these pictures first . . . in terms of unexpected confrontation, those pictures are striking, aren't they?*

BERTON: *Well, they are no more striking than [what] you can obtain for two dollars of rent in any adult video store in this or any other Canadian city, and show to yourself in colour and in motion. These are still pictures in black and white, and here is a Customs guy saying we have to check with Ottawa on this, when he can go around the corner and see the same thing on a movie screen.*

DURING the early weeks of the Little Sister's trial, the annual Vancouver International Writers Festival was unfolding a few blocks away; a local *bon mot* was that the most impressive literary line-up was appearing in Courtroom 65.

Little Sister's had spent years building their case and the writers came. Nino Ricci, winner of a Governor General's award for fiction and past president of PEN Canada, took the stand. Author and broadcaster Pierre Berton, regarded by many as a genuine Canadian icon, was asked to lead off his testimony with a lengthy recitation of his awards. Sarah Schulman, celebrated American novelist, arrived after receiving a single phone call a few weeks before the trial. But the writer most anticipated by the Little Sister's fans was Jane Rule, who waited patiently in the public gallery.

Jane Rule's official courtroom role was to testify to the artistic merit of several works of lesbian fiction, including Pat Califia's novel *Doc and Fluff.* "Artistic merit," and "educational, scientific or medical purpose" are important mitigating factors, according to the *Butler* decision, in assessing whether a work is criminally obscene. But along with her literary stature, Rule's personal integrity and indomitable presence were being called upon. She was no stranger to controversy, having spent a lifetime exploring some of the most disputed issues in the lesbian and gay community, including a vigorous defence of Toronto's *Body Politic* magazine during censorship attacks in the 1970s and 1980s.

Jane Rule also had first-hand knowledge of Canada Customs' excesses. She had lent support to Little Sister's owners Jim Deva and Bruce Smyth during their earliest battles with Customs. And she had witnessed detentions of her own books, in her own province and her own country.

Contract with the World (1980) was the most recent detention—the spring of 1993; a Customs inspector had first suspected it was "hate propaganda," then obscene. *The Young in One Another's Arms* (1977) received the Canadian Authors Association Award for best novel in 1978 and a detention in early 1990. It wasn't just Rule's books that fell afoul of the border guards. The movie based on Rule's novel *Desert of the Heart* was also detained by Canada Customs. *Desert of the Heart* was written in 1964, shortly after Rule moved to Vancouver from the U.S. It immediately became a classic, especially beloved by Rule's lesbian readership. *Desert Hearts,* the 1985 movie by director Donna Deitch, circulated freely in Canadian movie houses and video stores for years before being detained by Customs en route to Little Sister's in 1993.

In fact, Jane Rule's novels tended to circulate freely around the world, in translations and foreign editions. Although many of her works were available from homegrown publishers, some Canadian booksellers liked the convenience of ordering from her American publishers, notably Naiad Press in Florida (Naiad is as much an institution to lesbian publishing as Rule is to lesbian literature). Rule's books sat peacefully in almost every mainstream Canadian bookstore and library, yet had the occasional dust-up at the border, especially when ordered by a gay bookstore.

Arthritis has slowed Rule down and she testified sitting in a wheelchair. She no longer writes full time, living in retirement with her lover, Helen Sonthoff, on Galiano Island, their home for almost thirty years. Rule's testimony had the characteristic wit and authority her readers have come to expect from her pen.

Arvay started by asking her about the criteria for judging books, and about the consequences of banning them.

"There are no set rules . . . because literature is so various," said Rule. "As scholars and critics, we try to read a book and let the book dictate

how we will deal with it . . . We try to ascertain the intent of the novelist . . . not only the artistic intent, but often the social intent, the insights
that the novelist called to our attention . . .

"I think great errors in judgement can be made when a person who is
judging a work for [the purposes of] banning it [misses] the cultural context of the book, because books are not born out of nothing. They live
inside the traditions of our culture. And our culture is not only a North
American culture, a contemporary culture, but reaches back into the lit-
eratures that we have studied and modelled our own upon.

"Therefore, if you were going to deal with questions of humiliation, of
sexual explicitness, we would have to know that we are dealing with
[works] such as Dante's *Inferno,* the Marquis de Sade's work, as well as
dealing with writers of our own time . . . There have always been writers
who have been preoccupied with the darker sides of human experience,
who are perhaps best equipped to give us the insight into those very
troubling and often horrifying things that go on in the world today . . ."

Rule articulated a defence of the "author's intention."

"I think it's quite easy to draw a distinction between the artistic purpose and the artistic merit," said Rule. "Let me give you an example of
Moby Dick. It is probably the worst-built novel ever written, in terms of
what [Melville] should have done. He started out to write a novel, he
ends up writing a play, and then he's writing an essay. He's all over the
map. It's probably one of the greatest failures of our inheritance, [yet it is]
a better book than most well-made books. As a structure it fails, but it's a
brilliant, brilliant book . . . [Melville's] intent is so enormous."

Later in her testimony, she reflected on Pat Califia's purpose and merit
in *Doc and Fluff.*

"I think it is a moral book . . ." said Rule. "For myself, Pat Califia is not
a fine stylist . . . She can be sentimental, she can be over-simplistic, but
she is asking all the right questions. She is asking about the nature of
power, she is asking about the nature of bondage . . . And if we don't
agree with some of her answers, we have to admit that the questions are
the right ones."

Arvay's final question concerned Rule's reaction to the detention of her
work.

"Ms. Rule, were you aware that [*Contract with the World*] was detained
by Canada Customs and subsequently released . . . in 1993?"

"Not until yesterday," Rule replied.

"Now, as a writer in Canada," asked Arvay, "and particularly one whose books have been detained—not prohibited, but certainly detained—by Canada Customs, what are your concerns and what are the implications to you of having Canada Customs detain your work on the grounds that it may be obscene?"

Rule thought for a moment, then began speaking in an almost offhand tone. But she swiftly drew her audience in, providing the Little Sister's trial with one of its most compelling moments.

"Some cynics have said, 'Isn't it nice to get all that attention,'" said Rule. "But in fact, it's the kind of attention that . . . would very possibly cut me off from the general audience for whom I write. It is the kind of [attention] that does not simply last for that week or a month, but labels me for the rest of my professional life . . . as someone who is probably a pornographer. Because, you know, if they held the books, there must be something in them that they don't like.

"Now, there are a number of people in Canada who do know that *The Young in One Another's Arms* won the Canadian Authors Association Award for the best novel of 1978. [But] there are a great many *more* people in Canada who know *The Young in One Another's Arms* was detained by Customs. And that is what I have to carry. I have to carry a reputation created by this charge for which I have no way of defending myself . . .

"And I bitterly resent the attempt to marginalize, trivialize and even criminalize what I have to say because I happen to be a lesbian. I happen to be a novelist. I happen to have bookstores and publishers who are dedicated to producing my work. The assumption is, therefore, that there must be something pornographic because of my sexual orientation, and I think that is a shocking way to deal with my community.

"Of course we have writers who are writing erotica and so we should. I celebrate that. But we are not a community churning out sex tracts. We are a community speaking with our passion, our humanity in a world that is so homophobic that it sees us as nothing but sexual creatures instead of good Canadian citizens, fine artists, and brave people trying to make Canada a better place for everybody to speak freely and honestly about who we are."

Little Sister's has certainly brought me some fame, if no fortune. Midway through the trial, I received a phone call from one of Canada's national

JANINE

dinosaurs, er, institutions: the TV game show *Front Page Challenge,* thirty-eight years old and one of the longest-running programs in North American television history.

Would I be their Mystery Guest, answering questions behind a screen while four panellists, esteemed Canadians of an older generation, attempted to guess my identity and the associated headline news story?

I was a bit reluctant. *Front Page Challenge* was a little like apple pie and vanilla ice cream—mondo straight. Then the face of my late grandmother, who watched *Front Page Challenge* all her life, floated before my eyes. Nanny would never have forgiven me. I'm sure that she and Gordon Sinclair, the crusty original panellist who passed over to the Final Edition, were watching the show together, every Friday evening.

My lover Julie and I arrived for the pre-taping as instructed: at the rear door of the Canadian Broadcasting Corporation (CBC) in Vancouver (this was to avoid a chance meeting between me and the four panellists). I was promptly whisked into the green room, while Julie was deposited in the studio audience, in a specially reserved chair affectionately called the "mom seat." They patted me down with a variety of foundations and an understated lipstick; then I sat like a porcelain doll—okay, a large porcelain doll—waiting my turn behind the screen.

I was the show's first Mystery Guest because I had to return to court as quickly as possible. There was a quick run-through on what I could expect—sound check, visuals—and then it was the real thing. (To the viewer at home, *Front Page Challenge* looked totally automated; in reality, the special effects consisted of a worker cranking something backstage, or heaving a lever to twist the guest around. All those budget cuts at the CBC . . .)

From behind my screen, I listened while the panel was introduced, trying desperately to keep my upper lip from getting stuck to my top gum—my mouth had dried out. But after seven national media interviews, I felt ready for anything—even the reliably cantankerous Jack Webster, jowls and eyebrows and all.

Most of the panellists were veteran journalists or broadcasters, and most had been with the show since time began. So too, the ever affable host Fred Davis, who announced: "And for viewers at home and in the studio audience, here's our first headline . . ." While the panellists sat in sensory deprivation, the audience was let in on my identity: "The rolling press may symbolize free speech, but in Canada it's not for everyone. Border book seizures continue, as Canada Customs rules on what Canadians can read. The Little Sister's bookstore in court now battles Big Brother for the right to import books and magazines. Please welcome the woman who is challenging the government and our panel: bookstore operator Janine Fuller!"

I proved to be an easy meal. Once the panel pinpointed Vancouver as the story's location, panellist Pierre Berton guessed "Little Sister's" faster than you could say *Quiz Show*. This left a considerable amount of time for questions. After the obligatory commercial break, Fred Davis helped me down from my perch and over to the hot seat. (Fred helped everyone down, as a precaution after someone took a spill. I'll let you in on another FPC secret: the panellists were provided with a sealed envelope containing details about the Little Sister's trial and sample questions they could ask. This was to guard against embarrassing dead air, in case all the panellists were unfamiliar with the Mystery Guest or the news story, which apparently happened once. Now you know.)

The show aired the following evening and, though I didn't watch it myself, I was amazed by who and how many did. I'd be in my West End grocery store and a stranger would approach me and rather sheepishly admit to seeing the show. Someone else would be renting a porn video at the bookstore and they'd say, "Well, I was channel surfing and I just happened to catch it." The gay and lesbian community was finally coming out as aficionados of *Front Page Challenge*.

The CBC cancelled the program a few months later, despite its huge popularity. Time's up, they simply said. I wasn't surprised. I know from considerable personal experience that very good things get stopped in their tracks, all the time.

In Which Mr. Berton Defends Mr. Mapplethorpe

The morning after the taping of *Front Page Challenge*, Arvay introduced the day's first witness with unusual fanfare.

"My lord, I thought it might be appropriate to have the next witness testify behind a screen," said Arvay, "and give your lordship twenty questions to guess his identity. But then I thought maybe it wouldn't be appropriate. So my next witness, without any concealment, is Pierre Berton."

At seventy-four years, a robust six-foot-three, with trademark bow tie and white hair, Pierre Berton reeks of Canadiana. After almost forty years on network TV, Berton's face was deeply embedded in the mainstream consciousness; he was also a prolific print journalist. But it was Berton's literary accomplishments that formed the bedrock of his national reputation: several Governor General's Awards for popular histories (notably, his saga of the CPR railroad, *The Last Spike*), plus a Stephen Leacock Medal for humour (*Just Add Water*).

It would be hard to imagine a personality better equipped than Pierre Berton to lend a respectable air to Little Sister's case. While solidly liberal and urbane, he also represented an orthodoxy: that of the white, middle-class, heterosexual man. The side of Berton that emerged during his Little Sister's testimony—perhaps less well known to his game show audience—was his strong commitment to civil liberties. For Berton, the Little Sister's case was inescapably linked to his experience as a soldier in World War II.

"I spent four years of my time, partly because I was drafted, but also because [we] felt that for once we were involved in a just war," he testified. "We were attacking the very people who burn books and destroy books, either in public or in secret, and I have been opposed to that ever since."

Berton's allegiance to a civil libertarian viewpoint came with all the attendant contradictions. Earlier in 1994, he had been part of a furore that erupted around the Writing Thru Race literary conference scheduled for that summer. The milestone Vancouver conference—organized by, for and about people of colour, with evening sessions for the general public—was sponsored by the Writers Union of Canada. As a member, Berton had disagreed on principle with the union sponsoring an event for some members only. (He wasn't the only high-profile, mainstream writer who disputed the conference's structure.) When a member of Parliament from the right-wing Reform Party spoke against government funding for the "exclusive" event, the Liberal government caved in and abruptly withdrew its financial support—yet another example of (indirect) state censorship. Writing Thru Race was thrown into crisis and a massive fundraising effort was launched; the conference eventually went ahead on schedule, to great success. Among many others, Pierre Berton and Little Sister's made donations to the cause.

Berton spoke effortlessly on the merits of Richard D. Mohr's *Gay Ideas*, published by Beacon Press in 1992 and seized by Canada Customs in April 1993. A philosophy professor at the University of Illinois, Mohr had difficulty finding a publisher for the academic text, which covered scandalous topics like civil rights and the politics of culture and identity. *Gay Ideas* was originally scheduled for Canadian distribution by Oxford University Press, but they declined the book. The apparent problem? Mohr's analysis of the erotic photographs of Robert Mapplethorpe, which were reproduced in the book, made *Gay Ideas* a likely candidate for a Customs seizure.

After exploring *Gay Ideas,* Arvay asked Berton to step back and consider the impact of censorship on the community.

"Well, I'm a member of a large constituency," Berton said. "It is a constituency of people who write books and read books. We believe that books are the essence of our culture, that without a literature, a country has not only no soul, it has no reason for being . . . Literature . . . will be the basis on which we are judged as a civilized community, and we are very upset when people try to infringe upon our freedom either to write or to read."

"You mentioned literature," said Arvay. "Do you draw some distinction between literature and pornography?"

"I don't think you can draw a distinction," Berton replied. "I think anything that is written down is literature . . . You can say whether it is bad literature or good literature or whether the author doesn't achieve his purpose or whether he is ungrammatical, but I don't think you can make moral judgements on literature. You can make judgements of taste. That is quite a different thing."

Arvay invited Berton to "to tell his lordship [anything more] about this issue."

"Well, I should say more exactly where I stand on censorship," said Berton. "I don't think it is necessary in democracy. I think that books deserve to be judged the same way as a human being is, because books are just as important . . . as human beings and some may be more important. I think a book has to face a jury of its peers, and through cross-examination and evidence and statements, people on the jury or the judge himself make up their minds as to whether that book is breaking the law, which are the obscenity laws in this country . . . But it must have its day in court."

The following day, Berton's testimony was quoted in flattering terms by newspapers and broadcasters across the country. Not surprisingly, many of Little Sister's lesser-known witnesses would receive no media mention at all, let alone respectful coverage. Even Jane Rule's appearance was barely recorded, despite the drama of her testimony.

Art on Trial: Eli Langer vs. the Kiddie Porn Law

Berton's remarks about a book deserving to face a jury of its peers came, prophetically, at the exact time that some Canadian culture was indeed propped up in a courtroom, awaiting judgement.

The sensational Toronto trial of art works by Eli Langer ran concurrently with the Little Sister's case. An artist in his mid-twenties, Langer's haunting canvases and pencil drawings showed boy and girl children, some in sexualized scenes with adult males. In December 1993, forty pictures were seized from the Mercer Union Gallery by the Toronto porn squad. Langer and gallery director Sharon Brooks were charged under Canada's six-month-old child pornography law, despite the conspicuous fact that the art was a painful exploration of child sexual abuse, rather than an endorsement of child sex. The personal charges were eventually dropped but, in a bizarre legal twist, the art itself was charged under rarely used laws of forfeiture. If found "guilty," the works would be destroyed. Throughout the Langer trial, the paintings and drawings sat in the dock.

As in the Little Sister's case, a parade of artists appeared as "character witnesses" to the artistic integrity of Langer's work, his technical skill, and the role of serious art in provoking discussions that may offend, even frighten, some members of society. In the end, Justice David McCombs was persuaded by Langer's arguments, accepting the statutory defence of artistic merit. The paintings and drawings were set free.

The Langer trial, like the Little Sister's case, seemed to highlight the inability of officials to make sensitive, nuanced judgements about sexual materials—especially those of a controversial nature. In Toronto, the Crown charged Langer as a child pornographer, oblivious to his intentions as an artist. Across Canada, Customs officials routinely detained gay and lesbian materials, often s/m, unaware of the cultural milieu from which they arose. By offering the testimony of critics and scholars, Arvay hoped to undermine the notion that an easy, reliable test for obscenity existed, despite *Butler's* assured language. Arvay's strategy was not, however, to "prove" to Justice Smith that the books in question were not legally obscene, but rather to demonstrate the flaws in Customs' decision-making processes.

Heads Up: Critical Theory Takes the Stand

Just how inadequate Customs' processes were was amply demonstrated by Lorraine Weir, professor of English literature at the University of

British Columbia. Weir offered an eloquent artistic defence of some s/m texts, notably Geoff Mains' *Urban Aboriginals: A Celebration of Leathersexuality.*

But first, she took Courtroom 65 on a brain-teasing excursion through critical theory's heavier waters. Like that of another scholarly witness—Bart Testa, semiotics and cinema instructor—Weir's testimony was hardly the stuff of cocktail party chatter. Even the most learned spectators struggled to keep up with them—as, no doubt, did the lawyers and the judge.

"Professor Weir, can we start by having you identify the [two] main schools of literary theory . . . which address the question . . . [of] whether any particular book may be degrading or dehumanizing, and the effect of that book?" asked Arvay.

Weir patiently spelled out "hermeneutics" for the court reporter. "And the second school is deconstruction," she said.

"Can you explain to his lordship, in language I can understand, what hermeneutics is?" asked Arvay.

"It's really not that difficult," said Weir. "Hermeneutics is what most of us in everyday life define as 'interpretation' . . . [The basic principle] is that there is a relationship of what literary theorists call 'transparency' between the text and the reader. The reader will be affected in some way by reading the text . . ."

"Now, likewise in a very simple way, can you describe what deconstruction is about?" asked Arvay.

"Well, we can get at deconstruction quickly by saying that it makes problematic the definition of hermeneutics which I just gave," said Weir. "The security and certainty that underlies the notion of the text and the reader and meaning in hermeneutics—all of those are questioned . . . In deconstruction, the understanding of *who* the reader is and *how* one experiences understanding is made problematic. You can think of it as substituting very clear, crisp boundaries in hermeneutics for fuzzy ones, plural meanings, plural possibilities, in deconstruction."

Arvay and Weir spoke at length about the two contrasting methodologies, then turned their attention to *Urban Aboriginals*. Published in 1984 by Gay Sunshine Press and prohibited by Canada Customs in April 1993, after an appeal by Little Sister's, *Urban Aboriginals* is a serious inquiry into the gay leather community and its explorations of consciousness through s/m practice. Author Geoff Mains was trained in biochemistry and ecology at the Universities of Toronto and British Columbia. He took this scientific knowledge and integrated it with his experiences in the leather scene in Vancouver and San Francisco. Mains died of AIDS in 1989.

Using the deconstruction method, Weir noted that "words don't turn into sex acts"—contrary to the assumption of some sociological and feminist perspectives.

"[*Urban Aboriginals*] is not concerned to persuade us that we ought to go out and adopt any particular formula or recipe," said Weir. "The text is powerfully concerned, in the elegance of its writing . . . to convince us that those who do practice leathersexuality, in Mains' terms, are engaging in an activity that has a kind of nobility. In Mains' terms, that serves as a way of accessing for him and for those in the community . . . a kind of truth.

"I called it transcendence earlier . . . a kind of higher experience that could not be had in any other way . . . Some of our key words are pilgrimage, transformation, the notion of therapy, the therapeutic exploration . . . But the purpose is not harm, the purpose is not pain . . ."

Bart Testa teaches semiotics and film studies at the University of Toronto. An intense, sardonic man, he described semiotics as the study of signs: linguistic signs ("natural languages" like English) and specialized signs ("visual languages" like photography, film, painting or gestures). Signs are codes that people use to send one another messages—to communicate; we are constantly encoding/transmitting and decoding/receiving, depending on our community(ies) and assumptions. By carefully studying a system of codes and its relationship to a text or image, a person can grasp the meaning of a work and its intended message. In essence, Testa wanted to show how easy it is to make simplistic, and erroneous, judgements about, in his words, "what a pornographic message is."

He spoke about the one-dimensional view of pornography held by most people.

"I think [this view] corresponds to our common sense of pornography," said Testa. "It has many echoes . . . about the notion that pornography is bereft of ideas, is an obsessive genre concerned only with sex and is therefore completely uninteresting from the broader human perspective. Some critics have even set up a notional ideal of pornography which they call 'porntopia.' This portmanteau word means a represented sexual utopia where there is nothing but sex, nothing else interrupts the sex . . .

"It is this pornographic ideal that has led many to say that pornography is worthless because it excludes ideas, it excludes art, it excludes psychology . . . Now, against this we can suggest that there may be other messages, other codes at work in any text, including the pornographic text."

Testa spoke about the codes embedded in the works of S/M authors like Pat Califia, and his message to the court was clear.

"I do not believe that judgements can be made by Canada Customs agents in isolation and using criteria that are so very detached," said Testa, "from the persons and groups who use [the books] and find in them purposes and meanings that [Customs'] criteria do not begin to address."

Before the trial began, even before the media started zooming in on Little Sister's, I tried to keep my family alert to what was coming up in my life. Not as a warning to leave town—my public persona just might cause them a little embarrassment—but because I had convictions about what I was doing. My parents brought me up to say what I felt and stand up for what I believed. Of course, they hadn't imagined it would be as a lesbian activist fighting censorship, but you don't always choose your battles.

J A N I N E

My coming out had been about as painful and painless as it is in many families, but after fifteen years and several girlfriends, my mother and father had warmed to the idea. During the trial, I was concerned they might catch some backlash on my behalf—they may very well have, but they spared me the news. They phoned whenever they read an article on the case. My father would say how horrible it was for the store to be treated that way (too much government regulation, that kind of thing), then he would take the clipping and read it to my mother. She was in the latter stages of Huntington's disease and, after twenty years of living at home under my father's care, she had been admitted to the palliative care unit of Toronto's Sunnybrook Hospital.

My dad visited me in Vancouver two months after the trial, the second time he'd ever taken a long holiday away from mom. My friend Bernard had taped all the TV news stories about Little Sister's, including the *Front Page*

Challenge episode, and my father flew home with a copy, carrying it as though it were the Hope Diamond.

"There's a VCR at the hospital, Erne will love this," he said. (My mother had the misfortune of being named Ernestine, and she was not at all disappointed that none of her offspring would name their children after her.)

A few days later, Dad called from a hospital pay phone to say they had watched it together. I felt sorry for my mother, completely wheelchair bound and unable to speak very much, when I imagined my father enthusiastically playing the video clips over and over again, freeze-framing at an annoying rate. Dad held up the phone so my mother could speak.

"I love you," she said in a watery, gravelled voice.

"Let's go watch the video again," I heard my father say.

In the spring of 1995, after some fundraising at the American Booksellers Association conference in Chicago, I touched down in Vancouver for a change of underwear, en route to Toronto for the Canadian Booksellers Association conference and a quick visit with my family. I was especially looking forward to seeing Mom.

The phone rang as I was unpacking. It was my father, calling to say that my mother had died of a heart attack that morning. Julie and I caught the red-eye to Toronto. A week later, we were fundraising again, sitting behind a book table with Jim Deva, trying to act like this never happened. My father took the video tape home from the hospital and watched *Front Page Challenge* again, but I'm sure it had lost its charm.

The Mastery of John Preston

Author John Preston was not unfamiliar with the storms that churned around his work. True, he had enjoyed mainstream recognition as the editor of anthologies published by Penguin: the three-part *Flesh and the Word* series, and *Members of the Family* and *Hometowns*; with American lesbian author Joan Nestle, he had co-edited *Brothers and Sisters* for Harper Collins. But his gay S/M story collections were intensely scrutinized by Customs, with the result that some of these other books also succumbed to detentions. *Hot Living*, erotic short stories about safer sex, was prohibited by Customs in 1987. Preston's *Masters* series—*I Once Had a Master, Entertainment for a Master* and *In Search of a Master*—had Customs' rap sheets that would have made a hardened criminal blush. These books had all been prohibited at the highest level of Customs' appeal process.

In a letter to Preston confirming his appearance as a witness at the trial, lawyer Joe Arvay summarized Preston's relevance: "*I Once Had a Master* and *Entertainment for a Master* are what started the litigation, it is very significant that you are able to attend the trial." But after the numerous delays and postponements, Preston would not attend. He died of AIDS in the spring of 1994. He did, however, provide a written account of his evidence—entitled "My Life as a Pornographer"—based on the Jon Pearson Perry Lecture he delivered at Harvard in April 1993.

Nino Ricci, leading Canadian novelist and winner of the 1990 Governor General's fiction award for *Lives of the Saints*, defended John Preston's work instead. In the last few months leading up to the Little Sister's trial, with Preston's health deteriorating, Ricci began to read Preston's work; Arvay had requested that he testify about *Entertainment for a Master.*

Ricci's prominence as writer, teacher and literary activist made his presence another coup for Little Sister's. (Ricci was PEN Canada's "rep" at the trial.) He was not, after all, an obvious choice to defend the artistry of gay and lesbian S/M fiction. Besides Preston's work, Ricci testified about *Afterglow,* a lesbian fiction anthology edited by Karen Barber, and Pat Califia's *Melting Point.* Within these books, Ricci testified, he found strategies for community building, for self-affirmation and the creation of proud lesbian and gay identities—the replacing of shame with celebration. Ricci described this as "validation literature," the necessary expression of any self-respecting minority. As the son of Italian immigrants, these themes were at the heart of much of his own work.

Turning to Preston's work, Ricci described a story from *Entertainment for a Master* that revealed Preston's ability to write porn that radically engaged his readers on complex, intellectual levels. "An Education" explored the ironies and limitations of using theoretical discourse to portray the intricacies of queer lives. Ricci's telling had an eerie resonance in the muffled walls of the courtroom, a setting almost archetypical of Preston's premise.

"There is a scene in the story 'An Education,' " said Ricci, "in which the narrator and two of his lovers go to a panel, a panel on sadomasochism at a conference. And while the panel is going on in a fairly abstract sort of way, they begin to engage in sexual behaviour in the conference room. I think what's going on here—and what eventually happens—is that the people who are in the panel and part of the conference are not able to deal with this. Even though they are supposedly dealing with sadomasochism, they're not able to confront sexuality directly when it's before them.

"As in *Afterglow*, what's going on here is the insistence on acknowledging a sexuality that has been traditionally marginalized, traditionally stigmatized, traditionally dismissed as unnatural. The tension between the academic and scientific, and the sexual and visceral—between the rational and the irrational—[is what] informs the text . . ."

Girls, Visions and Testimony

Sarah Schulman responded readily to a last-minute plea to testify as a literary expert on Preston's work. Novelist, teacher, journalist and all-round bright light among the lesbian literati, Schulman's own book, *Girls, Visions and Everything* (1986), had been detained by Canada Customs en route to Vancouver's Women In Print. Her credentials were impressive: a 1994 Fulbright fellowship; awards from the American Library Association and the 1990 Gregory Kolovokos Award for AIDS Writing; articles in the *London Guardian,* the *New York Times* and *Mother Jones*. Schulman's special status in queer circles came not just from her vivid, on-the-pulse fiction, but from her willingness to stand and be heard on difficult political issues.

John Preston and Sarah Schulman had not been close friends, though they had often participated at the same events; one of her favourite memories of Preston was taking a ferry trip together to Victoria, during the 1990 Gay Games in Vancouver. In testimony, she described him as "an extremely charismatic and gentlemanly person . . . well-regarded in literary circles as well as in the gay community at large." Arvay presented Schulman as a writer and teacher qualified to express an opinion as to whether Preston's novels *Entertainment for a Master* and *I Once Had a Master* were degrading or dehumanizing, and whether they created a substantial risk of harm, or had literary, artistic or other purposes.

Crown lawyer Van Iperen immediately objected to Schulman's ability to testify to the question of harm, arguing she was not a social scientist. Arvay addressed the issue.

"Much of [the testimony] is designed to inform your lordship as to the kind of evidence that might be before a trial judge in an obscenity trial," said Arvay. "The trial judge is going to have to decide difficult questions of whether something is degrading, difficult questions of whether it causes harm, difficult questions about artistic merit. Surely the assistance that the court will look to with respect to the first two is not going to be limited to social sciences or forensic sciences. Surely since, at the end of the day, the court has to determine whether something is degrading or dehumanizing or causes harm, those are concepts which persons from various walks of life and various disciplines may have an opinion about that may be useful to the court . . ."

Thus began an engrossing exchange between Arvay and Justice Smith about the obscenity law, an exchange that seemed to step outside the already unreal ambience of normal court procedure and leave the public, and possibly the Crown, in its wake.

"The terms degrading, dehumanizing and risk of harm are, in a sense, legal terms now as a result of the *Butler* decision," said Smith. "There has to be a finding of these things . . . in order to classify literature as obscenity."

"Yes, but no more or less than the concept of literary merit," said Arvay. ". . . They're all part of the test . . ."

"Whether there's a risk of harm, for example, sufficient to conclude that a work is obscene," asked Smith, "would depend on findings of fact based on evidence of harm . . . Isn't that so?"

"It's difficult even to know what has to be proven," Arvay replied. "It may be it requires extrinsic evidence, it may be that you look at the work itself. I think it's a complicated question . . . That's where the literary person, the person who is versed and skilled in matters of art and writing and literature, will look at the question of harm perhaps very differently than a psychologist, who might look for some sort of causal connection between the work and some sort of anti-social . . . harmful behaviour."

"But, ultimately the question of whether there is harm is one for the court [to decide]," said Smith ". . . And the finding has to be made on the basis of evidence from which an inference of harm can be drawn."

"But it may be made from the text itself," said Arvay. ". . . I [obviously] won't ask Sarah Schulman to opine on whether, from a psychological point of view, for instance, someone reading this book is about to go out and commit acts of non-consensual sado-masochism or something . . . It's probably too soon after *Butler* to know with any degree of certainty how one proves harm, how 'fact specific' it is, or whether it's something else . . . What I suggest, my lord, is all you have to do is recognize that this might be the kind of evidence that a trial judge in an obscenity hearing might want to hear . . . What we're trying to demonstrate is that this is one of many questions that should be asked . . . in the course of deciding whether books are obscene, and they aren't the kinds of questions that are presently being asked."

Arvay was reaching for an understanding of *Butler* that would accommodate all his witnesses' testimony about the "risks of harm"; the testimony not just of the behaviorists and social scientists, but also of artists, S/M practitioners themselves, openly gay men and women in every field— the experts, in fact, who could describe in graphic detail the harm their community endured because of state-sanctioned homophobia. In the end, Justice Smith ruled that Schulman not be allowed to advance an expert opinion on the legal question of harm. Nevertheless, harm was a key theme in her testimony.

Schulman focused on the autobiographical authenticity of Preston's work, its historic importance in the enrichment of gay writing, and its witnessing of a time before AIDS.

"[Preston's novels] have become literary historic documents of a period of time which is over and of the lives of people, many of whom we've lost," said Schulman. (Crown lawyer Van Iperen strenuously objected when Schulman made statistical references to AIDS, disputing her qualifications to speak on such a scientific matter.)

Schulman addressed gay male S/M with a candour one might have expected from Preston himself.

"It's my opinion that neither of these books contain depictions of actual violence," said Schulman, "primarily because there's no physical injury, no one is violated, there's no physical harm. It does contain the pretence, the mutually agreed upon pretence, of the threat of violence as mutually determined by the participants. However, no actual violence ever takes place. The only threat of actual violence that's ever seen in these books is exhibited by people outside the realm of the relationship who express hostility towards homosexuality.

"I think it's clearly [Preston's] point of view that depriving people of access to community or information about their sexual lives would, in a sense, be a degradation by the society. And that providing this information is positive and mitigates harm, particularly for gay men."

On the stand, Schulman voiced her concerns about being a lesbian or gay writer in a world that had no room for, or acceptance of, your reality.

"The development of gay and lesbian literature is a very fragile development," said Schulman, "because it's about people's truly lived experiences, and the willingness and bravery of the writers to express those experiences in a hostile environment. Now, obviously, anyone . . . who chooses to be openly gay or lesbian in their work will face professional liability. There is still social stigma, and John Preston was certainly willing to shoulder the burden . . . of that stigma in order to tell the truth about how people were living."

For all their differences of style, Sarah Schulman, like Jane Rule before her, revealed a deep, bodily knowledge of the conditions borne by gay and lesbian artists.

"As an openly lesbian writer for fifteen years," said Schulman, "I'm very familiar with the social manifestations of homophobia, how they impact on literature. And we see that homophobia is an anti-social behaviour that has anti-social consequences that isolate people from the society and destroy family relationships. It's a cause of violence, and [our] literature identifies and coalesces gay peoples as people who deserve social equity and dignity."

Schulman had neatly turned the question of harm to her own purposes: the issue in Courtroom 65 wasn't that harm flowed from pornography, but that harm flowed from *homophobia*. Lest Justice Smith forget, that's what the Little Sister's trial was about.

SIX

Lies, Damn Lies and Statistics

JOSEPH ARVAY: *Now, Dr. Marshall, you say [in your study] that the "lack of ill-effects may be seen as puzzling"... And you therefore have come to a conclusion ... which is contrary to your working hypothesis.*

DR. WILLIAM MARSHALL: *That's correct.*

ARVAY: *And your working hypothesis is based on some research that has been done by some social scientists in this field?*

MARSHALL: *That's correct.*

ARVAY: *And you would agree that the research that has been done by social scientists in this field is largely inconclusive on the question of proving a connection between pornography and harm?*

MARSHALL: *I would have thought that previous evidence suggested harmful effects for some types, limited types of pornography.*

ARVAY: *On some viewers?*

MARSHALL: *On some viewers, exactly.*

ARVAY: *It's fair to say that there are many reputable, very well-qualified social scientists working in this field who would question even that proposition?*

MARSHALL: *That's correct.*

THERE are only two kinds of witnesses: the expert and the not. To not be an expert meant you were a mere Anybody—an artist or a bookseller, a writer or a publisher, a Canada Customs inspector or a vice squad police officer. Such witnesses could give "opinion" evidence. But to be an expert witness at the Little Sister's trial, you had to be a Somebody with an advanced academic degree, preferably that of a social scientist. As Crown lawyer Neena Sharma explained, "The [*Butler* decision] said that in determining whether a prohibition [based on obscenity] under the Criminal Code . . . was constitutionally valid, it was reasonable for Parliament to rely on social science evidence that indicated there was harm, even if that evidence was inconclusive." So that there was no misunderstanding, Sharma emphasized that "it has been [the Crown's] position in this trial that whether that social science is valid or not [is not] relevant."

The deified, yet haphazard, nature of social science evidence had been commented on by Carole Vance earlier in the trial. She had given a droll account of her attempt at statistical analysis during field research into people's reactions to pornography.

"As the interviewer, I simply tried to elicit from my interview subject some thoughts and comments about the images in question," said Vance. "The range of reaction to the same image was extraordinary, from the most brutal degradation to the most happy reception. It sometimes reached almost comic proportions if the people were all in the same room and felt it was possible to actually offer their comment, which is not such an easy thing to do. But when they did, it was almost an hilarious cacophony of totally different reactions to the same image.

"It's a bit of a joke, but from this [research] I coined the term 'Vance's One-Third Rule': that if you take any image and show it to an audience, one third of the audience will think it's funny and ridiculous, one third will think it's disgusting, and one third will think it's erotic."

Vance's One-Third Rule notwithstanding, the relevance and relativity of social science evidence were central to both the Crown's and Little Sister's cases. The presence of Drs. Becki Ross and Gary Kinsman for

Little Sister's, and Dr. William Marshall for the Crown, signalled that scientific evidence would be used to "prove" *something*: either Little Sister's accusation of homophobia within Canada Customs or the Crown's claim that pornography had harmful effects.

Becki Ross entered the arena of the Little Sister's trial with more premonition of what she was up against than anyone would want. In 1993, she had served as a key witness for Glad Day Books in the *Bad Attitude* case (*R. v. Scythes*) and she was still smarting from the Crown's relentless cross-examination. Things were not going to be any easier in Courtroom 65. The liability of being an expert witness with social science credentials was that you were seen as a worthy target: a menace to be contained, undermined and refuted at all costs.

As the first Ph.D. in lesbian studies in Canada and author of the forthcoming work *The House That Jill Built* (1995), the first book-length treatment of Toronto's contemporary lesbian-feminist culture, Ross was very much in demand at obscenity trials. She had recently moved from Toronto to teach at Cariboo College in Kamloops, B.C.; soon after the move, she had accepted a full-time position in the sociology department at the University of British Columbia. Ross usually made a dramatic impression, even during courtroom appearances, with her brazenly artificial henna rinse, matching slash of red lipstick and stylish outfit. She represented a youthful, postmodern lesbian sensibility, unafraid to challenge certain feminist dictates of sexual conservatism and lesbian identity.

Ross was also committed to a radical sociological perspective—sociology *for* the subject—that challenged the traditional concept of the neutral observer. Ross' methodology, based in part on the work of Canadian feminist theorist Dorothy Smith, called for explicit recognition and encouragement of the dynamic between observer and subject group. In court, Ross identified herself as a lesbian, and she acknowledged this identity as integral to her sociological analysis of the dyke community. The government lawyers, not surprisingly, took aim at Ross' ideology and honesty in an effort to tarnish her credibility.

Arvay presented Ross as an expert in the sociology of women's studies and lesbian representation, and also on the differences and similarities between heterosexual and homosexual images and text. She started by sketching a brief history of homophobia in everyday Canadian life.

"I think that there has been a fear or loathing of lesbians and gay men that has pervaded all societal institutions for centuries," said Ross, "and this has been manifested through stereotypes of lesbians and gay men as sinners, as sick people, as criminals . . .

"The relationships that lesbians have with each other, and also gay men, have never been equally respected. There are about eighty court challenges before the federal government at the moment, introduced by lesbians and gay men, that put forward claims to equality and a revising of state policy with regard to pensions, health benefits, bereavement leave, immigration, marriage, for example . . ."

The unique value of Ross' expertise lay in her knowledge of contemporary North American lesbian culture. She was capable of drawing meaningful distinctions between lesbian and heterosexual porn, and of authoritatively describing the social context of dyke erotica. In fact, few people were better qualified than Ross to discuss lesbian sexual materials, including s/m porn, in the sociological language the courts were happy to hear. But Ross' task was difficult. She needed to illustrate the singular qualities of lesbian porn without implying that heterosexual porn deserved condemnation or censorship.

Ross began by considering the experience of women, straight and lesbian, who were working against the commonplace misogyny of the hetero-porn industry.

"I think heterosexual pornographers are realizing that women and female sexual pleasure constitute a very, very significant phenomenon," said Ross. "And as women have become more articulate and more vocal and more demanding in expressing their need of sexual images, heterosexual women have begun to devise their own images and their own vehicles for imagery. Not to be outdone, heterosexual male pornographers are realizing this is a market in terms of dollars and cents."

Arvay asked her opinion on whether mainstream pornography degrades or dehumanizes women.

"As far as my experience and research has told me," said Ross, "there is no monolithic, singular, uniform entity that we might be able to define as heterosexual pornography . . . [There is] a multiplicity of sub-genres . . ."

Ross reflected on the stark differences between the occasional "lezzie spread" in mainstream porn magazines like *Hustler* and lesbian-produced images.

"[In hetero-porn,] the women are typically, though not always, constructed as to be primed or ready for heterosexual intercourse, initiated and controlled by the male reader," said Ross. "So the male reader then is invited into the scene and the women's bodies are positioned to maximize his arousal and their compliance with his sexual need. They exist on the page, then, to service men."

By contrast, lesbian porn includes women models, photographers and producers in a collaborative process, recording sexual situations that are as much for themselves as for their intended readership; in fact, said Ross, the lesbian audience simply widens the circle of sexual exchange initiated in the original scenario. This kind of production, as Ann Scales also noted, has a profound impact on the images created. They are concerned, said Ross, "with female sexual subjectivity, female sexual empowerment and liberation, and female sexual self-determination."

The issue of lesbian s/m was never far away during Ross' testimony. Arvay launched into the topic directly.

"Can lesbian material, in your opinion . . . be degrading and dehumanizing, or dehumanizing to women?" he asked.

"I maintain that nothing that I have seen or read [of] lesbian sexual imagery—s/m imagery or not—can be classified under the category of degrading or dehumanizing," said Ross.

"Can you explain briefly why that is so?" asked Avray

"I believe that we know that female sexual self-knowledge, pleasure and desire have been systematically denied and repressed in this culture. In my opinion, contrary to the interpretation of lesbian s/m materials as degrading, these materials contribute to an emerging lesbian sexual literature and knowledge that seeks to embrace lesbian sex as healthy and articulate rather than unhealthy and non-existent . . ."

Bucking the *Bad Attitude* Attitude

Ross revisited evidence she had presented in the *Bad Attitude* trial, creating an uneasy sense of déjà vu; the Toronto trial, after all, had ended in a damaging obscenity conviction. But it was essential that Ross establish a sociological defence of s/m practices, in order to upset the heterosexist premises about consent and degradation that the Crown, and *Butler,* relied upon. Her job was to articulate the reality of lesbian sexuality from within its own framework.

"I would like to emphasize the consent established between the two female characters in the lesbian s/m fantasy [in *Bad Attitude*]," said Ross, "which is absolutely essential to accept as the motor which drives the image and the story . . . In actual lesbian s/m sex and in lesbian s/m fantasy, the bottom actually dictates the scene . . . By orchestrating the sexual encounter, the bottom disrupts the popular conception that she is passive, a victim, submissive and exploited. The objective of the top, by contrast, is to provide her bottom with sexual pleasure."

When Neena Sharma and Frank Falzon cross-examined Ross, their strategies were aggressive and effective, laying bare the competing versions of reality offered by the government and Little Sister's. Crown lawyer Sharma was intent on demonstrating a link between lesbian S/M porn and violence against women, apropos of *Butler.* "Consent" was the grounds on which Ross and others would salvage lesbian S/M materials from the taint of violence and degradation. But *Butler* had changed how judges could look upon the appearance of consent, since contrived consent, in the words of the Supreme Court, "makes the depicted acts even more degrading or dehumanizing."

Sharma and Ross immediately clashed, the Crown's hardline equation of S/M with harm running up against Ross' unconditional assertion that consent existed in all lesbian S/M encounters. Sharma went straight to Ross' identity, as well as her expertise.

"Would it be correct to describe you as a lesbian feminist?" asked Sharma.

"Yes," said Ross.

"And I take it that your testimony today and your opinion comes partly from that description, is that right?"

"Yes, I think so. I'm not . . ."

"I think that was a simple question."

"Yes. I think it was, too. I think it is a simple answer," Ross shot back. Sharma continued.

"You stated that there was nothing inherently demeaning about lesbian sexual activity, including S/M activity. Is that your view?"

"That is my view," said Ross.

"I take it that is assuming the activity is consensual, is that right?"

"All lesbian S/M fantasy and activity is consensual."

"Well, Professor Ross, you don't actually know that, do you?"

"I can tell you," Ross said, "that I can base that statement on fifteen years analyzing lesbian S/M subculture, lesbian S/M material, and my close relations with lesbian S/M participants and the lesbian S/M subculture in a number of different cities."

"But you would agree with me that—and I don't mean to be flippant—but you would agree with me that in some circumstances, it's possible there may be a problem with consent in lesbian s/m activities, is that fair?" asked Sharma.

"No."

"Not at all? Not ever?"

"No."

"Is that your view?"

"That is my view."

"You are not testifying today that you know of every lesbian person who engages in s/m activity, are you?"

"No, I am not," said Ross, "and I did not say that I was speaking as a representative of all lesbian s/m participants or all lesbian subcultures."

The Crown was obviously taken aback by what they characterized as Ross' "categorical" stance. For them, acceptable evidence needed to be based on conventional social science research, especially the kind that showed a link between porn and harm. Ross' opinion, in contrast, was formed deductively from the best available evidence about the lesbian community, with which she was intimately associated as a researcher and community member. For the Crown, Ross' approach was irrelevant, and their inability to grapple with her findings was both strategic and, possibly, sincere.

Ross was somewhat shaken by the end of Sharma's combative cross-examination. There was more to come from Frank Falzon.

The Attorney General's counsel acknowledged that social science had found "no conclusive evidence to demonstrate a causal link between [sexually violent] material and violence against woman," citing the 1985 Fraser Report (Canada) on heterosexual pornography. Falzon then asked Ross how she could make her unequivocal claims about lesbian s/m.

"I need to state that lesbian pornography has never been of interest to social science researchers," said Ross. "They have not made the study of lesbian pornography a priority, and so my testimony has been based on my own personal knowledge of [and research into] . . . the import, significance and meaningfulness of lesbian s/m imagery to that community."

"But you can't prove," Falzon asked, "based upon the work that you have done, that there is no harm, can you?"

"I'm not going to assume that there would be harm . . . So questions of harm or coercion or violence, as you might frame them, do not apply," said Ross.

After the *Bad Attitude* case, Ross had observed that the word lesbian had been mentioned probably no more than five times throughout the entire trial. She was evidently determined not to be silenced a second time. Yet courtrooms tend to smother certain messages, such as the small matter of sexual pleasure as a value in its own right. For the government, the Little Sister's trial was about obscenity and control, not bodies and pleasure. Even Joe Arvay, in his effort to prove that sexually explicit materials were a form of meaningful speech, concentrated on legal arguments, steering clear of desire.

But in one of the most emblematic moments of the trial, Ross was forced to remind the court that sex was at hand. Falzon was interested in the practice of fisting because "fisting was one of the activities . . . that the court in the [*Bad Attitude*] case held to be obscene." He asked Ross if she "could please describe fisting for his lordship?"

"Fisting is a sexual practice . . . [in which] a woman inserts her hand into the vagina of another woman," said Ross.

"When that is consensual, you are of the view that is not degrading or dehumanizing?" asked Falzon.

"Exactly the opposite," said Ross. "I would have to say that it is about sexual pleasure, and the experience can be very transporting sexually and extremely pleasurable and stimulating . . ." Falzon then asked Ross to read the fist-fucking passage from "Wunna My Fantasies," the *Bad Attitude* article that had been judged obscene.

For some people watching the cross-examination, this exchange with Falzon itself bordered on the degrading. Jim Deva considered it the low point of the trial. "Can you imagine the Crown's expert, William Marshall, having to explain some intimate sexual activity under cross-examination?" said Deva. But the moment had another dimension as well. Ross had made herself vulnerable by having the courage and willingness to deal with these questions, not simply in her role as a social scientist, but as a lesbian committed to her community. Ross' forthright answers, dismissed as the advocacy of an admitted "lesbian feminist" by the Crown, were, in fact, tremendously uplifting to many spectators in the public gallery.

The 1993 *Bad Attitude* obscenity trial—its messy execution and dispiriting defeat—was not just personally haunting to Ross. The case had also given legal weight to some dangerous sociological "evidence" about lesbian and gay pornography. Like a bad dream, that evidence was resurfacing in Courtroom 65. In *R. v. Scythes,* the Crown had called upon Neal Malamuth, the University of California (L.A.) professor whose research into the connection between pornography and sexual aggression is the most cited in the field. (For example, Malamuth's research was used by LEAF in their brief to the Supreme Court in the *Butler* case.) The Crown had asked him to prepare a response to the fundamental question—also at stake in the Little Sister's trial—as to whether "homosexual pornography may cause harm even if it is distinct from heterosexual pornography."

Malamuth was content to summarize his findings on the effects of heterosexual pornography, conducting no new research on gay porn or gay subjects. He asked himself three questions: (1) Are the messages contained in homosexual pornography critically different from those in heterosexual pornography? (2) Are the minds of homosexuals fundamentally different from those of heterosexuals? and (3) Are there problems relating to social conflict, including sexual and non-sexual aggression, within the homosexual community?

Malamuth had told the *Bad Attitude* trial that the similarity of content in homosexual and heterosexual porn would suggest that "To the extent that one can conclude that messages within heterosexual pornography might affect attitudes regarding the acceptability of acts, it may be reasonable to assume that similar processes and effects would occur when such messages are incorporated within homosexual pornography."

Furthermore, Malamuth argued, "considerable research" suggests "that processes for social influences, attitude change, normative effects, consequences of arousal, etc. do not differ fundamentally as a function of a person's sexual preference," and that therefore "comparable theoretical models" could be applied to the mind of either the homosexual or the heterosexual.

Malamuth's answer to the third question, about violence in gay relationships, became the inspiration for the AG's cross-examination of Ross on the question of consent and violence in queer porn. Falzon read out a statement from Malamuth's *Bad Attitude* testimony:

> In recent years [there] has been increasing scientific research indicating that some of the behaviours that might be related to exposure to some types of pornography are a serious problem within the gay community as well as within the heterosexual one. For example, there are studies suggesting that within homosexual interac-

tions the frequency of sexually coercive acts as well as non-sexual aggression between intimates occurs at a frequency quite compara-ble to heterosexual interactions . . . Furthermore, there are many similarities among gay and straight people in motives for various behaviours, including sexual activity, and in problems of sexual and non-sexual coercion.

"As a social scientist," asked Falzon, "do you accept that this is a rea-sonable statement by Dr. Neal Malamuth?"

Ross' answer was characteristically fiery.

"I do not. I think there is absolutely no scientific validity to the state-ment whatsoever," said Ross.

"As a social scientist, Professor Ross," said Falzon, "I put it to you that it would be at best, given the state of the social science research, it would be at best premature to express the categorical statement that you have just made."

"I fundamentally disagree," Ross answered. "As a social scientist, one of the principles that we operate from is the principle that we do not generalize from research carried out in one specific context for a specific set of purposes and objectives to another context. This is an absolute vio-lation of the principles of social scientific research."

"Notwithstanding any similarities between those two contexts?"

"Exactly."

Towards a Gay Sociology

When Dr. Gary Kinsman answered Falzon's same question, he was more diplomatic. But his assessment of Malamuth's claim was the same.

"I would suggest that this type of methodology," said Kinsman, "which suggests that, because you have done research in a certain area with a certain population, you can also generalize to another grouping, another population—that this is quite suspect and is often challenged within social science research."

Since publishing *The Regulation of Desire* (1987), the first and, so far, only history of gays in Canada, Gary Kinsman has been one of few out male scholars visible beyond the scattered pages of academic journals or the gay press. Now an assistant professor in the sociology and anthropol-ogy department of Laurentian University in Sudbury, Ontario, Kinsman has long balanced the roles of academic and activist. In Toronto in the

early 1980s, he was a co-founder of *Pink Ink* and *Rites,* two important lesbian and gay national newsjournals, and of the Canadian Committee
Against Customs Censorship (CCACC), which was originally formed
around the detentions at Glad Day Books. Because of his longstanding
resistance to Customs censorship, especially through the CCACC, the
Crown was suspicious that Kinsman's testimony would be that of an
"advocate" rather than of a neutral expert. But Kinsman adapted easily to
his role as the reliable narrator of gay legal and sociological history in
Canada, letting the facts speak for themselves.

As Kinsman explained, the complete criminalization of all male homosexual activity, consensual or not, was introduced in the 19th century
and continued without interruption until the Criminal Code of Canada
reforms of 1969. (These Liberal reforms, contained in an omnibus bill
called C-150, decriminalized sexual acts in private between two consenting adults aged twenty-one years or older.) Throughout Canada's history, criminal sanctions against gay sex were justified under many varying
doctrines, just as Carole Vance had earlier outlined: from moral to medical
and criminal and back again.

"In Canada, there were laws in the 1950s that were referred to as
'criminal sexual psychopath' laws," said Kinsman. "In the 1960s, they
were referred to as 'dangerous sexual offender' legislation . . . During this
period, all engagement in homosexual activity was criminalized.
Offences for either criminal sexual psychopaths or dangerous sexual
offenders included gross indecency and buggery, the main sexual
offences that could be used against men for engaging in sexual activity
with other men. So during this period, it was possible that someone convicted of gross indecency—even if it was consensual, it would still be
illegal—could actually at the time of sentencing be processed as a criminal sexual psychopath or a dangerous sexual offender, and that would
mean they could actually be put away indefinitely."

Kinsman tried to convey how this history impacted on contemporary
beliefs that gay porn, and gay sex itself, was inherently degrading.

"The historical legacy is a series of legal, social and moral [traditions],"
said Kinsman, "that have established male homosexuality—sex between
men—as already having a more criminal . . . or a more immoral or a
more indecent character than similar representations of heterosexual
activity."

The historical context also directly impacted on Canada Customs'

position. As Kinsman pointed out, the criminal offence of "gross indecency" (the code word for gay anal sex) wasn't abolished until 1988,
despite the 1969 reforms. Throughout the 1970s and beyond, however,
Customs routinely detained materials showing anal penetration between
consenting male adults. Their guidelines, it seemed, were firmly lodged
in pre-reform values.

Until Kinsman's testimony, the Crown rarely had to address Canada's
legislative record on gay and lesbian rights. Institutionalized homophobia was not a matter they wished to explore, since an essential premise of
their defence was that rules and regulations were, *prima facie,* impartial
and nondiscriminatory. Indeed, Memorandum D9-1-1 made absolutely
no mention of homosexuals or lesbians; nor did the obscenity provisions
of the Criminal Code, the basis for the memorandum. To the Crown, this
meant Little Sister's had no grounds to cry "discrimination." If they were
unhappy with some decisions by Customs, they were welcome to use the
perfectly adequate appeal system.

When Crown lawyer Van Iperen cross-examined Kinsman, he zeroed
in on Kinsman's statements about homophobia in the Criminal Code.

". . . What I am particularly concerned about is whether there is a bias
in your opinion," said Van Iperen. ". . . I'm putting to you that the
Criminal Code section itself, on the face of it, is not directed at homosexuals. Is that correct?"

The simplicity of the question caught Kinsman off guard.

"But it—yes, that is correct. I mean it does not specifically refer to
homosexual acts," said Kinsman, "but it's important to point out that the
clause in it referring to acts of indecency has been used and interpreted
by police forces to lay charges against gay men for engaging in consensual sexual activities behind locked cubicle doors . . . which I would
understand as being [in] private . . ."

When it was Angela Westmacott's turn to cross-examine Kinsman, she
fixed her sights on his claim that there were important distinctions
between lesbian and gay porn and heterosexual porn. As co-counsel for
the Attorney General, Westmacott took a palpably hard line, much to the
dismay of Little Sister's supporters.

In general, the province's intervention in the trial felt like a betrayal.
B.C.'s New Democratic Party government could usually be counted on to
take a fairly progressive stand on gay and lesbian rights; they had added
sexual orientation to the province's *Human Rights Act,* provided core

funding to the Vancouver Lesbian Centre and increased support for AIDS services. But in Courtroom 65, the AG's lawyers were often the fiercest interrogators of Little Sister's witnesses. Their nominal interest was in protecting B.C.'s *Motion Pictures Act*—the regulation of films has been a provincial perk since the beginning of the medium—but Westmacott and Falzon seemed to go out of their way to argue forcefully against Kinsman's and Ross' queer-positive perspectives.

Kinsman took a complex approach to the question of harm and pornography. He understood the feminist concern that some heterosexual porn reflected and reinforced the power imbalances between women and men in everyday life. But he strenuously argued that lesbian and gay porn couldn't contribute to those imbalances, for the simple reason that queer porn doesn't depict sex between women and men, and therefore, can't depict women being victimized by men.

Westmacott, however, was relentless in her attempt to show that the (heterosexual) risk of harm was directly translatable into lesbian and gay relations, and that the risk was especially evident in the rituals of gay S/M.

"Dr. Kinsman, is it not the case that violence is violence, regardless of the biological capabilities of the persons involved?" asked Westmacott.

"I would agree that actual violence is always actual violence," said Kinsman.

"You say that gay male S/M is not actual violence, but it's ritualized or theatrical use of pressure, constraints, discipline, punishment?"

"That's correct."

"That's also true of heterosexual S/M, is it not?"

"That's correct," said Kinsman, "but in the added social context of also being shaped by very pervasive forms of gender inequality."

"From a sociological point of view, Dr. Kinsman, is there not a reasonable concern that a medium which encourages and eroticizes aggression as a sexual practice will reinforce and indeed promote abuse in society?" asked Westmacott.

"If it is S/M you are referring to," said Kinsman, "I don't agree that that is what characterizes gay male S/M. It's not about aggression . . ."

Earlier, Westmacott's cross-examination had veered onto extremely questionable ground, when she seemed determined to make a causative link between gay domestic violence and S/M practices. Westmacott approached the issue by discussing various American studies of battering in gay male relationships.

"Did you consider the issue of domestic violence in same-sex relationships in forming your opinion that gay s/M does not raise the same troubling issues as the heterosexual s/M?" Westmacott asked.

"Yes, I did," said Kinsman.

"You would agree that this is a significant issue which has some bearing on the issue of gay s/M?"

". . . In terms of the research . . . I have done, there's no significant correlation or connection between gay s/M and these problems of domestic violence," said Kinsman. "Far more often what you will find are problems with alcoholism, problems with people feeling not fully comfortable about themselves as being gay . . . There is no relationship in any direct linear way between practices of gay s/M and the forms of domestic violence and the abuse you're describing."

"You're making that statement categorically?" asked Westmacott.

"In terms of the studies that have been done, that's the suggestion," said Kinsman.

The Little Sister's case, as a constitutional challenge, hinged in part on the issue of equality, as defined in the *Charter of Rights and Freedoms*. Arvay was arguing that Little Sister's owners, as gay men, were being discriminated against on the basis of their sexual orientation. The Attorney General, however, took a decidedly different—and regressive—run at the question of equality, tapping into the oft-heard accusation that "gays' rights are special rights."

"You're critical of the fact, understandably so, that homosexual people have been singled out for unequal legal and social treatment throughout Canadian history. Is that correct?" asked Westmacott.

"Yes, I'm very critical of that," said Kinsman.

"But now you're suggesting that gays and heterosexuals should not be treated equally in terms of the regulation of pornography, is that fair to say?"

"No, I don't think that's what I'm arguing at all," said Kinsman firmly. "What I'm suggesting is that the historical legacy has been that gay sexual representations have actually been treated differently than heterosexual ones . . ."

The government lawyers' characterization of Kinsman and Ross as "categorical," "lesbian feminist," "biased" and "advocate" was a tactic to neutralize their expert testimony. The cross-examination of both witnesses was lengthy, aggressive and often frustrating, for lawyer and witness alike. But the clashes over Little Sister's sociological evidence set the tone: advocacy and bias would be ferreted out and exposed, if necessary, when the Crown's own expert took the stand. The Crown probably hoped *their* sociologist would win back some lost ground by casting Customs in a more benign light. If so, they were going to be sorely disappointed.

After all of Little Sister's witnesses were duly examined and cross-examined, there was a week's break in the proceedings while the Crown geared up for their defence. This was Arvay's opportunity to review his cross-examination strategy—in theory, at least. In practice, Arvay used the week's recess to immediately fly to Ottawa and argue the Egan-Nesbitt case before the Supreme Court of Canada.

Jim Egan and Jack Nesbitt are an elderly gay couple—over forty years together—who now live on Vancouver Island. (Egan is a Canadian gay rights pioneer—in Kinsman's words, "the only homophile activist in 1950s Toronto.") They were demanding equal treatment under the Old Age Security act, which provides a pension benefit to spouses of OAS recipients—but only if the spouse is of a suitably opposite sex. While Irene Faulkner stayed behind to organize Little Sister's final weeks in court, Arvay wrestled yet another gay rights case, this time in the highest court of the land.

Vancouver has many unforgettable sights: the majestic mountains . . . the ocean at sunset . . . the towering cedars of Stanley Park . . . Joe Arvay burning a trail of wheelchair rubber down Vancouver's

J A N I N E   rough 'n tumble Granville Street, on a porn hunt, his crew of helpers in hot pursuit . . .

They moved like a SWAT team from one smutty store to the next, leaving perplexed cashiers in their wake. Did the clerks suspect cleverly disguised undercover cops? Joe's team included his colleague Irene, her stepson, Mark, Mark's lover Mark—why do people with the same name insist on becoming lovers?—and Jim Deva. Joe shepherded them through pornland, scouring one magazine after another for evidence to present to witnesses, ours and theirs. Bondage, violence against women, anything that might—should?—attract the attention of Canada Customs and Memorandum D9-1-1. Other customers, having secretly stolen away from home during their children's homework hour, looked on rather nervously, perhaps expecting to be featured in a local media exposé.

After hours of searching in the pouring rain, they called it quits. The team had gathered plenty of magazines, but they still lacked a crown jewel, the image that would have made the soggy night completely worthwhile. Still, enough was enough.

But the next morning, Arvay awoke dissatisfied. He made his way solo to a local corner store's adult magazine rack, where he was greeted by a stern Don't Read the Magazines sign. Ignoring it, Arvay started his search. He soon hit pay dirt: a spread in *Hustler* magazine that strongly suggested violence against women. Loading up with enough copies for everyone in Courtroom 65—excluding the public gallery—Arvay approached the cashier. "All in the line of duty, all in a day's work," I'm sure Joe thought, as he watched the clerk watch him, no doubt thinking less than flattering thoughts.

Throughout the trial, I never knew what kind of rabbit Joe would pull out of his hat. He would get a twinkle in his eye, gesture me quietly over to his side and explain the highlights of what was to come. Sometimes I would detect troubled waters underneath his calm surface, but Joe at the helm of our little boat made us seem as solid as a tanker. I would be having a bite with Irene and the phone would ring. "It's for you, Irene," the waiter would call out. It would be Joe again, with another idea, another expedition, another book to track down in the middle of the night, another witness to convince to come out and testify. But because Joe seemed to be doing the impossible, I thought I could too. If he had asked me to dress up as Catwoman to help the case, I would have been preening my whiskers in no time.

The witnesses who appeared for Little Sister's also went above and beyond the call of duty. Besides the ordeal of testifying, many of them sat on panels, attended fundraising receptions and were generally run ragged from the moment they arrived in Vancouver. There was the benefit bash at the Pitt Gallery by the Writers Union of Canada and the B.C. Federation of Writers, and another at the Kootenay School of Writing—a funky venue perched atop a veritable Everest of stairs. And Simon Fraser University organized a two-part evening series called Forbidden Fruits, at their comfy-corporate downtown campus.

The first panel brought together witnesses Nino Ricci, Bruce Ryder (a Toronto law professor), Persimmon Blackbridge and Sandra Haar. A week later, the second panel included Pat Califia, Gary Kinsman, Becki Ross and

Bart Testa. I was in awe of these men and women. How did they find the stamina to speak so eloquently after a day on the stand? I could do little more than sit in respectful silence. Both panels were lively discussions about censorship, sexuality and resistance—and the difficulties ahead. One voice from the audience left some sobering thoughts.

"We are all talking about 'when this trial is over,' but this struggle will never be over," said filmmaker Aerlyn Weissman. "It doesn't stop just because you win or lose the Little Sister's case."

After the second panel, many of us made our way to the last social event of the trial. A delectable spread had been whipped together at the Kootenay School, courtesy of the epicurean talents of my friend Jules and my lover, Julie. I staggered up the stairs and through the door, expecting a cheese tray at best. Julie and Jules leaned back, cool as cucumbers, the serene hosts. At the party's end, most of the panellists returned to their B & Bs, except Pat and J.C., who drove back to Seattle. Julie and I scraped the remains of the food into a green garbage bag, thanked all the volunteers at the event and made our way home. Of course, my duties weren't really over.

The following week, Sarah Schulman would be at the Kootenay School, doing a hastily arranged reading. I needed to prepare for my own at-long-last turn in the witness box and I had clearly run out of stair-climbing steam. I'm sure Sarah had read b-u-r-n-o-u-t in my eyes when she graciously offered to go to the reading alone. I went home, determined to bone up on my testimony as if it were an exam. But in the time it took to open a page of my notebook, I was on the couch, passed out.

In Which the Crown Gets Snookered

Dr. William Marshall was easily the most experienced witness at the Little Sister's trial. After citing at least fifteen court appearances, he admitted to losing track of how many times he had testified. Marshall was like the government's "house" sociologist, serving the prosecution in many important Canadian obscenity cases, including the Eli Langer trial and R. v. Scythes, the Bad Attitude trial; he was also one of few Canadians invited to contribute to the American Meese Commission on pornography in the mid-1980s.

Although a recognized authority—professor of psychology at Queen's University, Kingston; prominent clinical psychologist; founder of the first treatment clinics for sexual offenders in Ontario and New Zealand—

Marshall was refreshingly free of professional arrogance. Tentative and precise about his findings and their implications, acknowledging that it was the "nature of theorizing that you're wrong a lot of the time," the Australian-born psychologist showed a stronger allegiance to actual results than to his own, or anyone else's, assumptions.

Since the late 1980s, Marshall had met several times with Customs officials in Ottawa to discuss, as he said, "the effects of pornography . . . [the sessions were] partly a morale booster, or maybe to sharpen their understanding of issues, too." In 1991, he was approached by a senior Customs administrator who was concerned that the well-being of Customs inspectors was perhaps being eroded by their workplace exposure to porn. Marshall was asked to test ninety volunteers, representing all bureaucratic levels and all degrees of exposure. His study consisted of a detailed, multi-levelled questionnaire that delved into the beliefs, attitudes and personal reactions of the Customs officials. Marshall also did face-to-face interviews with groups of workers. On completion, he submitted the "Report of the Study of the Effects on Customs Officers of Reviewing Pornography" to Revenue Canada.

At the Little Sister's trial, the Crown intended for Marshall to highlight only a small fragment of this wide-ranging study: a subset of the questionnaire that dealt with Customs officers' attitudes towards lesbian and gay porn. These findings were considered good news by the defence; the number-crunching apparently demonstrated that Customs officers did not have an especially censorious attitude towards queer porn. The Crown most certainly did *not* want to explore the study's central finding: that Customs officers seemed unaffected by their prolonged exposure to porn. But when Joe Arvay commenced his cross-examination, the Crown learned, to their considerable dismay, that the scope of Marshall's testimony would be far beyond their control.

Crown lawyer Neena Sharma guided Marshall to the section of his study that showed Customs officers weren't inclined to detain or ban more materials than they already did, despite the fact that some officers had strong negative reactions to homosexuality itself. The Crown believed this indicated a healthy professional environment at Customs, where one's personal prejudices did not interfere with one's job description.

The subset had posed three questions. The first asked the officers: "Regardless of your responsibility to administer departmental guidelines as contained in Memorandum D9-1-1, which of the following depictions do you personally feel should not be available for distribution?" Twelve sexual depictions followed, both explicit and implicit in nature, including male couples kissing and petting, and a female couple using dildos. The second question asked the respondents to estimate how common various kinds of lesbian and gay sex were among the general adult population, on a five-part scale from very rare (less than 10 percent) to very common (better than 90 percent). (Marshall suspected there was a correlation between believing homosexuality was uncommon and being homophobic.) Finally, officers were asked to "indicate how much you would desire to engage in each of the listed [gay] sexual activities," on a five-part scale from "very desirable" to "repulsive."

"Our overall intent," said Marshall, speaking of the subset, "was to get an idea of whether [the Customs officers] were rather censorial about sexual matters altogether, and whether that had anything to do with their own desires or feelings of repulsion and so on . . ."

"So, Dr. Marshall," asked Sharma, "what is your opinion about whether Customs officers are homophobic?"

Marshall's answer exemplified the cautious, meticulous—and impartial—tone of his testimony.

"This group of Customs officers," said Marshall, "did not appear to me to be homophobic with respect to those particular items indicated in the context of this particular study."

"Are there portions of the questionnaire that assisted you in assessing whether Customs officers were overcensorious?" asked Sharma.

Marshall described the officers as "willing to tolerate some sexual depictions that they themselves found undesirable, if not even repulsive, personally—a fairly tolerant view, I would say." He also pointed to the one area where officers' attitudes "differed from departmental guidelines: violence independent of sexual matters. Most of them thought that should be censored, something like 70 percent of them."

When Arvay and Marshall dissected the study more closely, Marshall declared that approximately 20 percent of the officers were found to be personally homophobic. Yet the question that gauged personal feelings seemed to suggest a different story. A detailed analysis of those responses showed that over 70 percent of the officers felt that "homosexual acts" were repulsive.

"The fact that a very large proportion considered homosexual acts repulsive, what did you draw from that?" asked Arvay.

"I was surprised at that," said Marshall, "to be honest, that so many of them found it to be repulsive. But I was surprised by the fact that [this] didn't seem to affect, profoundly affect, at all their judgement as to whether these materials should be available for other people."

In effect, Arvay was able to demonstrate that Marshall's study lent itself to two very different interpretations: the Crown's, which was that Customs officers' feelings about gays and lesbians had no bearing on their on-the-job performance, and Little Sister's, which was that homophobic attitudes appeared to be alive and well at Canada Customs.

But it was on the question of porn's relationship to harm that Arvay really scored, with a solid professional assist from William Marshall.

"The interest here," said Arvay about Marshall's study, "was whether or not increases in the levels of involvement in pornography reviewing would produce harmful effects . . . on the officers' functioning. In fact, few negative effects were observed."

Crown lawyer Sharma interrupted.

"We have never taken the position that that issue is relevant in this trial," said Sharma. The Crown, she said, hadn't tendered Marshall "for that purpose and we've consistently taken the position it's not relevant evidence." This was the first of many skirmishes between Sharma and Arvay about how much of Marshall's expertise was admissible in the Little Sister's trial.

Arvay replied to the issue of relevancy.

"Simply put, my lord, the basis upon which the federal government defends this [Customs] legislation is that pornography, specifically obscenity, is harmful." said Arvay. "If, in fact, I can show through Dr. Marshall that those persons who read or view pornographic material day in and day out, for an extended period every time, including pornography of the most explicit sort, do not suffer negative effects, then this is information which should be relevant in the constitutionality of this legislation . . ."

Sharma tried to persuade Justice Smith that "asking [Marshall] his opinions about the effects of pornography goes beyond the expertise that this witness was qualified to give an opinion on . . ." But the Crown's urgent attempt to restrain their own expert witness failed, and Arvay was soon presenting Marshall with a series of damning claims from his own study. Marshall was happy to report his findings.

"Now, Dr. Marshall, in your study," asked Arvay, ". . . you also express this opinion: . . . 'reviewing pornography had no effect on job satisfaction or satisfaction with life generally, nor did it affect most of the features of intimate relations or general aspects of social relations.' "

"That's correct," said Marshall.

". . . And then you say: 'Beliefs about how humiliating certain sexual behaviours are were unchanged by . . . reviewing pornography' . . . ?"

"Correct."

"And you say: 'Similarly, the desire for conventional, unconventional or hurtful sexual behaviours was unchanged as a result of reviewing pornography.' "

"Correct."

". . . And you express this opinion: 'Their own sexual lives seem unaffected by their work. They are not haunted by deviant thoughts or desires; they are not worried about what they might do sexually . . .' "

"That's correct."

. . . And Then Snookered Again

During the first day of Marshall's testimony, amidst an earlier clash between Sharma and Arvay, the psychologist had mentioned a letter he had received from the Crown's previous counsel, an H. J. Wruck, dated September 29, 1993. Wruck had been preparing the government's defence for the Little Sister's trial scheduled that year and later postponed; he had since dropped out. In the confusion over the correspondence—whether it was inadmissible as a privileged exchange between solicitor and witness—Marshall revealed that the letter was tucked away in his briefcase. Irene Faulkner walked over to the stand, Marshall politely handed her the document and in no time it was in Arvay's possession. The Crown had neither seen, nor could they have guessed at, the letter's contents.

The next day in court, the bonanza of this fluke disclosure became apparent. Wruck had asked Marshall to "review a number of the expert reports prepared by various experts that Little Sisters Book Store [sic] intends to call as witnesses. I require your assistance in order to assist me in attacking and refuting their expert report evidence . . ." Wruck listed the Little Sister's witnesses he needed ammo against, including Thomas Waugh, a film studies professor at Concordia University in Montréal, and Dr. Bill Coleman, a Vancouver psychologist whose court appearance was proving very difficult to schedule.

What was extraordinary was that Marshall had handwritten a draft of his reply on the back of Wruck's letter. Despite strong efforts by the Crown to have this evidence declared privileged, there was no way of keeping Marshall's reply under wraps. As Arvay pointedly said, "Well, my lord, clearly any privilege that attached has been waived. I have the letters, I can't spill from my brain the information I have in it."

Justice Smith agreed.

Wruck seemed especially concerned about Little Sister's expert evidence on anal penetration. He commented on Coleman's report. "I question whether in today's society," wrote Wruck, "given our knowledge of AIDS, that many gays are practising fellatio and anal penetration. I also have no idea of whether S&M and bondage is generally practised by 7 percent of gays . . ."

"Now Dr. Marshall," said Arvay, "as I understand it [from reading your reply], you carefully looked at Dr. Coleman's report and you could find no grounds to disagree with his conclusions, and indeed concluded his reasoning was sound."

"I did, yes," said Marshall.

Besides putting the Crown in an exceedingly embarrassing position—their own expert was clearly agreeing with Little Sister's expert—the reference to Coleman's report offered Arvay an irresistible opportunity. He immediately tendered Coleman's report as an exhibit, neatly solving the problem of fitting the psychologist into the packed schedule of witnesses.

Wruck had also asked Marshall for help refuting Waugh's submission. (Waugh had testified earlier for Little Sister's.) "Mr. Waugh suggests that anal intercourse is a standard sexual practice within the gay male community," wrote Wruck. "Is this an accurate statement given the advent of AIDS?" Arvay asked Marshall to read a portion of Waugh's statement aloud. Waugh's earlier testimony had caused Arvay some concern—he had answered a Crown question about snuff films in a troublesome manner—but his written paean to gay anal sex was now redeeming the oft-maligned act:

> Anal intercourse is a standard sexual practice within the gay male community. Exalted by classical Greek and Arabic poets, as well as by modern artists from Rimbaud and Ginsberg to Pasolini, anal intercourse evokes all of the romantic and erotic connotations within

gay culture that "missionary position" coitus does within mainstream culture. To use anal intercourse as a criterion for inadmissibility because of its presumed degradation of the participants discriminates against minority practices, values, and cultural traditions. Furthermore, unprotected anal intercourse having in recent years been established as a high-risk sexual practice in the context of the AIDS epidemic, the interdiction of the verbal and visual representation of anal intercourse constitutes an embargo on the import of "Safe Sex" guidelines within the Canadian gay community.

"I take it, Dr. Marshall," asked Arvay, "that you could find no reasons to disagree with Professor Waugh's conclusions . . . and indeed considered his reasoning sound?"

"Yes, I did," said Marshall.

Marshall made this same reply again and again, having found no basic disagreement with the Little Sister's witnesses the Crown had asked him to disagree with. When Arvay further investigated Marshall's own published work, he discovered this open-minded attitude was, in fact, a motif of Marshall's professional life.

"Dr. Marshall," asked Arvay, "I take it that it is your opinion that pornography is only an exaggerated and blatant expression of the anti-female and anti-child sentiments that pervade the media, [especially] advertising?"

"That's my view, yes."

". . . And in 1988 you joined a list of researchers who would emphasize that we have not found that exposure to violent pornography is a correlate of sexual aggression against women in natural settings [rather than in laboratory experiments]."

"That's correct."

Under Arvay's dazzling cross-examination, the neutrality of the Crown's star witness had come dangerously close to conversion to the Little Sister's camp. Sharma scrambled to retrieve something useful from Marshall's evidence, but the government had been snookered. With Marshall's testimony completed, the Crown began presenting their next witnesses: Customs employees and police officers. Although less glamorous, they at least promised to be less unpredictable—perhaps. With Arvay at the height of his game, even that was no longer a sure thing.

□ SEVEN □

Strange Customs

JOSEPH ARVAY: *So it is your understanding that if the Customs Inspectors are doing their job properly, before they prohibit a book, they should read that book from cover to cover?*

JOHN SHEARER, Director General of the Tariff Programs Division: *They should.*

ARVAY: *Is it your understanding that that occurs?*

SHEARER: *. . . if a Customs Inspector is experienced in doing his work and has done a detailed examination of a book, he can or she can obtain a good, or should be able to obtain a good, understanding of whether the book can be found to be obscene or whether it can be saved by any literary or artistic merit through a good close perusal of the work.*

I am not sure that they need to read every single word in the book but certainly they have to read a good portion of the material before them.

ARVAY: *Do you know of any instance in which a Customs Inspector has read a book from cover to cover, prior to ruling on it and prohibiting it?*

SHEARER: *Personally, I do not say that I do, no.*

ARVAY: . . . *Do you personally know whether a Tariff Value Administrator has ever read a book from cover to cover?*

SHEARER: *No, I couldn't say I personally know that they have.*

ARVAY: . . . *Do you personally know whether Tariff Administrators read books from cover to cover?*

SHEARER: *Yes, I do.*

ARVAY: . . . *Give me an example of a book that a Tariff Administrator has read thoroughly from cover to cover . . .*

SHEARER: . . . *I can tell you that* American Psycho *has been read from cover to cover . . .*

IN the fall of 1994, while the Little Sister's team was neck deep in prep-arations for the October trial, the bookstore's owners braced for the inevitable. Even newspaper reporters were buzzing the store: Would there be another abrupt turnaround, an eleventh-hour phone call sig-nalling the Crown's next motion to adjourn—or to dismiss the case alto-gether? After years of postponements and other delaying tactics, no one could label Little Sister's paranoid for believing the government might be cooking up something.

Sure enough, on September 29, 1994, a mere two weeks before the trial date, a government fax squeaked into Little Sister's back office. Bruce Smyth and Jim Deva weren't especially surprised by the message. Canada Customs had revised Memorandum D9-1-1 so that anal penetra-tion—box (g) on Customs' notice of detention—was no longer listed as grounds for prohibited entry. The timing was hardly coincidental.

The B.C. Civil Liberties Association and Little Sister's immediately issued a press release. The headline said it all: "Too Little, Too Late." The bookstore predicted that next to nothing would change and that Customs would simply use the remaining categories to detain the same books and magazines. Legal experts from across Canada, they noted, had called for the elimination of anal penetration from D9-1-1 for years, to no avail. Changing the memorandum on the eve of the trial was certainly not an act of good faith as far as Little Sister's was concerned.

Indeed, both Little Sister's and Glad Day Books in Toronto continued to have their shipments opened and inspected by Customs as frequently as before. If the booksellers had hoped the September amendment might trigger a speedy release of the mountains of magazines and books already detained for anal penetration, they were quickly brought back down to earth. Deva and Smyth could recall only a single title, *Roman Conquests,* from Alyson Publications, being returned to the store that autumn.

There was a small sense of victory, however; Customs had clearly wilted in the heat generated by the upcoming trial. But people who had had close encounters with Canada Customs remained wary.

"You can change a form, but it doesn't change the system," Janine Fuller told the media. "It doesn't change the attitudes that have allowed this discriminatory regulation to be used in the first place, and to remain unchanged for so long. If they think we are going to fold up our tents and go home because of a change to a Customs memorandum, they have misjudged our community's commitment to be heard."

After Dr. William Marshall's cross-examination, the government turned to another crop of witnesses: Customs officials. Many of these officials were actually appearing at Joe Arvay's request, with Crown lawyer Hans Van Iperen graciously agreeing to call them at the government's expense.

The Crown started as close to the top as they could get. John Shearer, the Ottawa-based director general of the Tariff Programs Division, was a high-altitude bureaucrat, two notches down from the deputy minister of National Revenue. He was followed by Linda Murphy, the director of the Prohibited Importations Directorate in Ottawa. Next came various regionally based Tariff and Value Administrators (TVAs), Commodity Specialists and, finally, a Customs Inspector. The Crown hoped these witnesses would give Justice Smith a succinct picture of Customs' screening and detention processes and the two-tiered appeal system. Van Iperen wanted to shed light on the complexities and scope of Customs' work, to give a human face to Customs employees and to offer plausible explanations for the prohibitions and detentions before the court. He didn't feel a need to prove that Customs ran a flawless ship or was absolutely consistent in its practices. In his closing arguments, Van Iperen would suggest to Justice Smith that Customs had some internal bugs that could be worked out without totally dismantling its system of prior restraint.

Arvay's goal with the Customs witnesses was three-pronged: to show widespread inconsistencies, to highlight ongoing abuses and to demonstrate that even Customs officers were themselves confused about how the bureaucracy worked. But Arvay wasn't trying to paint Customs workers as simply inept or unsophisticated; he wanted to expose the unreasonable burden and stress placed on their shoulders in trying to enforce and make sense of Memorandum D9-1-1. His cross-examination of defence witnesses would untangle some of Canada Customs' messy web and draw out some of the trial's most controversial evidence.

Follow the Bouncing Book—Again

Canada Customs' web starts at a "point of entry"—a border crossing, an airport, a post office, a Customs warehouse, a seaport. Books or magazines are examined by a uniformed Customs Inspector at this first level of operations. If the inspector suspects that a publication is obscene, seditious, treasonous, hate literature or child pornography, according to Memorandum D9-1-1, he or she can detain the book for further scrutiny. The importer will be sent the top portion of a legal-size document called a K 27, a Notice of Detention/Determination. This notice merely indicates which title(s) is being held for review and nothing more.

Next, a "thorough" review is performed either by the same Customs Inspector or by a Commodity Specialist, one step up. If the publication is deemed to be obscene, then the full K 27 form is mailed to the importer. A cursory explanation is provided in the shape of boxes to tick off: (a) Sex with violence; (b) Child sex; (c) Incest; (d) Bestiality; (e) Necrophilia; (f) Hate propaganda; (g) Anal penetration (now scratched out); and (h) Other. When (h) is used, a simple one-word explanation may be written on the line below—"degradation" or "bondage" are common— or nothing may be indicated. This process is known as a Section 58 decision. The vast majority of Customs detentions are for suspected obscenity. The bureaucracy estimates that 90 percent of Ottawa-level appeals involve obscenity; the other 10 percent involve suspected hate literature.

The importer—let's say Little Sister's—then has the option of appealing the prohibition. (If they don't appeal, the goods may be either exported, abandoned to the government or forfeited—potentially at the importer's expense.) Little Sister's fills out a B2 form requesting a Section 60 appeal. A regional Tariff and Values Administrator (TVA), a more specialized official, reviews the banned publication. If he or she upholds the prohibition, a final Customs appeal is possible: in Ottawa, at the deputy minister's level (Section 63 level) in the Prohibited Importations Directorate (PID). Again, Little Sister's fills out exactly the same B2 form, altering only the appeal level. Customs forwards the offending book to the PID where it is again reviewed, this time by a Tariff Administrator. A final decision to prohibit must be authorized by three senior civil servants, culminating in the director general of the Tariff Programs Division, John Shearer.

But the book has one more avenue. After all Customs appeals have been exhausted, the importer can pull out their cheque book and drag Canada Customs through the courts, which is exactly what Glad Day Books did in 1987 over the banning of *The Joy of Gay Sex* (see Chapter 1).

Customs' regime appeared to be relatively straightforward in theory, if not draining and discriminatory in practice. But even the theory had its weaknesses. For example, at the lowest level of determination, a Customs Inspector may seek the opinion of a regional TVA; if the inspector's banning is disputed by the importer, the same TVA could handle the Section 60 appeal. As Arvay put it to John Shearer, "the decision of the Customs Inspector would be appealed to that very same [TVA]? Is that the case?"

". . . it could happen," said Shearer. A similar duplication could happen at the higher appeal levels as well. Indeed, Arvay was convinced that Customs' whole appeal apparatus was faulty, with officials at the highest level often "signing off" a decision based largely on the notes provided by the lower-level workers. Throughout their testimony, the witnesses from Customs' upper echelon would defend the thoroughness of the review process and the integrity of their officers, but Arvay was often able to show how arbitrary and sketchy the procedures were.

The sheer scope of Customs operations also lent itself to uneven rulings. Shearer, who looked as though he could have played major league football in an earlier career, estimated there were over 250 points of entry in Canada and about 4,000 uniformed inspectors. With that many inspectors, Arvay questioned how Customs could assess publications in a consistent manner.

"So one Customs officer can look at the same material as another Customs officer and come to a completely opposite decision about it?" asked Arvay.

". . . that's possible," said Shearer, in his clipped manner. "That's why we have the appeal system." Arvay then reminded him that "very, very few of the [appeals] reach the deputy minister's level . . ." because importers often throw in the towel.

Customs had made some effort to keep track of its decisions via a computerized technical reference system (TRS) that identified materials that had been prohibited. The data base was used by Customs workers at points of entry and by TVAs at regional offices, but the TRS had problems. For example, Dorothy Allison's novel *Trash* was detained at the border when a Customs Inspector punched its title into the TRS and was fed information about a publication with the same name. Even more problematic was the fact that the TRS only identified titles that had been prohibited, and not necessarily the thousands of books and magazines that had been detained, reviewed and *released*. The most notorious example was Pat Califia's *Macho Sluts*—detained, prohibited, reviewed and released at the deputy minister's level on five separate occasions while en route to Little Sister's. (The most recent ministerial decision was August 30, 1994, ten weeks before the trial began.)

Arvay recited the almost comical train of *Macho Sluts* seizures to Shearer.

"My question to you, sir," he asked, "is, is there anything about that treatment of *Macho Sluts* that you consider to be a bit worrisome?"

"Well, certainly it's a situation . . . [that] is not something we would want to see happen," said Shearer.

"Any explanations for it?" Arvay mildly asked.

"Without doing an investigation on the facts . . . no, I wouldn't want to offer an answer other than that mistakes do happen, obviously," said Shearer.

Customs also made mistakes keeping track of time. The *Customs Act* states that a first-level determination must be made within thirty days of a publication's detention or the title is automatically deemed admissible. Arvay was able to document many cases where the deadline was either missed or fudged. One example involved twenty copies of *The Scoutmaster's Minute*, destined for Glad Day Books when it was detained on April 3, 1990. Eighty days later, June 21, 1990, a decision on the book was rendered.

Scratching Some Big Boys' Backs

Arvay was eager to talk with Canada Customs about its pre-screening system, the mechanism used to ensure that Madonna's *Sex* and scores of hetero-porn magazines, among other notable publications, had a relatively breezy ride across the Canadian border. In particular, Little Sister's lawyer wanted to focus attention on the system's imbalances and its function as an ersatz censor.

Linda Murphy, director of the Prohibited Importations Directorate in Ottawa, was self-assured and decisive throughout her testimony, answering Arvay's lengthy cross-examination with a perkiness that seemed relentless. (Murphy had been working in another government agency since October 1992, but she still retained her "substantive position" as PID's director.) Her testimony was scheduled to last a few hours, but after the first session, Arvay remarked, "This is going to take a while."

Murphy described how foreign exporters and Canadian importers—anyone, in fact—can ask Canada Customs for "advice and guidance in understanding the Customs guidelines" on obscenity. For instance, a publisher can submit an advance copy of a book to the PID, which will offer suggestions about where and how the book may be in contravention of Memorandum D9-1-1. A common practice is for mainstream porn publishers to send Customs a dummy version, or blue line, of their magazine.

"The whole reason for the pre-approval process," asked Arvay, "is for the . . . publishers to know what will or will not be acceptable to Canada Customs, correct?"

"Yes, that's correct," said Murphy. ". . . We'll go through and itemize in a listing, page by page, any areas of concern . . . But we will not go through and mark up a magazine. We don't do that."

"You may not mark on the magazine, but on the separate piece of paper you will tell the publishers on what page of the blue line there is an unacceptable depiction or description of sex?" asked Arvay.

"Yes, we will do that," said Murphy.

"And it's because of that that the publishers then will go about blocking out the offending, or possibly offending, text or picture, right?"

"Yes," said Murphy.

While Murphy was adamant that "[Customs has] never asked that anything be deleted . . . We would [only] point out any areas of concern in the magazine," gay men who have purchased porn in Canada are all too familiar with the ubiquitous black dots and slashes concealing depictions of anal sex, whether in words or pictures. Arvay found it rather amusing that this fervent blackening out didn't actually hide what was going on. The prohibition wasn't just against gay anal sex; Arvay read several passages from a heterosexual porn magazine, including ". . . When I felt she was suitably lubricated, I lodged my dick against her 'blank' crevice and propelled it directly into the tight pit . . ."

"Now, Ms. Murphy, there's really no doubt in your mind that all those blanks refer to anal penetration or anal intercourse of some sort?" asked Arvay.

"Some of them may, some of them may not," said Murphy. "I just couldn't tell you what some of those blanks were in reference to."

". . . And if those blanks were done as a result of Canada Customs' concern with anal penetration, would you agree that the blanks have really accomplished nothing?"

"Well, the guidelines have to do with explicit descriptions of anal penetration," said Murphy. "It had to do that. It certainly has removed it."

"But did [the removal] accomplish anything?"

"It depends. I don't know," said Murphy. "I suppose that . . . the magazine would have been prohibited entry if it hadn't been done."

Little Sister's had never engaged in Customs' pre-screening process, nor have most small-scale booksellers or publishers. Inland Books once made a stab at it, in a fruitless effort to alleviate their Customs woes. In 1993, the distributor submitted twenty-nine books to Ottawa for pre-screening; after a two-month wait, Inland was informed by Customs that four titles were problem-free, but the other twenty-five would probably be found to contravene Customs guidelines. None of the books were ever returned. Pre-screening gives a publisher "suggestions," said Murphy, not guarantees. A book "suggested" to be A-okay by the PID's pre-screening staff might very well get bounced back to Ottawa, to the same office, months or even years later, having been prohibited by Customs staff at the border and beyond.

Murphy testified that the PID did somewhere between 3,000 and 3,500 advance reviews every year. She provided Arvay with an interesting example.

"We were requested to address the editorial staff of *Penthouse* magazine," said Murphy. ". . . *Penthouse* invited us to come down to their offices and to go over the guidelines thoroughly with their staff." She flew to New York with a PID colleague, a trip paid for by the Canadian government.

"And what was accomplished with that visit?" asked Arvay.

". . . [*Penthouse*] . . . had a large number of new staff—they have quite a large staff," said Murphy, "and they wanted to have everyone understand our guidelines. So they asked us if we would go through the guidelines point by point, with the editorial staff . . . There would be, I'd say, thirty or forty people in attendance . . ." Murphy seemed unaware of the irony of this disclosure: Canadian taxpayers paying Customs to tell big-time pornographers in New York how to peddle their wares; in fact, she seemed to almost relish the story as proof of Customs' professionalism.

Earlier, Arvay had asked Murphy if she was aware of a magazine called *Bad Attitude*.

"Yes. I am," said Murphy. "I'm familiar with that title."

"It's a small publisher?" asked Arvay. *Bad Attitude* is very small indeed, almost a one-woman operation.

"I don't know who publishes *Bad Attitude*, actually," said Murphy.

"I see; you've never visited the editorial staff of *Bad Attitude*?"

"I've never been invited," said Murphy. "I would have gone if I'd been invited."

Customs' most high-profile foray into pre-screening occurred in 1992, when media conglomerate Time/Warner arranged a preemptive strike for Madonna's *Sex*. Employing the services of a high-profile Toronto legal firm—among whose luminaries was former Tory cabinet minister Ronald Atkey—Time/Warner spared no expense in ensuring that Customs' blessing was bestowed on *Sex*. Atkey prepared a sophisticated, almost feminist argument for why *Sex*—replete with text and photos of Madonna's fantasies about rape, bestiality, kiddie porn, water sports and whipping—should not be banned in Canada.

". . . in a number of places in [*Sex*]," wrote Atkey, "it is the woman who assumes the dominant role over the man; it is clear that the book portrays a woman who freely and self-confidently explores a variety of sexual attitudes [and] that the publication would not create a substantial risk of harm identified in *Butler*, i.e., the subordination and dehumanization of women."

Like most affairs involving Madonna, the fuss over *Sex* was considerable.

"[The publisher] had a high degree of security around the book itself," testified John Shearer, "and wanted to make arrangements to have the book delivered for review under armed guard." But even more telling was evidence that Customs had faithfully advised the Privy Council Office of the review's status. The PCO is the eyes and ears of the prime minister and the federal cabinet, the government's most senior agency. Between August 28 and October 1, 1992, the PCO was repeatedly informed—seventeen times—of *Sex*'s progress.

"What role does the PCO play in your decision-making process?" Arvay asked Shearer.

"None whatsoever," said Shearer, ". . . but they do have a role in keeping government advised of issues that are likely to be sensitive or controversial." Unable to cite another firm example of the PCO's involvement, Shearer speculated that *American Psycho* may have received similar attention.

Linda Murphy was also closely questioned about *Sex*. Like Shearer, she denied there had been any political interference in Customs' pre-screening process, but she did shed light on Customs' political skittishness. Arvay quoted from an internal memo that Murphy had helped draft; entitled "Communications Strategy Secret Final," the memo warned that the review of *Sex* had the potential to "resurrect and refocus the continuing debate of whether the government should be in the censorship business." Murphy had issued a similar caveat when *American Psycho* was under review.

Although *Sex* was ultimately found to be admissible under Memorandum D9-1-1, Murphy was unable to supply a written version of the decision; incredibly, the paper trail simply didn't exist. As Arvay said, "one clear inference to be drawn was that there was no principled decision" made about *Sex*.

When Arvay escorted Murphy through the book, page by page, she was also unable to provide either a credible or consistent accounting for *Sex*'s "innocence." Murphy agreed that many of the images seemed to involve the "undue exploitation of sex," yet she was frequently evasive. Arvay read from a passage in which Madonna describes having sex with a teenager: "Sex with the young can be fun if you're in the mood . . . One of the best experiences I ever had was with a teenage boy. I think he was a virgin. He hardly had any pubic hair . . . he was so young . . . he wasn't big. He was just a baby. See, I'm not a size queen . . ."

Did Murphy consider this to constitute a depiction of sex with a juvenile? Arvay asked. She replied that the situation was unclear because the boy's age was not given. Frustrated, Arvay asked her how many teenage boys she knew who "hardly had any pubic hair" yet were of legal age. Closing off this round of cross-examination, Arvay suggested that the motivation for allowing *Sex* and *American Psycho* into the country was that prohibiting those books would have put Murphy's entire department out of business.

"I don't . . . I can't answer that," said Murphy.

In 1991, the arrival of Bret Easton Ellis' horrifically sexist novel, *American Psycho,* had been anticipated by an anxious Canada Customs.

"Well, we knew that *American Psycho* was a very controversial work in the United States," said Shearer, ". . . so we had an interest in being prepared for its importation and obtaining a copy of the book for review." He was minimally involved in the actual pre-screening of the book because he was away from the job at the time. Nevertheless, Arvay questioned Shearer carefully about Customs' process.

"Mr. Shearer, was there a concern . . . that the reason *American Psycho* should be let in was to simply avoid the resurrection and refocusing of the [Customs censorship] debate?" Arvay asked.

"That was not at all my understanding in the limited involvement that I had," said Shearer.

"What was your understanding, then . . .?" Arvay asked.

"My understanding is that, upon . . . application of D9-1-1, it was determined that this was a good that would, in fact, fall outside the provisions of Tariff Code 9956, as simple as that," said Shearer.

After establishing the rather surprising fact that Shearer had never read any of *American Psycho,* Arvay asked him to read aloud several of the novel's most disturbing passages. The recitation of Ellis' grotesque accounts of the sexual torture and murder of women was one of the trial's most anguished moments, leaving many people in Courtroom 65 in numbed silence.

"Do you agree that these passages read in isolation of the entire text are in clear violation of Memorandum D9-1-1?" asked Arvay.

"Yes, I would."

"Did you have any idea that those passages were in this book?"

"Not having read it, no."

Like Murphy, Shearer was unable to say why Customs had decided *American Psycho* didn't violate their guidelines.

". . . I don't know the details of the support for that decision," said Shearer, "but I do understand that that decision was reached."

The Story of Oh-Oh

The Story of O, the French classic by the pseudonymous Pauline Reage, had an altogether different pre-screening history. (Reage's novel, considered by many to be a lyrical portrayal of sexual possession, includes many scenes of bondage and domination.) Arvay questioned Linda Murphy at length about her key role in the book's 1987 banning, a cross-examination that revealed just how provincial and lax the Customs mindset could be.

Although the novel had circulated freely in Canadian bookstores and libraries for about twenty years, *The Story of O* was sent to Ottawa for review at the request of an unnamed importer. As head of the PID, Linda Murphy initialled the 1987 report that determined the book "would fall within the prohibitory provisions . . . and importation to Canada would therefore be prohibited." By 1994, however, Murphy appeared to have no memory of the process; in fact, she and Arvay tussled over whether the 1987 decision involved a comic book or some other version of Reage's work.

In cross-examination, Murphy acknowledged that she had not read *The Story of O* in its entirety, but had simply reviewed the passages that a Tariff Administrator had identified as contravening Customs guidelines. Arvay directed her attention to the Translator's Note (by Sabine d'Estree) at the beginning of Grove Press' 1965 edition of the book: ". . . Pauline Reage has done what all good artists aim for and, when they are successful, accomplish: To arouse us from the lethargy of our set ways . . . prick us into consciousness . . . ; in short, to make us think."

"Now, I take it, Ms. Murphy," asked Arvay, "that that paragraph itself might be useful for you as the director of the PID to have read in judging the overall merit of this book?"

". . . Yes, I think it would be helpful," said Murphy.

Earlier, Arvay had asked her about the impact of Customs' negative pre-screening review.

". . . The purpose and effect of [Customs'] opinion was to therefore discourage that exporter/importer from bringing this book into the country, isn't it?" he asked.

"No, that wasn't the purpose," said Murphy. "It was simply to give the person some advice and some guidance that in our opinion it could . . . it would fall within the prohibitory provisions of the tariff code."

". . . All right. And if you were the person who received this [opinion], isn't it fair to say, Ms. Murphy, that you would not bother trying to bring this book into the country."

Murphy was apparently oblivious to the immense strain that a Customs seizure places on a bookseller.

"Not necessarily," she said. "I would come back and say . . . 'I intend to import it because I think that's an incorrect decision. I'm going to import it and if that's what happens [at the border], I'm going to ask for a redetermination . . .' "

On the Front Lines

After the top brass, the court heard from Customs officers who staff the front lines. Under Arvay's cross-examination, they soon rounded out the picture of Canada Customs as an oft-times confusing, inconsistent workplace. Witnesses from central Canada testified that they read books in their entirety before deciding to ban them; later, witnesses from western Canada would testify that they were seldom able to read entire books due to the overwhelming volume of goods they encountered every day.

Corrine Bird is a tall, resolute woman who testified as a Commodity Specialist at Fort Erie, Ontario. Her name appeared on many K 27 forms received by both Little Sister's and Glad Day Books; Bird was on guard when Inland Books shipped their large, consolidated order in May 1993. Arvay had originally intended to briefly cross-examine her, but her performance in the witness box soon confirmed she was a goldmine of evidence for Little Sister's—even if her reticence made her a slow strike.

Bird outlined how determinations were made at Fort Erie and what prompted her to detain a book. Like other Customs officers, she would survey the shipper's invoices to figure out which books were packed in which boxes. (Bird claimed that "who the goods are going to is not a factor.") In a consolidated shipment, she would be confronted with between fifty and two hundred invoices.

". . . How would you know, with respect to an invoice, which titles might be problematic or not?" asked Arvay.

". . . Well, we wouldn't know," Bird replied. "We would just look down the invoices . . . I just look at the titles and if it suggests to me a sexual theme that might be of concern to us, it might be an idea to take a quick look at it . . ." Some of the titles detained by this method were *Girls, Visions and Everything* by Sarah Schulman, *Herotica* by Susie

Bright, *Gay Ideas* by Richard Mohr, *The Gay and Lesbian Reader* edited by Henry Abelove et al., *Tales of the Dark Lord* by John Preston, *Leatherfolk* by Mark Thompson, and *Gay Roots: Twenty Years of Gay Sunshine* edited by Winston Leyland.

Although Bird's name appeared on numerous K 27 forms entered as evidence, her testimony was riddled with statements like "I don't specifically remember the book"; "I don't remember"; "I don't recall. It's over a year ago"; "My colleague released it, I didn't." Arvay was not surprised to learn that a signature on a K 27 didn't mean a Commodity Specialist had actually done anything more than some paperwork—or had they? Why decisions were made and by whom was becoming increasingly difficult to pinpoint.

Arvay asked Bird why she had detained Jane Rule's *Contract with the World* in a 1993 Inland shipment. She remembered the details of this seizure.

"My colleague and I, when we saw that title, we actually didn't think that it might have a sexual theme," said Bird. "We were actually more concerned . . . that it might be hate propaganda."

"And why would that title suggest hate propaganda to you?" asked Arvay.

"Just sounds like it might have a political theme to it," Bird responded rather casually. ". . . I scanned the back [cover] synopsis."

"And was anything there that would in any way suggest that it was hate propaganda?" asked Arvay

"No," said Bird, "there's nothing there. But it does discuss eroticism, so I continued to detain it to ensure that it didn't contain any sexually explicit material." Bird admitted she was unfamiliar with Jane Rule's name or work.

The back-cover blurb was not obviously calculated to make a pulse race: "*Contract with the World* is a powerful panorama of life in all its complexities and contradictions, a novel of possessiveness and jealousy and eroticism, a novel filled with extraordinary . . . portraits of an awakening new generation and the dimensions and the fascinating eccentricities of their art, their lives, their love . . ." Bird's supervisor, Frank Lorito, caught her mistake when he spotted the novel among a pile of detained books in their office.

"[Lorito] recognized Jane Rule's name as being a fairly mainstream author," said Bird, "and he suggested [it] was probably going to be admissible . . . so we released it without further review, accepting his expertise in this matter."

Bird revealed the different treatment meted out to nonfiction anthologies, short story collections, magazines and novels.

"We found anthology-type material . . . usually involved the reproduction of excerpts from prohibited material . . . such as the book *Gay Ideas*," said Bird. "So we had some concerns always with anthologies because they normally contained material which was of a prohibited nature." However, said Bird, an anthology deserved to be judged by its overall theme, like a novel. But short story collections could be prohibited on the basis of a single tale.

Magazines were assessed, Bird said, "on a segment-by-segment basis" and were also vulnerable to detention on the basis of a single, offending paragraph. (Linda Murphy had earlier testified about the quaint sensitivity Customs had to the freedom of *commercial* speech: since the late 1980s, Customs did not apply D9-1-1 to magazine advertisements. Murphy was unable to recall the rationale behind this policy. Even if a magazine contained nothing but advertisements that explicitly contravened Customs guidelines, it would be free to enter Canada.)

The Umpires of the Senseless
One of the huge headaches for the Customs officers responsible for making Memorandum D9-1-1 determinations was the sheer volume of materials they faced. Frank Lorito testified as a Tariff and Values Administrator stationed in Fort Erie.

"At any given time you can look out the window and see trucks backed across the bridge [from the U.S.]—2,000 to 2,500 trucks a day," said Lorito. At the border, the uniformed Customs Inspectors acted as the bureaucracy's "eyes and ears," said Lorito; however, decisions to prohibit books were no longer made by them, as in the past, but were the purview of Commodity Specialists like his colleague, Corrine Bird. Lorito proved to be a forthcoming and relaxed witness, intent on giving an honest and full account of how his office functioned. As Arvay soon discovered, he was able to provide a close-up of the difficulties a TVA confronted when applying D9-1-1, especially to works of a literary nature. Lorito's role in the detention and release of Kathy Acker's novel *Empire of the Senseless* became a focus of Arvay's cross-examination.

Acker's book was en route to L'Androgyne, Montreal's gay and lesbian bookstore, when it was detained at Fort Erie and later prohibited by a Mr. Wilkinson, Commodity Specialist, in November 1988. As the regional TVA, Lorito was responsible for reviewing the book's prohibition, which was appealed by Lawrence Boyle, L'Androgyne's owner. A veteran of Customs seizures, Boyle had immediately challenged the outrageous detention; unknown to Canada Customs, Acker's book was widely regarded as a dazzling creation that took a hard, no-holds-barred run at sexual abuse and oppression.

Boyle didn't protest to Canada Customs alone. He also fired off a press release denouncing the prohibition to every major newspaper, literary association and publisher in Canada. Boyle wrote to Frank Lorito, too, in December 1988, offering him scholarly commentaries on Acker's work, reviews from several magazines, including the *Village Voice,* and an article condemning the seizure in Montréal's *Le Devoir.* Lorito testified that he was influenced by the reviews because he didn't feel he was "really well versed in literary [matters], but when someone tells you that it has literary merit and they're experts in the field, then I think you pay attention to what they say."

In his letter, Boyle outlined concerns about what Mr. Wilkinson, the banning Commodity Specialist, had written on the K 27 and later said in conversation:

> You claim the book to be obscene in that it promotes incest, anal penetration, and sex with violence. I have, by the way, only verbal affirmation of that fact, as no one filled in the appropriate spaces on the form . . .
>
> After having only "skimmed" (Wilkinson's word) the book, he found passages depicting sexual violence, in particular incest, rape and sodomy (sic). When I asked if the context of such scenes made any difference to their merit, he said "No," that rape was rape. When I asked if he had ever read the Bible, which contains numerous scenes of sexual violence, he admitted that the context could make a difference, but that Acker's novel "sensationalizes" these acts, thereby outweighing its merits as a work of art.

While awaiting the appeal of *Empire of the Senseless,* Boyle reported that other books in the same shipment were also held back for almost three weeks, despite being clearly admissible; the authors included Truman

Capote, Jean Cocteau, William Burroughs, Ursula K. Le Guin and David Leavitt, as well as copies of the landmark book for incest survivors, *The Courage to Heal.*

Boyle's leveraging of the media got results.

". . . Knowing that the media was sort of watching what you were doing, you would act more quickly?" Arvay asked Lorito.

"Correct," said Lorito. In mid-December, Lorito wrote back to Boyle. His letter revealed, in rather time-consuming language, the pressure-cooker of Customs' work environment: "Restraints placed on our time by the requirement of expedition sometimes precludes us from devoting the necessary time to conduct an exhaustive review."

Boyle again wrote to Customs in late January 1989, after the book had been hurriedly released, further outlining his bookstore's experiences with Canada Customs:

> Since this detention, every shipment crossing the border and destined for L'Androgyne has been opened and inspected, repacked (badly), and resealed with Customs tape. In our 15 years, this has rarely happened. Have I drawn too much attention to myself? Is there indeed a list of bookstores that customs agents have been asked to be particularly thorough with? . . .

Arvay asked Lorito to describe his own process reviewing *Empire of the Senseless.* The TVA first acknowledged that the Commodity Specialists at Fort Erie were doing a less than rigorous examination of detained books.

"[Wilkinson] did not read the book from cover to cover," said Lorito. ". . . We were under some time constraints and . . . their work was falling behind and at that particular time they were . . . more or less perusing the books."

In the rush to review Acker's work, Lorito took *Empire* home for the weekend. He hadn't quite completed the novel when a phone call came Monday morning from headquarters. Ottawa, smarting from Boyle's actions, was eager to know the TVA's assessment. Lorito testified that he had told his superiors " 'I'm not quite finished. I'm almost finished and I'm likely to uphold the prohibition but I haven't made a final decision yet.' "

But his opinion of *Empire of the Senseless* did a 180-degree shift when he hit the final sentence in Acker's book. Arvay invited Lorito to read aloud the passage that had changed his mind.

" 'And then I thought that, one day, maybe, there'd be a human society in a world which is beautiful, a society which wasn't just disgust,' " Lorito read. Then he explained his reasoning. "It's almost like a disclaimer that, 'yes, this is what it is and I don't like it.' "

Lucky for Kathy Acker and her Canadian readers, Lorito had gotten the point. Arvay would later characterize his sudden conversion as "absurd . . . many of the previous passages must have made it clear that the book was a serious work."

Lookouts! Heightened Scrutiny and Hot Indicators . . .

Lawrence Boyle's contention that L'Androgyne and Canada's other gay and lesbian bookstores were the subject of Customs surveillance was carefully explored by Little Sister's counsel. Arvay cross-examined Linda Murphy and others, gradually prying from them an authentic rendition of Customs' intense scrutiny. Murphy, true to character, initially denied there was any targeting of queer stores.

"So gay bookstores are not treated any differently than other bookstores in Canada," asked Arvay.

Murphy indicated that they were not.

"To the extent that there are inspections, detentions and prohibitions of books destined to gay bookstores," said Arvay, "it's your evidence . . . that that is just a result of random inspections?"

"I wouldn't know if I would say it was just random," said Murphy. ". . . But if material has been found to be prohibited in shipments [to a] bookstore, then it would be likely that that bookstore's shipments would be looked at again."

"Ms. Murphy, doesn't that mean that the bookstore then is being targeted?" asked Arvay.

"No, it doesn't. That's not targeting," she said.

"What is targeting?" asked Arvay. Murphy's answer was surprisingly perceptive, though she seemed unaware that she was describing the experiences of Little Sister's, Glad Day and Inland to a tee.

"It would be focusing on a particular company, on a particular importer, for a particular reason," said Murphy.

Arvay struggled to find an agreeable word—more neutral than targeting—to describe how Canada Customs responded to shipments to a store like Little Sister's. Suppose there was a gay bookstore that had imported books that had been prohibited in the past, maybe two or three

times, he said. Would they be under "heightened scrutiny"? he proposed
to Murphy.

"Yes, I think that would be appropriate," said Murphy.

". . . Did you know that bookstores such as Glad Day in Toronto and
Little Sister's in Vancouver were being subjected to heightened scrutiny?"
asked Arvay.

"Yes," said Murphy.

". . . Can you name one bookstore in Canada, other than a gay and
lesbian bookstore, that was subject to regular scrutiny?" asked Arvay.

". . . I'm not sure if we received any letters or any concern expressed
by other bookstores," said Murphy.

"Did Customs officials tell you that any other bookstore in Canada,
other then gay and lesbian bookstores, was subject to heightened
scrutiny?" asked Arvay.

"I don't think anyone ever told me that, no," said Murphy.

Murphy's boss would be more frank about the reality of targeting.
Under questioning by Crown lawyer Hans Van Iperen, John Shearer
divulged fresh news about the status of Little Sister's—fresh to him, that
is. Upon arriving in Vancouver for the trial, Shearer had seen fit to make
inquiries about whether local Customs officials observed any special
notifications or "lookouts" regarding the bookstore.

"I did find that there was a general lookout in the Vancouver
[Customs] mail area for importations by Little Sister's," said Shearer, "just
to make new staff aware in the mail facility that Little Sister's was an
importer of . . . on occasion, of obscene materials as defined in Tariff
Code 9956."

Under cross-examination, Shearer's actions looked distinctly shaky, if
not bizarre.

"When did you make those inquiries [about the lookout]?" asked
Arvay.

"I made them yesterday," said Shearer.

"Had you heard before yesterday that Little Sister's was of the view
that it was being targeted by Canada Customs?" Arvay asked in a master-
piece of understatement.

"I have heard that reported in the media," said Shearer. Arvay questioned why he had not made inquiries earlier.

"I had no reason to make those inquiries, no," said Shearer. "It is a
normal practice of our law enforcement approach, if there is an indica-

tion of an importer who has a history of . . . [offending] some provision of the law, indeed, those kinds of lookouts are put out at the discretion of the people involved in putting them in place . . . That was a local discretionary lookout."

"Is that a decision that you assume no responsibility for?" asked Arvay.

"Correct."

Shearer's response left many in the courtroom shaking their heads in disbelief. Under oath, one of Customs' top bureaucrats had admitted he didn't find it necessary, or even prudent, to concern himself with the fact that local officials had "looked out" for Little Sister's so persistently that the government itself had ended up on trial.

Later on, Corrine Bird described how her Fort Erie workplace dealt with the nuances of lookouts and Customs' other trigger, "hot indicators." Arvay asked her about the status of Inland Books.

"Inland is the subject of a lookout, is that correct?" asked Arvay.

"A hot indicator," said Bird.

"Is there a difference?" asked Arvay.

"Yes. A lookout is normally more of a high risk, when we have reason to believe, for example, that a trucking company is smuggling liquor in a load," said Bird. "[A lookout] is . . . pretty much a mandatory examination. A 'hot indicator' is an indicator put into our computer system that triggers a message to the Customs Inspector [about the importer] . . . It doesn't necessitate a mandatory examination; it just indicates that there's a concern there, to be aware of it."

"And why was there a concern for Inland?" asked Arvay.

"Because they were known to import [sic] material which fell within the prohibitory guidelines of Tariff Code 9956," said Bird.

In the summer of '94, Joe Arvay asked me to observe a meeting with himself, three Customs officers, two Crown lawyers (Neena Sharma and Dan Kiselbach) and one of his articling students. This was to

JANINE be a disclosure session, wherein Customs would spill their operational beans to Little Sister's and the Crown, preparatory to the court case. It was a beautiful summer day and, naturally, the meeting was indoors at Customs' office building. I met Tamara-the-articling-student outside and we rode the elevator together. For me, this was the coming together of the Great Unknown and the Oh-So Familiar. For the first time, I would be meeting different Customs agents at the different appeal levels, face to face.

Tamara and I were buzzed into the office, like some high-ranking diplomats on official government business. A Crown lawyer emerged and we chatted about the gorgeous weather and other important things people say when they're excruciatingly nervous. Sure, I'd spoken with Customs people on the phone but I'd never actually seen one of them, except for a five-minute clip on TV that wasn't exactly flattering: two hefty men pulling up a roll-top door to reveal where Customs stashed their seized books.

My adrenalin was racing. What if they didn't like me? What if we didn't get along? "Pull yourself together, this isn't camp," I told myself. One by one, the others arrived and we were introduced to the Customs officers. The first agent was nice, neither fanged nor buttoned up tight, a woman I had spoken to on the phone. She explained Customs' procedures, I interjected the odd question, I got frowned upon by the government lawyers—after all, I was only supposed to observe. So I clammed up and took notes.

The Customs woman was quite funny. I could almost imagine where she'd go for a drink on Fridays at the end of the work week. She was just doing a job, one that was not always to her liking, as she had revealed during our occasional phone calls. I felt the two of us had somehow, through fate, landed in our opposing positions, but maybe in another time, another place . . . and suddenly it was lunch time. I daydreamed some more and then we were back to work, hearing from another official. I listened half-headedly to more of the bureaucratic rigamarole—who did what and when and how— and then I was hearing something that made my heart stop. There were, the Customs officer was saying, two appeal levels that used *the same application form*. The same form—B2—for both Section 60 *and* Section 63 appeals.

A harsh reality started sinking in, like lead boots to the bottom of the ocean. I, Janine Fuller, had failed to grasp this simple administrative fact. I had believed the B2 from the Section 60 appeal was automatically forwarded to Ottawa for the Section 63 appeal. In effect, over all these years, I had never actually applied for the final appeal. I sat dead still. In my mind's eye, I was so small a fly would have needed eyeglasses to see me. And so I stayed for the rest of the afternoon.

My fly brain was busy enough, though, contemplating the thick folder back in Little Sister's office, overflowing with all the appeals I *thought* I had filed. The next day I couldn't bring myself to look at it. Days passed. Jim and Bruce quietly watched as I sulked around the store as though my entire being had been sucked up by the Customs vacuum cleaner. Finally, I found the stomach to talk. We were all together in the back room, I slid open the filing cabinet, pulled out the folder and made my grand announcement.

"Guys. I've fucked up, big time."

Of course, Jim and Bruce were as supportive as ever. And as realistic, too. I'd been hammering myself with "Couldn't I even fill out a form properly?" But as they pointed out, why did the people at Customs say "your stuff is going right to Ottawa"? With that message, how could I have known to fill out the exact same B2 form that I had already filled out?

The court date was fast approaching and I was talking to Irene Faulkner or Joe almost daily—as Julie joked, "I must be having a threesome." But even with such intimacy, I couldn't bring myself to 'fess up to the lawyers, imagining I had ruined the whole case by blowing this evidence. What burned the most was the feeling I had messed up for everyone—my community, my friends, the bookstore, Jim and Bruce, and especially Joe and Irene. All these years I had organized the files, written up my phone calls with Customs, recorded the banned books on the relevant invoices, charted where the titles had originated, who they were distributed by, the dates, the forms, the files—all carefully tracked. But I hadn't filled out the goddamn B2 form properly.

Way back when, I had wrestled with my first-ever Customs appeal on the front steps of Michael Bushko's home. Michael was a friend who had genuine Customs know-how; he worked for a company that imported crystals and had also worked at Little Sister's. I figured he could decipher the B2, which had almost a hundred possible boxes to tick off or fill out. The B2 was like a Christmas present that came unassembled, only worse: it lacked any instructions. Michael and I mulled it over and he eventually figured out some of the codes and how to proceed (do it in triplicate, as someone had said.) On another occasion, and another detention, Michael made me a glorious offer when he learned I was heading out of town.

"I'll do it," he said, a cigarette hanging from his pearly white teeth. Michael had the most dazzling eyes, almost too beautiful to be real. He brushed his thin dark brown hair back through his fingers and behind his ears.

"Get out of here, have a good holiday and don't forget to get me something," he shooed me off.

When I returned, Michael was sicker then I'd ever seen him. The grey sweat pants he would normally not have worn outside his room were now his staple outfit. After dawdling a little, somewhat at a loss, I thanked him for doing the Little Sister's appeal. Michael lifted his head up from the bed-pan he'd "borrowed" from the hospital

"I forgot to do it," he said.

"Don't worry, we'll do it another time," I said, probably trying to convince myself that Michael would be better than he was ever really going to be again. I tackled the forms as best I could, following Michael's first appeal. But I was often wrong. Different points of entry don't fill out the forms in exactly the same way. An item may appear at the top of one form and in a totally different place on another. When I sent that second appeal in, I attached a letter explaining my plight and confusion. I never received an answer and the form was rejected for not being filled out correctly.

Later, when Michael was in what people call the latter stages of AIDS, he was still always there to support me and Little Sister's. Just before the case was scheduled to begin in 1993, I was looking after him along with Julie and some other friends. A phone call came through for me at his home, an interview about the upcoming trial. I perched myself on Michael's front steps, fielding the interviewer's spirited questions through a cordless phone.

"So, do you think you can win?" he asked. My answers were almost robotic. Half of me was inside with Michael and the other half was doing politics with the media. When the interview ended, I absentmindedly tried to hang the phone up in a nearby tree. One minute you're shooting someone up with morphine, the next minute you're on national radio. As my friend Shawna would say, "Go figure."

As the summer of '94 dwindled, I knew I had to tell Irene and Joe about the nonexistent appeals. Irene and I met in Victoria one day, and I finally heaved out the words.

"Irene, I've got something to tell you."

Irene listened, nonplussed, as I explained the whole tortured story. Don't worry, she simply said, and we got down to work. At the end of the long day she drove me down to the harbour and the waiting sea-plane.

"It says a lot about Customs if you can't figure out their forms," said Irene. As I boarded the plane, I noticed how much lighter I felt. The trip to Victoria had purged me of my burden; maybe now I'd be getting a few good nights' sleep.

Penetrating the Anal Penetration Maze

My Biggest O is a 1993 anthology celebrating the best sexual experience of various gay male writers. Edited by Jack Hart, the book presents diverse snapshots of the gay community's sexual appetites: there are playful and passionate scenes of oral and anal sex, light s/M, water sports and a few accounts of sex with young men and boys. Canada Customs found only a diversity of obscenity in its pages. *My Biggest O* failed at the uppermost appeal level and appeared doomed to permanent "banned in Canada" status unless some would-be importer was willing to haul Customs into court.

To be exact, *My Biggest O* was prohibited on July 26, 1994 by Joel Oliver, the acting director of the Prohibited Importations Directorate in Linda Murphy's absence. Oliver upheld the decision of a regional TVA, agreeing that the book violated D9-1-1 provisions relating to anal penetration, sex with pain and sex with juveniles (the book does not advocate sex with children). When the September 29, 1994 amendment to D9-1-1 removed anal penetration as a prohibited category, Little Sister's again attempted to have *My Biggest O* deemed admissable. But on October 11, 1994, during the trial, a regional TVA once again upheld the book's obscenity. Joe Arvay intended to use the book as an example of Customs' more incomprehensible processes.

Joel Oliver was like an *éminence grise* at the Little Sister's trial, sitting up front with the Crown lawyers, conferring with Van Iperen and his collegues. He was originally slated to appear after the other Customs officials, but Arvay decided at the last minute that Oliver's testimony would not be needed; Little Sister's case, he believed, had already been strongly established. Nevertheless, Oliver was to play a dramatic role in the trial.

On the last day of testimony, before Justice Smith had entered the courtroom, Van Iperen walked over to Arvay and informed him that Customs had just reversed its position on *My Biggest O*; the anthology was now admissible. Arvay was incredulous.

"Who was responsible for this decision?" he asked Van Iperen. Joel Oliver, the Crown lawyer said. As the top bureaucrat, Oliver had decided to overrule his own decision—and that of the regional TVA—in light of the change to D9-1-1. There was, of course, no paperwork offered for this process, nor was there an explanation for what had become of Customs' concerns about "sex with pain" and "sex with juveniles." When Arvay reacted to Van Iperen's news with chagrin, Oliver leaned over and suggested that he could just as easily prohibit *My Biggest O* again, if that's what Arvay wanted.

A number of spectators overheard the sarcastic comment, but no one laughed. For Little Sister's, Oliver's arrogance felt like a re-run of what they had endured years earlier, when the government simply changed their minds about prohibiting *The Advocate* magazine. It was as though the weeks of testimony hadn't impacted on Oliver at all—a reminder that Customs' arbitrary and opaque methodology was still very much alive.

There was one more revelation to come. The fact that Memorandum D9-1-1 hadn't been amended in a timely fashion after the 1992 *Butler* decision was a question that loomed large for Little Sister's. Arvay wanted some answers from the upper-level Customs officials. In cross-examination, he set off to discover what legal opinions Customs had entertained prior to the September 29, 1994 decision to lift the ban on anal penetration. Arvay suspected that advisors from the federal Department of Justice had probably come knocking on Customs' doors soon after the Supreme Court decision.

Arvay's explorations led him to *Quim,* a British magazine; the No. 4 (1992) issue had been prohibited en route to the Toronto Women's Bookstore. *Quim: For Dykes of All Sexual Persuasions* typified the lesbian porn "industry": a small, irregularly published magazine that depended on its grassroots readership for submissions. The feminist bookstore had sought some heavy-duty legal help from a pair of law professors at Toronto's Osgoode Hall: Brenda Cossman, a noted anti-censorship feminist, and Bruce Ryder, an expert on Customs censorship who had testified earlier at the Little Sister's trial. Cossman and Ryder had sent a blunt letter to Customs in early 1993:

> We would like to reiterate our view . . . [re:] the detention of *Quim,* that it is extremely difficult, if not impossible, to prepare an effective appeal . . . without knowledge of the legal basis for Canada Customs' actions . . . Most importantly, we request that we be informed of the legal authority for the conclusion that descriptions of anal penetration are obscene according to Canadian law.

In another letter, dated June 2, 1993, the professors had addressed their concerns directly to the minister of National Revenue, Otto Jelinek:

In particular, the Supreme Court's decision in the *Butler* case . . . makes clear that depictions of non-violent, non-degrading consensual expression between adults is not obscene.

We look forward to hearing from you as to what action you will take to correct this situation.

Cossman and Ryder were hitting the nail on the head: Canada had no law that explicitly labelled anal penetration as obscene; moreover, the *Butler* decision, with its alleged emphasis on "harm to women," should have rendered at least gay and lesbian anal sex harmless. Arvay asked John Shearer about these matters.

"Did you recommend to the deputy minister that after *Butler,* Memorandum D9-1-1 should be amended to repeal the anal penetration provision?" Arvay asked.

"I don't recall a recommendation that specific," said Shearer. "We provided an analysis." Arvay asked if their analysis suggested the removal of anal penetration.

"No, we did not," said Shearer. ". . . As I recall, we took a fairly neutral position."

"What is a fairly neutral position?" asked Arvay.

"The jurisprudence wasn't clear, was my understanding of the [*Butler*] decision," said Shearer. He then went on to describe how Customs closely watched the *Glad Day v. Canada* case, the post-*Butler* decision that ended in a disastrously homophobic ruling by Judge Frank Hayes. Shearer described the case as being "decided in favour of [Customs]."

"Our analysis," said Shearer, "was that D9-1-1 was in conformity with the *Butler* decision."

". . . Was that analysis formed on the basis of advice from the Department of Justice?" asked Arvay.

"Yes, it was, in my recollection," said Shearer.

"So how did it come about then in [September] of this year that D9-1-1 was amended?" asked Arvay.

"There was a second Supreme Court case that was brought to our attention . . . the *Tremblay* decision," said Shearer. The 1993 *Tremblay* decision did not concern obscenity *per se*, but involved a club where nude female dancers would perform a sexual "dance" in a private cubicle for a paying male customer, who usually masturbated. The ruling had commented on community standards around indecent acts, observing that activities like group sex and anal sex were considered acceptable by Canadian courts; as Arvay later pointed out, the *Tremblay* decision's position on anal penetration was, in fact, drawn from a 1985 Supreme Court ruling—*R. v. Towne Cinema*—a decision Customs would have been fully aware of.

Arvay continued to dig deeper, determined to sniff out any hard evidence that Customs had resisted earlier advice to update their memorandum. He asked Shearer if the analysis from the Department of Justice had been in writing.

"Yes, it was," said Shearer.

"Was there more than one legal opinion?" Arvay was fishing.

"I only recall one off the top of my head," said Shearer.

"Who?" Arvay asked gingerly.

"Mr. Vern Brewer," said Shearer.

It seemed like an insignificant moment, but the name Vern Brewer was all Arvay needed to request a copy of the legal opinion that the justice department had given Customs. After a lengthy contest with Van Iperen about whether the letter could be released, and then several days awaiting the judge's decision on the matter, Little Sister's triumphed: Justice Smith ruled that Brewer's letter could be disclosed.

Brewer's letter revealed that, as early as 1990, two years *before* the *Butler* decision, Customs had received advice from the justice department that anal penetration in and of itself was not obscene, unless depicted in a context that was degrading or dehumanizing. (Ironically, Brewer had been the senior Crown counsel prosecuting the *Glad Day* case.) Arvay's instincts had been dead on: Canada Customs had been unwilling to heed the advice of the government's top legal experts at the justice department. And Little Sister's skepticism was dead on, too: Would Memorandum D9-1-1 ever have been amended if the bookstore hadn't dragged Canada Customs into court?

ABOVE: *Little Sister's bookstore.* RACHEL ROCCO

BELOW: *Janine Fuller with some of the books previously detained en route to Little Sister's.*
KIMBERLEY FRENCH

ABOVE LEFT: *Jane Rule.* AVIVA LAZAR

ABOVE CENTRE: *Ann Scales.*

ABOVE RIGHT: *Pat Califia.* PHOTO COURTESY OF CLEIS PRESS

BELOW: *(l. to r.) Becki Ross and her partner, Ingrid Stitt, display a little wedded bliss on Gay Pride Day in Toronto, 1992.*

ABOVE LEFT: *Carole Vance.* JEAN LLEWELLYN

ABOVE CENTRE: *Sarah Schulman.* AVIVA LAZAR

ABOVE RIGHT: *Pierre Berton.* DENISE GRANT

BELOW LEFT: *Persimmon Blackbridge.* HEATHER FAULKNER

BELOW RIGHT: *Aerlyn Weissman, videotaping outside the courthouse, October 1994.* AVIVA LAZAR

ABOVE LEFT: *Joe Arvay, the lawyer for Little Sister's and the B.C. Civil Liberties Association*

ABOVE RIGHT: *Irene Faulkner (r.), Arvay's assistant, and her partner, Brock Macdonald.* JULIE STINES

EIGHT

Watching the Detectives

JOSEPH ARVAY: *Would you agree, leaving aside your abhorrence that this material might be in the mail, that you can accomplish the same from a law enforcement perspective if the material is allowed to go to [a] post office box?*

DETECTIVE NOREEN WOLFF: *No . . . it's prohibited material. I look at it no differently than any other item [that's prohibited, like] drugs or guns . . . It's evidence that, if you just put it back into the [mail] system, it's not controlled as to how or where it's going . . .*

ARVAY: *Whether it's child pornography or adult pornography?*

WOLFF: *That's correct.*

ARVAY: *And yet you understand there is a very big difference between adult pornography, and guns and drugs, don't you?*

WOLFF: *No . . . What I'm doing is enforcing the laws and I'm just saying that this material is prohibited just like these other items . . .*

ARVAY: *You're aware, Detective Wolff, that the possession of obscene material of the adult pornography variety is not a crime? Are you aware of that?*

WOLFF: *Yes, I am.*

ARVAY: *Possession of drugs is a crime, right?*

WOLFF: *Yes, that's correct.*

ARVAY: *Possession of certain weapons is a crime?*

WOLFF: *That's correct.*

ARVAY: *So if you were to allow adult obscenity, for want of a better expression, to go from Customs to a person living at [the fictious] 222 Burnaby Street, no crime would be committed, you agree?*

WOLFF: *No, I don't agree . . . The legislation . . . has said that it's prohibited material in Canada. And to allow it in [would be] . . . contravening what the legislation is . . . We don't want to see this type of material in Canada.*

IF the Crown had put considerable stock in witnesses from Canada Customs, they also had high hopes for the expert testimony of police officers. Detectives from vice and pornography squads would be called upon to extol the virtues of Canada's border guards and, in particular, to show the interdependency between the two enforcement bodies. The Crown intended to show that Customs functioned as the nation's ever-vigilant watchdog and an invaluable source of police intelligence. Without the long arm of the Customs officer, they would say, the police would be stuck with very short arms indeed, unable to reach or even be aware of the obscenity creeping into the country. The highly emotional child pornography card would be played here, despite the fact that kiddie porn was not really an issue in Little Sister's detentions; owner Jim Deva was not even cross-examined on the subject.

Arvay had anticipated this line of the government's defence and was prepared to unravel it. He would undermine the legitimacy of Customs' role by showing how little impact they actually had on the porn trade in Canada, especially on child pornography. But more importantly, Arvay would advance one of Little Sister's central arguments: that crimes relating to obscenity and child pornography could, and should, be dealt with under the Criminal Code of Canada, not through Customs.

Little Sister's point of view was straightforward: When the crime of obscenity was suspected, the police could make an arrest, the Crown could lay charges, the case would go to trial, a verdict would be rendered and the guilty party would be punished. The justice system was designed for this job, with built-in checks and balances—albeit flawed—to protect individual freedoms and society's interests. Customs, on the other hand, had few checks and apparently little balance, despite having the ability to violate Canadians' right to freedom of expression.

Detective James Maitland, with thirty-three years on the Vancouver police force, was the first officer to take the stand. Maitland accepted Justice Smith's polite invitation to "have a seat if you like"—police officers usually testify on their feet as a sign of respect for the judge—and then proceeded to prove himself every inch the veteran, answering questions in a kind of tough-guy "been there, done that" tone.

Crown lawyer Dan Kiselbach extracted Maitland's relevant work history: a stint with Vancouver's vice squad in the mid-1970s, then reassigned to the unit from 1986 to the present. In the 1970s, Maitland testified, vice had "twenty investigating members attached to the squad," but times had changed. By 1994, only eight officers battled the city's vices, including obscenity, prostitution, gambling and liquor violations. With this loss of personnel, largely due to budget allocations, the department's nature had also changed. In their heyday, said Maitland, "we had the luxury of being able to seek out and investigate matters . . . At present, because of manpower, we are more reactive rather than proactive." The squad's main concern was child pornography; in 1993, the new child pornography law had made possession of kiddie porn illegal, along with its production, distribution and sale.

Kiselbach went directly to the Crown's central points.

"How much of the obscenity you have seen as a police officer is of foreign origin?" Kiselbach asked. Maitland estimated the figure at "somewhere in the vicinity of 85 to 90 percent."

"Has the nature of the obscenity you've seen changed over time?" asked Kiselbach.

"Yes," said Maitland. "I would say that there is now more material coming into the country right now that is of a violent or bizarre nature."

"Is much of the child pornography you've seen as a police officer of foreign origin?" asked Kiselbach.

"Yes," said Maitland.

The Crown hoped to demonstrate that Customs and the police were essential allies in the war against obscenity. (Unintentionally, however, Customs often came across as the informal back-up for staff-starved vice squads.) Maitland referred to Canada Customs and U.S. Customs as "a first line of defence to protect the country from what I would consider to be an open invitation if they weren't there." He described how Customs contacted him "maybe once or twice a month" regarding materials they had intercepted at the border and the post office; Maitland later described the frequency of contact as "fifteen calls a year, or something like that."

"I would say about 50 percent of the [obscenity or child pornography] cases I have investigated in the last three or four years has been as a result of an information I received from Customs and other sources," said Maitland.

Under cross-examination, the role Customs played in Maitland's vice squad world would become far less well-defined. But the first fact Arvay quickly established was that Little Sister's had never been the subject of any criminal investigation.

"I take it you've never had any complaints that Little Sister's bookstore is a purveyor of child pornography?" Arvay asked, confining his question to the material Maitland was most concerned about.

"I personally haven't, no," Maitland said, "and I don't recall any [about] that particular store."

Arvay also wanted to show how the diminishing police response to adult pornography was a sign that this material was simply not a high priority. Maitland testified that his department would only investigate adult stores "if we have a complaint."

"Aside from child pornography," Arvay asked, as though to remind the court, "it's not an offence in Canada to possess obscene material, do you understand that?"

"To possess, that is correct," Maitland replied.

Then Arvay used Maitland's years of experience to illustrate Customs' lack of accountability. He asked the detective to outline how an obscenity charge was laid, including the role of outside experts and local Crown prosecutors. Crown prosecutors, it became clear, didn't like to proceed without a high degree of confidence that a charge would stick.

"We don't very often go to court with the opinion of [only] the one officer involved," said Maitland. "It's generally a compilation of various . . . people who make up and formulate an opinion." He cited resource people at the B.C. Film Classification Branch, the former Periodical Review Board and other police officers. In essence, Arvay was letting Maitland show that the police and Crown prosecutors were well aware that their actions would be strictly tested in a court of law—and that the onus was on them to prove guilt. In contrast, Customs was entitled to ban a book without any formal legal advice, within a system of "reverse onus" where a bookseller needed, in essence, to prove the book's innocence.

Arvay also wanted to show that the police used Customs as a kind of duly constituted snitch, not so much a source of obscenity convictions as a source of where to look further. This was especially true of child pornography.

"So you will use the initial seizure at the border as some evidence to justify the obtaining of a search warrant?" asked Arvay

"Exactly," said Maitland.

"And in every one of these instances you are dealing with private persons, persons who may be in possession of child pornography, rather than distributors?" asked Arvay

"For the most part, that is correct," said Maitland. Earlier, Arvay had established that the police mainly used Customs to gain entry into the murky underworld of child pornography—not the above ground, adult porn market that Little Sister's represented.

But Customs didn't simply make it easier for the police to obtain a search warrant; they enabled the police to skip that stage altogether.

"Detective Maitland, when you seize material at the border," Arvay asked, "I take it you have to obtain a search warrant first?"

"No," said Maitland. "The material has already been detained by Customs . . . I believe the Customs are empowered under legislation to make a detention of that nature and turn it over to us." Arvay didn't pursue this point, letting it stand as a sinister reminder of how little scrutiny Customs enjoyed; unlike the police force, Customs officers had no need to jump through the time-honoured hoop of proving "reasonable cause" when applying for a search warrant.

Courtroom 65 was already packed when the two elderly women entered and scanned the aisle for standing room. Watching their predicament, another spectator and I offered our seats. There's a better view at the back, anyway, I told myself, but I was perplexed by these latecomers. Throughout the trial, the public gallery had been peopled by the regulars, plus a steady stream of drop-ins: school kids studying the justice system (they arrived during a very graphic presentation by the Crown); German tourists curious about a Canadian courtroom. Yet I couldn't place these two old ladies. I found myself especially rivetted to the tall, attentive woman who now sat in my seat. She seemed captivated by every exchange. "Probably from some Fraser Valley watchdog group," I thought, "monitoring the smut and the homos and reporting back dutifully to her local chapter or church."

J A N I N E

When the courtroom broke for lunch, I looked towards her the way a fighter eyes their opponent coming out of the corner. Then I noticed that Irene Faulkner was also eyeing the old woman. "Oh-oh," I thought, "maybe she's one of those legendary court watchers who haunts the most salacious trials . . ." Irene came over to me and, just as I was about to whisper, "Who *is* that woman?" she said, "Thanks for giving my mother your seat, Janine." Oh, you're welcome, I thought to myself.

Irene and I had become friends. Night after night, we debated and discussed the trials of the day (pun intended) and life in general. We weren't alone. An assorted group of friends, new and old, would get together to chew over the most recent testimony, often at our local watering hole, the Parkhill. Anyone looking for us knew to search the four-block radius around Irene's West End hotel.

Meeting in her room was impossible. Every square inch was covered in "evidence"—books, magazines, witnesses' statements, enough black binders to supply a back-to-school shopping spree. In fact, Irene's hotel room became so crowded that her partner, Brock Macdonald, was recruited from their Vancouver Island home to help solve the crisis. I was curious to meet this Brock character. I'd come to really like his son, Mark, and if there had been any Irene Faulkner trading cards, I would have collected 'em all.

Brock arrived one weekend with armloads of shelving and went to work. He is a shy, handsome man with a beautiful mane of fluffy white hair, and he toiled unobtrusively while Irene and I went over my evidence. Then he stayed on for the week, helping Irene, making sure she ate, getting to know some of the Little Sister's crowd. Of course, he also did time in Courtroom 65, getting a rare look into his son's reality and community. Some parents actually read the coming-out books their kids give them, but how many are willing to sit through days of testimony about almost every aspect of gay and lesbian identity?

Brock is a psychologist by trade and he was intrigued that my mother had been one, too. During countless heart-to-heart talks, he began to explore some of the unasked questions: What being gay was really all about . . . What he felt as a father . . . How he could move on with Mark . . . For many of us, the after-hours of the trial became an opportunity to talk about who we truly were, unburdening our family histories. For Brock and Mark, it was like a bulldozer clearing the debris left by years of misspent communication between son and father. But the trial was also one of those interludes in life that is heightened and almost surreal—and who knows if we would be able to sustain any of our new understandings?

Standing on Guard for Thee

The Crown's next witness was Detective Noreen Wolff, an eighteen-year veteran of the Vancouver Police Department who had joined the Pornography Portfolio in June 1992. She had clearly taken to the assignment; with her shoulder-length, salt-and-pepper hair and a kind of grim energy, Noreen Wolff was one of trial's most unforgettable participants. Unlike the other detectives, Wolff remained standing throughout her lengthy testimony, steadfastly directing her answers towards Justice Smith. Even the cool-headed Joe Arvay was unnerved by her forceful presence—and especially by her refusal to look him in the eye.

Wolff was a member of the Coordinated Law Enforcement Unit (CLUE), a joint Royal Canadian Mounted Police/Vancouver police operation with province-wide jurisdiction. The Crown expected her to bolster the view that Customs had an indispensable role in helping the police combat obscenity.

"[We do] investigations around prohibited pornography which include child pornography or adult pornography with bestiality and bondage, sex with violence, degradation—those type of pornography investigations," Wolff told Crown lawyer Kiselbach. Like Detective Maitland from vice, Wolff's main focus was child pornography.

"The majority of [child pornography] we have been dealing with in the unit has been from . . . detentions through Canada Customs, and it's all foreign," said Wolff. ". . . 95 percent of what I and my partners have done over the past two years have been as a result of detentions from . . . Customs."

Also like Maitland, Wolff had nothing but gratitude for Customs' part in the anti-obscenity play. "I don't feel there is the remotest possibility that we could do what Customs does," she said.

In cross-examination, however, Arvay was not about to let Wolff's version of Customs' role go unchallenged. He hoped to show that Customs' powers of prior restraint amounted to overkill, even as far as the police's needs were concerned. Why, Arvay wanted to know, couldn't Customs simply alert the police when they came across some potentially obscene material.

"If you had a person who was willing to come forward and swear . . . a statement that he or she saw material that he or she believed was child pornography, would that provide the basis for a search warrant?" Arvay asked.

"No," said Wolff. "There would have to be a fairly in-depth investigation into that . . . the Justice of the Peace wouldn't give us a search warrant unless we had some fairly concrete evidence to go on."

". . . Why wouldn't you accept the opinion of the Customs officer that [something was] obscene?" Arvay asked. Wolff reiterated that more "in-depth information" would be required.

Again and again, Arvay tried to hammer home the idea that identifying and prosecuting individuals in possession of child pornography was not dependant on border seizures, and that the information from Customs was only a small portion of a police investigation. He cross-examined Wolff for hours, trying to demonstrate that the police, upon notification by Customs, could simply track a parcel's arrival to its destination, rather than rely on Canada Customs' detention and review powers.

"Detective Wolff . . . my question is: Why is it necessary for Customs to *seize* the material and *maintain possession* of the material for the police to know the identity of the persons or person to whom the material is directed?" asked Arvay.

Crown lawyer Kiselbach interjected, arguing that Arvay's question was heading into a realm of privileged information about police investigative techniques. Arvay countered Kiselbach's objection.

"It's highly unfair that we wouldn't be allowed to test the conclusions and the very strong assertions made by this witness," he told Justice

Smith. "The fact of the matter is, I haven't come anywhere close to treading on an area of Crown privilege or public interest immunity." The judge agreed and Wolff again faced Arvay's question. It became clear that Wolff was adamantly opposed to the law enforcement technique known as "controlled delivery," in which suspected materials are routed to a staked-out destination. (Later on, Detective Bob Matthews of Toronto's Project P would testify that controlled delivery was a viable practice in his bailiwick.) But in disputing the effectiveness of controlled delivery, Wolff let the court in on how Customs' practices could, in fact, actually *hurt* a police investigation.

". . . We have asked Customs to forward [a K 27] when we have been, in some cases, unable to identify . . . the person," said Wolff, referring to the Customs notice of detention. ". . . In that way, we can identify who the person is when they come to pick up the item . . . at a postal outlet."

"Sometimes you ask Customs *not* to issue a K 27 form?" Arvay asked, sensing he was on to something.

"That's correct," said Wolff. ". . . We feel, in many cases, that if the K 27 goes out that it will alert the person to a possible investigation by us, the police, and hamper it."

"Have you ever had a conversation with Customs officials to the effect that maybe the [Customs] legislation is getting in the way of your law enforcement objectives?" Arvay asked.

"No . . ." replied Wolff. By now, Arvay wasn't expecting any other answer from Detective Wolff; but he hoped Justice Smith would consider the ironic implications of the question.

Boiling over *Boiled Angel*

During questioning by the Crown, Wolff had been asked her opinion of *Boiled Angel,* a comic book by an American, Mike Diana. Customs had seized *Boiled Angel* when a student had been routinely searched at the Vancouver International Airport ("that person is subsequently under [criminal] charges relating to this publication," said Wolff). Kiselbach invited Wolff to "discuss" the portions of the comic that violated the child pornography law, probably believing he had an incontrovertible sample of what all good Canadians would want seized at the border.

Boiled Angel, an exposé of child sexual abuse, is filled with bizarre, troubling scenes of child rape, bestiality and necrophilia, among others. The fact that the comic book was Diana's attempt to alert readers to child abuse and to society's hypocrisy had evidently escaped the Canadian government, as it had officials in Clearwater, Florida, where Diana had been convicted on obscenity charges.

Initially, Arvay objected to Kiselbach allowing Wolff to comment on the comic's legality. He argued that obscenity was a matter for a court to determine, not a police officer. But the Crown managed to persuade Justice Smith that Wolff's opinion was relevant because, in Kiselbach's words, "she makes recommendations as to whether or not to proceed in criminal matters after taking a look at material such as this."

Kiselbach may have later regretted his persuasiveness. In Arvay's hands, *Boiled Angel* and Noreen Wolff became a revealing—and embarrassing—combination. In cross-examination, Arvay agreed with the Crown that Wolff's standpoint was relevant, and he told Justice Smith exactly why.

"My lord, this is a witness who has come to this court with very, very strong opinions about what is obscene," said Arvay, ". . . and it was part of her evidence as to why Customs is so important to the police. It's my submission that I should be entitled to test the foundation of that opinion . . .

"[Detective Wolff] has said that [*Boiled Angel*] is one of the worst things she has ever seen, or words to that effect. This all goes to her credibility and to the weight that you should attach to her evidence."

Arvay recognized *Boiled Angel* as a violent, punk 'zine attempt at social satire, and he wanted to show that Wolff had no apparent capacity to grasp this aspect of Diana's work. Rather than being the worst of the worst, *Boiled Angel* would become a vehicle to explore the issue of artistic purpose.

Wolff had been very deeply affected by *Boiled Angel*. She said ". . . [Its] drawings couldn't be more explicit, more graphic as to what's taking place in the publication, and it includes both child and adult pornography and very disturbing forms of it." When questioned by Arvay, she repeated that she "found the material quite disturbing."

"Well, it may be disturbing, Detective, but you appreciate that even disturbing matters may not be obscene?" Arvay asked. Wolff simply responded that she based her understanding of obscenity on the child pornography legislation.

The comic book is extremely disturbing. *Boiled Angel* has a deliberate, over-the-top style, yet Wolff seemed to register its contents on a strictly literal level. One scene shows a baby being raped by his adopted father; the baby is then forced into a shredder and canned as dog food.

"Do you really think [Diana] is really proposing that you grind up babies to sell to the A&P store?" Arvay asked Wolff.

"Do I really think this is something that I'd want in Canada for people to look at, to even give them remote ideas?" Wolff answered.

". . . That's not my question," said Arvay. "Do you believe that the author's purpose is to suggest that people should grind up babies and put it in tins and sell them as dog food?"

"Can you say he's not?" said Wolff. "I can't say that he isn't . . ."

Wolff's penchant for the literal was confirmed in a highly charged episode in Courtroom 65. During a brief break in Arvay's cross-examination, Irene Faulkner asked her partner, Brock Macdonald, to photocopy some illustrations that Arvay intended to pass out to the judge and government lawyers. (They were drawings by Mike Diana about the role of political satire and his struggle with American obscenity laws.) Observing Faulkner from the witness box, Wolff mistakenly concluded that she had handed Macdonald *Boiled Angel*—that Faulkner was, in effect, *distributing child pornography* in the courthouse. Wolff relayed her concern to Crown lawyer Van Iperen, who in turn informed Faulkner, who more or less shrugged off the matter in her haste to prepare for Wolff's further cross-examination.

But Detective Wolff was convinced she had seen the banned comic leave the courtroom. She dashed out of the witness box and into the hall, looking for Macdonald, who was photocopying a few floors down, unaware of the furore. In the meantime, Van Iperen again asked Little Sister's if *Boiled Angel* was being reproduced. Arvay, already exasperated by Wolff's overzealous stance, angrily asked the Crown to please control their witness.

Arvay presented interviews and reviews relating to Diana's work, including an anti-censorship story in the December 1994 issue of *Mother Jones,* a progressive American magazine. He was attempting to show the court, if not Detective Wolff, that these sorts of interpretive materials might be relevant during an obscenity trial. Not surprisingly, Wolff rejected Sean Harry's article in *Mother Jones* outright, after first admitting she was unfamiliar with the magazine. The article was "obviously [by] somebody who is a member of the civil liberties in the U.S." said Wolff. "It's not written by somebody here . . ." and therefore, she said, was irrelevant in a Canadian context.

Arvay hastened to give the judge a Canadian context for Wolff's dismissiveness.

"[This] shows that Detective Wolff is not interested in having Crown counsel be fully informed about the work of a person described as an artist in a relatively mainstream publication," said Arvay, "and would be intent on having the prosecution go forward without that information."

Arvay then quoted Mike Diana's own words from an interview in *Shadow* (No. 31), an American journal:

> I don't like child molesting or child abuse. I don't support the publication of actual photographs of child pornography, because that's real. That means real abuse is happening. But it's not going to go away . . .
>
> My drawings are saying "wake up and see that this is going on around you all the time." Why does it take me for you to get scared, though? What's obscene is that this stuff really goes on. Here I am just drawing a comic about it and they want to give me two years in jail for it. That's probably more time than they would give to the guys who are really abusing the children.

After establishing Wolff's belief that *Boiled Angel* was a clear-cut case of obscenity, Arvay wrapped up the cross-examination by asking her opinion of two other pornographic works: the December 1994 issue of *Hustler* and a humour book entitled *101 Uses for a Severed Penis*, apropos of the Bobbitt phenomenon. Wolff's responses showed both the bizarre nature of Canada's obscenity laws—and her unshakeable resolve.

Arvay presented the detective with several questionable pages from *Hustler,* including an ad advising lonely men to have sex with a Thanksgiving turkey. He then asked Wolff's opinion about another *Hustler* house ad.

"It shows a naked woman in a coffin . . . as if she was in a morgue, and it says: 'She's cold. She's stiff. She's our centerfold.' Would you consider that to be obscene?" Arvay asked.

"It wouldn't be obscene under the legislation that I know of," said Wolff.

"Would you not consider that to be a depiction of sex that is dehumanizing?" asked Arvay.

"There is a body lying in a body bag," said Wolff. "I can see no sexual

.context—the nipples are covered with the plastic bag. There doesn't appear to be any other sexual thing along with it."

Wolff did not consider any part of the *Hustler* to be obscene, and, legally speaking, she was entirely correct. Under Canada's obscenity laws, depictions of highly sexualized female corpses—in the absence of explicit sexual activity—are only guilty of bad taste.

Wolff and Arvay's exchange over *101 Uses for a Severed Penis* often sounded more like a comedy club routine than courtroom testimony. Arvay couldn't resist describing the first drawing in the absurd comic book.

". . . One of the uses for a severed penis is for a Supreme Court novelty gavel, for the benefit of your lordship," Arvay informed Justice Smith. (Canadian judges, Arvay knew, do not use gavels of any variety.) Then he asked Wolff if the image or suggestion were obscene.

"I don't think it would be . . ." she said. He then asked her about some of the other uses: a bandit, an eraser . . .

"You wouldn't consider any of these pictures depicting a severed penis as being obscene?" asked Arvay.

"Not under the legislation as I know it, but I haven't gotten through the whole book," said Wolff.

"Why is it not obscene?" asked Arvay.

". . . I can't think of where under the legislation it would be. They sell penis erasers in stores—"

"The [authors] *are* talking about a severed penis?" asked Arvay.

"Well, the way it's drawn here, it doesn't appear to me to be [a penis]. I don't know where it would be severed from or whatever," said Wolff.

"Most severed penises are from men, Detective Wolff. I mean, be serious," said an incredulous Arvay. ". . . The fact that there is a comic with a severed penis is not enough to make something obscene: would that be your evidence?"

"In this case, your honour," said Wolff.

Project P as in Pornography

Detective Sergeant Robert Matthews was almost a breath of fresh air after Wolff's intensity. He was direct, to the point and out of the witness box by lunch time. Matthews was another seasoned officer, twenty-seven years on the force and, since 1988, attached to the notorious Toronto-based Project P unit of the Ontario Provincial Police. Toronto's gay, lesbian and alternative arts communities were exceedingly well-acquainted with Project P's manoeuvres. A few months after the 1992 *Butler* decision, an officer from Project P had arrested John Scythes in the controversial *Bad Attitude* case; in the same time period, Bob Matthews himself had issued a warning to a Toronto restaurant, La Hacienda, for its display of homoerotic photos by Ron Giii and Bruce Eves.

In his testimony, Matthews described how the unit was formed in the mid-1970s to investigate and prosecute people who make, distribute and sell obscene materials and hate literature in Ontario. All but one member of the nine-person team worked on pornography investigations, said Matthews, who now heads the unit, and their "number one priority is child pornography . . . [Since] early 1993, 100 percent of our time is dealing with child pornography."

As Matthews explained, the unit formerly concerned itself with "investigations involving mainly penetration"—he didn't specify what kind; since *Butler,* Matthews claimed, "we don't lay any charges for material that involves simple penetration, consensual sex."

"So has the nature of the material you're investigating changed?" asked Kiselbach.

"It's changed dramatically," said Matthews. ". . . The material . . . is much more violent, and by that I'm talking about whippings, severe pain being inflicted on the human body, the use of foreign objects, the use of animals and reptiles, you name it . . . We have a tremendous amount of child pornography." Most of the material was produced outside Canada, although Matthews' later testimony left some confusion on this point.

Like the other detectives, Matthews painted an oft-times contradictory picture of Customs' role in Project P's operations. He told Kiselbach that "Customs is absolutely crucial to the operation of my unit"; he later described the number of investigations arising from the Customs liaison as "at least four or five" in the past year—hardly a compelling figure for a province-wide unit.

Like Maitland, Matthews viewed the child pornography trade as an underworld that relied on highly clandestine, interpersonal networks.

"Without a doubt, [child pornography] is under the counter, it's underground, and people do not openly sell child pornography," said Matthews. "And it's very difficult to purchase . . . The majority of the child pornography that we seize or that is produced in Canada is produced by paedophiles who are molesting children in Canada and trafficking in it within our own borders."

Matthews acknowledged that Project P mainly relied on Customs to point them in the direction of individuals who collected and exchanged kiddie porn.

"When child pornography is detected at the border and we become aware of it," said Matthews, "the key is: 'Who in our country is receiving or trying to receive the material?' That identifies someone who is likely, in my opinion . . . [to] already have possession of child pornography. So, therefore, that would spark an investigation."

Arvay wanted to explore the fact that kiddie porn rarely came across the border in ordinary commercial shipments, such as those destined for Little Sister's. Moreover, he suspected that Customs could hardly be seen as a deterrent to the sophisticated underground print market or the unregulated electronic networks, like the Internet.

"Would you agree that Canada Customs is not able to detect, let alone detain, all the adult or child pornography that enters the country?" Arvay asked.

"Oh, absolutely," said Matthews. "It's an impossible task."

". . . You will agree that people who are determined to smuggle . . . will attempt to do so, notwithstanding the presence of Canada Customs?" asked Arvay.

"Yes," said Matthews, but added, ". . . that [Customs] definitely does have a deterrent effect." Arvay and Matthews then agreed that Customs detected only a small percentage of the material entering the country.

Matthews had proven to be a useful and agreeable witness for Arvay. He gave evidence willingly, surprising the Little Sister's supporters who were aware of his reputation in Toronto as a tough foe of gays and lesbians. His testimony also had some unforeseen side-effects. Although it probably hadn't been his intention, Matthew's depressing evidence about the underground kiddie porn trade had cast doubt on Customs' role and effectiveness as a deterrent.

More importantly, Matthews and the other detectives had seemed quite unconcerned about a store like Little Sister's, which neither carried child pornography nor had ever been charged under the obscenity laws. If the police paid so little attention to Little Sister's, why, then, did Customs pay so much? The answer was either that the bookstore was indeed operating well within the bounds of the law, or that the police were relying on Customs' powers of prior restraint to do their own enforcement work. Whatever the answer, Arvay had made sure Justice Smith could see that this picture, to put it mildly, was not quite right.

Except for a few Vancouver Customs officials, the detectives were the final witnesses in the two-month-long trial. The mood of the courtroom had swung from grim to giddy and back again, as Arvay worked through his exhausting and often painful cross-examination of the law enforcers. Like the Customs officials in the weeks before, the detectives' testimony had given Little Sister's an unspoiled view of the assumptions and authority the bookstore had been up against all these years. To say the least, the experience had been disheartening.

NINE

Final Arguments
and a Very Long Wait

JOSEPH ARVAY: *The fact is that, notwithstanding their importance, sensitivity and difference from other goods, [books and magazines] are not treated any differently from other goods, whether textiles, electronics or vegetable oil . . .*

D URING the final weeks of November 1994, the Little Sister's trial threatened to drag into the new year. Joe Arvay had shown no intention of cutting short his cross-examination of the Crown's witnesses. Both Linda Murphy of Canada Customs and Detective Noreen Wolff of the Vancouver Police Department had been presented by the government in a few hours, yet each remained in cross-examination for several days as Arvay dissected their every assertion. But at the end of the month, the curtain was finally drawn on the witnesses and, for a week, the two sides withdrew from Courtroom 65 to prepare their closing legal arguments.

For Little Sister's team of two, it was a week of strenuous analysis and late nights. From the mass of evidence generated in over thirty days of testimony, Arvay and Irene Faulkner needed to distil the points that substantiated the bookstore's constitutional challenge. The Crown and the Attorney General's lawyers, with their considerable resources, were busy marshalling their defensive arguments. By December 5, the lawyers were again facing Justice Kenneth Smith, armed with their crucial closing submissions.

Not only did two profoundly different legal viewpoints emerge from the final arguments, but both differed fundamentally from the *feeling* of the trial itself. The emersion into a detached, legal realm seemed total. Gone were the theatrics of cross-examination, the probing into queer culture, the parade of witness-box personalities. Cool exposition was now the order of the day. In particular, the lawyers were deploying their weapons of constitutional warfare. Many Little Sister's supporters—even Jim Deva and Bruce Smyth—were probably mystified by the repeated references to the *Charter of Rights and Freedoms*' pivotal sections (to be exact, sections 1, 2(b), 15 and 24; see Appendix B), the Oakes Test, the doctrine of prior restraint, the *Constitution Act*'s section 52, the *Butler* decision (used by both sides), the nuances of Canadian, American and British jurisprudence, the remedies . . .

Yet these final weeks of trial also packed a unique punch, and the essence of what Little Sister's, the Crown and the AG had been trying to prove during the preceding weeks was often revealed for the first time.

Freedom of Expression Versus Prior Restraint

Arvay presented his arguments first. For Little Sister's, the "impugned legislation"—portions of the *Customs Act* and the *Customs Tariff Act*— was, first and foremost, guilty of violating the *Charter*'s guaranteed right of freedom of expression (s. 2[b]). Little Sister's conceded that the *Butler* decision entitled the government to use the Criminal Code to curtail that freedom by prohibiting obscene materials. But Canada Customs and Tariff Code 9956 were an altogether different matter.

Freedom of expression, said Arvay, was not a right to be trifled with. He quoted a 1989 Supreme Court of Canada ruling: "It is difficult to imagine a guaranteed right more important to a democratic society than the freedom of expression" (*Edmonton Journal v. Alberta Attorney-General*), and then offered an even more poetic formulation: "The diversity in forms of individual self-fulfilment and human flourishing ought to be cultivated in an essentially tolerant, indeed welcoming environment, not only for the sake of those conveying the meaning, but also for the sake of those to whom it is conveyed" (*Irwin Toy Ltd. v. Quebec Attorney-General [1989]*).

"The essence of this constitutional challenge," said Arvay, "is that the impugned legislation involves unconstitutional prior restraint of expression." The Crown, of course, didn't deny that Customs infringed on freedom of expression when it practised prior restraint. As Arvay knew, they would defend the Customs legislation as a justifiable limit under section 1 of the *Charter*; further, the Crown would try to discredit Little Sister's opposition to prior restraint by arguing that Canadians had a long and strong tradition of being restrained. The bookstore, they would say, had been bitten by an American anti-prior restraint bug and Justice Smith should just ignore their itching. Arvay was ready for this argument.

Prior restraint was recognized as a problem, he said, in Sir William Blackstone's *Commentaries* of 1803, a cornerstone of British—and hence Canadian—law. "The liberty of the press is indeed essential to the nature of the free state," wrote Blackstone, "but this consists in laying no previous restraints upon publications, and not in freedom from censure for criminal matter when published." To paraphrase Blackstone (and Little Sister's): don't stop the free flow of the printed word, because the courts can always be used to deal with any problems that may subsequently arise.

Arvay took some time to reiterate the damaging effects of Customs' powers. "Foremost," he said, "is the fact that the [Crown] cannot prove that the legislation results in the detention or prohibition of material that is only obscene and thus harmful. It is grossly over-inclusive." To illustrate his point, Arvay presented a startling figure, drawn from the case's Statement of Agreed Facts (facts accepted by plaintiff and defendant alike): in British Columbia, only fourteen obscenity charges were prosecuted under the Criminal Code between 1989 and 1992; during the same time period, Customs prohibited 34,748 shipments under Tariff Code 9956 (Arvay noted that a shipment usually included more than one item). This imbalanced ratio of obscenity charges to Customs prohibitions, said Arvay, demonstrated that Customs' "net" was stretched far too widely—and led to "results that defy rationality and fairness."

Under the Shade of the New Oakes Test

This language—rationality, fairness—was drawn from a pivotal legal principle used by both Little Sister's and the Crown: the Oakes Test. The test derived from a 1986 Supreme Court ruling on a drug possession case; *R. v. Oakes* created a benchmark for measuring whether a piece of legislation was constitutional, even though it limited or overrode a *Charter* freedom, like freedom of expression. The Crown would argue that Customs legislation passed the Oakes Test with flying colours; Little Sister's was arguing the opposite.

The Oakes Test is a sequence of mini-tests. First, the objective (purpose) of the questionable legislation must be found to be sufficiently *important* "to warrant overriding a constitutionally protected freedom." Second, the means chosen to limit the freedom—in this case, Tariff Code 9956 and Memorandum D9-1-1—must be *reasonable*; this involves a "proportionality test" that balances society's interests with the interests of individuals and groups, and is broken into three parts: (1) the means must be "rationally" connected to the purpose—not "arbitrary, unfair or based on irrational considerations"; (2) the means must "impair" the right and freedom in question as little as possible; and (3) there must be a "proportionality" between the means' impact and the legislation's purpose. Dry and obscure though it may appear, the Oakes Test is not only an indispensable factor in any constitutional challenge, it is an important protector of *Charter* rights.

Arvay was well positioned to use the proportionality test against Customs; he had, for instance, ample evidence that Customs legislation seriously impaired freedom of expression, and that its effects seemed disproportionate to its purpose. But a dramatic Supreme Court ruling in another case gave Little Sister's an unexpected and timely gift on December 8: a revision to the Oakes Test.

In *Dagenais v. the Canadian Broadcasting Corporation,* the Supreme Court was asked to rule on a lower court order that had banned the broadcast of a made-for-TV movie called *The Boys of St. Vincent.* John N. Smith's drama about child sexual abuse in a Newfoundland Catholic orphanage, based on a true story, had been temporarily banned in Ontario and Québec; lawyers for four Catholic Christian Brothers charged with sexual abuse in Ontario had successfully argued that their clients' right to a fair trial would have been jeopardized if the movie had been aired. In effect, the lower court had agreed that the men's right to a fair trial was more important than a temporary curtailment of freedom of expression. There was widespread outrage at the ban, especially among Canadian media.

The Supreme Court overturned the transmission ban and took a solid stand in favour of freedom of expression. In doing so, the court proposed a significant change to the Oakes Test. *Dagenais* came midway through Arvay's final submissions and he immediately took advantage of it, pouring over the decision and constructing his argument well into the night.

Arvay put *Dagenais* into plain English. (Chief Justice Lamar had written: "I would . . . rephrase the third part of the Oakes Test as follows: there must be a proportionality between the deleterious effects of the measures which are responsible for limiting the rights and freedoms in question and the objective, and there must be a proportionality between the deleterious and salutary effects of the measures.") Arvay explained that the Supreme Court had altered the Canadian common law tradition that emphasized the right to a fair trial over the right to freedom of expression, and had employed a new, improved Oakes Test to weigh the relative importance of those rights. *Dagenais* said that: "In the case of the publication ban at issue here, the specific freedom of expression interest engaged by the ban included: the film director's interest in the film; the public's interest in viewing the film; and society's interest in having the important issue of child abuse presented to the public." Applying the new Oakes standard to Little Sister's, Arvay argued that the right to view material considered not obscene by writers and other experts (and often by Customs themselves, after an appeal) far outweighed the possible threat that obscene items might enter the country and be sold by a bookstore.

Moreover, said Arvay, "the government's interest in prohibiting the entry into Canada of obscene material is not predicated on a constitutionally entrenched right or freedom. It is justified on the basis of *administrative considerations* . . ." (emphasis added).

Arvay also spoke at length about the built-in flaws in Customs' mandate and practices, drawing on the testimony of booksellers and Customs officials. He discussed the "chilling effect" the legislation had on publishers, booksellers and writers, and its "disproportionate impact on small publishers, many of whom cater to women and other minorities [sic]." Arvay hammered home that Customs legislation had unjustifiably harsh effects on "the written word"—on books and text, as compared to magazines and pictures—and that "there are few prosecutions for the written word in other democratic countries."

He also tackled the notion that Customs is the country's first line of defence against obscenity. The police, Arvay reminded Justice Smith, had freely admitted that adult pornography was no longer a priority. "The federal government cannot plead lack of resources as a justification for overriding a fundamental right when the police do not consider the problem a serious and pressing one," said Arvay. He then referred to

Oakes: "Accordingly, the present [Customs] system provides one of *the most restrictive means* that is justified by a failure of political will to provide better resources to the police."

Customs could still assist the police, Arvay said, by alerting them to suspected obscene items. "We are not saying that Customs should not be able to inspect materials," said Arvay. "We are saying that they should not be able to *detain* the material."

Arvay also looked at how Customs' approach to obscenity was badly out of step with *Butler's* concept of "harm." The Vancouver Customs Mail Centre, he noted, still used a document that defined obscenity as "offensive to prevailing concepts of morality or decency—indecent, disgusting, foul," and defined prurient as "having lustful cravings or desires, lewd." Not only did these definitions fail to conform to modern notions of obscenity as defined in *Butler,* they were throwbacks to a discredited Victorian standard. Despite the Crown's use of *Butler*-style terminology to justify the detention and seizure of lesbian and gay material, Arvay said, "There was no evidence that Customs officials even consider the question of harm . . ."

Discrimination for the (Queer) Nation . . .

The abrupt removal of anal penetration from Memorandum D9-1-1, mere days before the Little Sister's trial began, was perhaps the most damning evidence that Customs had failed to keep up with *Butler.* It was also a striking example of how Customs had discriminated against gays and lesbians. "But for this trial," said Arvay, "the change in the memorandum might have been ignored for an indefinite period of time." He reiterated that, as early as 1990, Customs had received legal advice from the Department of Justice that anal penetration *per se* was not obscene. "In the absence of any . . . contrary legal advice," said Arvay, "the only inference to draw is that Customs was acting in an unlawful and arguably a discriminatory manner, and committing an abuse of power."

The charge of discrimination against gays and lesbians was the other cornerstone of Little Sister's constitutional challenge. (The bookstore was also claiming that Deva and Smyth were personally discriminated against as gay men.) Sexual orientation, though not explicitly listed in section 15 of the *Charter,* is considered a prohibited grounds of discrimination—an "analogous" ground. That Customs discriminated against gays and lesbians seemed beyond dispute. The incessant targeting of shipments to Canada's few gay and lesbian bookstores had been shown, and Arvay repeated a few telling statistics, including the fact that, of the material reviewed at the Prohibited Importations Directorate, fully 25 percent is gay.

"This is particularly troubling," said Arvay, "given that gays and lesbians are a constitutionally protected community who are being systematically silenced by the impugned legislation. The evidence is overwhelming—and virtually uncontradicted—that gay and lesbian sexual imagery and text, including that which has been prohibited entry, is vital to gay and lesbian identity, dignity, self-worth, community formation, health and education."

Arvay argued that, though the Customs legislation was "neutral" on the subject of sexual orientation—didn't explicitly mention the subject—it clearly had a disproportionate impact on gay and lesbian pornography. He then addressed another key point.

"It isn't being argued that gay and lesbian material could never be obscene," said Arvay. "However, given the relative importance of this material to the gay and lesbian community, the likelihood that Customs will misunderstand homosexuality and the nature of this material, [and] the inherent differences of this material from mainstream, heterosexual pornography (particularly given the paradigm established in *Butler*) . . . it is submitted that the impugned legislation violates section 15 of the *Charter,* and is not justified under section 1."

. . . And Some Suggested Remedies

At the close of his arguments, Little Sister's lawyer needed to give constitutional shape to the bookstore's demands. Arvay proposed several legal remedies to Justice Smith—a kind of wish list that started with a "most wanted" option. First, he asked that the impugned Customs legislation be entirely struck down under section 52 of the *Constitution Act* (1982), which says that "any law that is inconsistent with the provisions of the *Constitution* is, to the extent of the inconsistency, of no force or effect." Little Sister's was asking Justice Smith to strip Canada Customs of its powers of prior restraint.

The bookstore's alternative demand was that Customs be deprived of a portion of its powers under Section 52: the ability to "detain, seize or prohibit the importation of books and printed paper" on the grounds of obscenity. This remedy reflected the idea that books, especially literature, were generally regarded as a more complex form of speech than pictorial representations, and hence were more difficult to evaluate for obscenity. It also reflected the reality that the Little Sister's case was mostly concerned with books, not videos or films, and that judges don't like to decide any more than they need to in any particular case.

The third alternative, for use with or in lieu of the second, was that Customs no longer be entitled to stop "the importation of books, printed papers, drawings, paintings, prints, photographs or representations of any kind that are alleged to be obscene but produced for a homosexual audience." This section 52 option was based on Little Sister's claim that gay and lesbian pornography was distinctive enough to raise many complex issues, and that Customs was incapable of making sound or fair judgements about its meaning.

As well, the bookstore requested a remedy available under the *Charter's* section 24: a declaration by the court that Customs had used their powers in a manner that violated the freedom of expression and equality rights of gays and lesbians. The practical impact of this declaration would be that Little Sister's would be entitled to seek a court award for special costs—in effect, to have the bookstore's enormous legal bills paid by the Crown.

The Crown: A Proud Tradition of Prior Restraint

Now it was the Crown's turn. The lawyers approached their singular task with a two-fold strategy. Their job was to defend Customs legislation, which they were well prepared to do even before the trial began. (Throughout the Crown's submissions, it often seemed as though Hans Van Iperen and his team hadn't really required the testimony of witnesses; instead, their arguments resonated with the voices of legal and constitutional authorities.) But they also needed to refute Arvay's points and destroy the credibility of Little Sister's case. For the bookstore's supporters, few of whom were present for the final arguments, this phase of the trial was a less than edifying experience.

Crown lawyer Dan Kiselbach presented what he called the "defendant's position in a nutshell," laying out the legislative foundation of Customs' mandate and the constitutional justification for Customs' actions: "*The Customs Act, Customs Tariff Act,* and Customs Tariff Code 9956 operate to prohibit the importation of material deemed to be obscene pursuant to section 163 of the Criminal Code of Canada. The

Supreme Court of Canada [in *Butler*] has held that the criminalization of obscenity . . . is demonstrably justified under section 1 of the *Charter* as a reasonable limit proscribed by law. It is submitted that, similarly, the civil regulatory prohibition of obscenity (which is anchored in the Criminal Code definition) is demonstrably justified under section 1 of the *Charter*."

Translated, Kiselbach's nutshell said: The Supreme Court has ruled that it's okay for the government to prohibit some pornography, even though this violates freedom of expression; therefore, the Crown asserts that it's okay for Customs to do the same.

The federal government, said Kiselbach, has a longstanding right and obligation to forbid the importation of "harmful forms of expression." As early as 1847, twenty years before Confederation, a tariff banned the entry of "books and drawings of an immoral or indecent character," and this wording, he observed, "remained intact for well over 100 years . . ."

In the 1992 *Butler* decision, said Kiselbach, the Supreme Court recognized that even the *Charter* "did not have the effect of dramatically depriving Parliament of a power which it has historically enjoyed." Throughout the Crown's and AG's arguments, the comfort given to Customs by the *Butler* decision was palpable. Yet it wasn't exactly the *Butler* pro-censorship feminists had fought for. When Kiselbach reflected on the issue of harm, he seemed to completely lose sight of *Butler's* supposedly feminist slant.

"The purpose of criminalization of obscenity," he said, "is in the national self-protection from harms caused by the exposure to obscene material." Customs served the same purpose in a civil, regulatory context and, said Kiselbach, "Both the criminal law and the Customs law are . . . based on the belief that obscenity has a detrimental impact on those exposed to it and, consequently, on society as a whole."

He then turned his attention to the issue of freedom of expression. In *Butler*, Kiselbach observed, the Supreme Court "indicated that obscenity does not stand on a equal footing with other kinds of expression which directly engage 'the core' of the freedom of expression values . . . It appeals only to the most base aspect of individual fulfilment, and is primarily economically motivated." Not only is obscenity a degraded form of speech, but the Supreme Court had found, said Kiselbach, that "the objective of avoiding harm associated with the dissemination of pornography is sufficiently pressing and substantial to warrant some restrictions on full exercise of the right to freedom of expression." In other words, the purpose of Customs legislation was *important* enough to meet the Oakes criterion and thus to allow the curtailment of a *Charter* freedom. The Crown, it became apparent, was not about to step outside the moralistic cage that traditionally enclosed pornographic speech.

Kiselbach went further into Oakes, considering aspects of the proportionality mini-test. Parliament, he said, intended Customs officers and the police to form a "two-pronged approach" to preventing the harmful spread of pornography. "The Customs officer's role in prohibiting the importation of obscenity . . ." said Kiselbach, "is *rationally connected* with the prevention of harm . . ." (emphasis added). For example, "Without the role of Canada Customs," said Kiselbach, ". . . police officers would have no practical way of investigating the existence and whereabouts of many child pornographers or collectors of child pornography."

Customs officers, he said, were given sound training and guidance about how to make decisions about obscenity, and the bureaucracy has created a reliable system of lookouts that catch repeat offenders. Taken altogether, said Kiselbach, Customs takes an experienced, focused approach to detecting obscenity, which results in the "minimum impairment" possible to freedom of speech. Moreover, he said, Customs has a "complete statutory code of appeal [that] provides importers with an informal, inexpensive procedure of requesting a redetermination . . ." Kiselbach's portrait of a competent and fair Customs was, of course, utterly astonishing to Jim Deva and Bruce Smyth.

Turning to Little Sister's claim that Customs prohibitions were seriously disproportionate to criminal obscenity charges—Arvay's 34,748 to 14 statistic—Kiselbach advised the court there was no cause for alarm. "It cannot be assumed that the bulk of [these] detentions and prohibitions have been in error," he said. Then he rejected Arvay's idea that the Criminal Code could do Customs' job by defending the bureaucracy's very wide net. "It is self-evident that if the same number of decisions regarding the tariff classification of goods had to be made by Canadian courts, the system of regulating the importation of obscenity would be brought to a standstill," said Kiselbach. "Once obscenity is imported into Canada, a system of subsequent punishment through criminal law enforcement is 'too little, too late'." Customs, therefore, is "the only practical means of preventing harm caused by the importation of obscenity."

Living with a Less than Perfect Customs

Kiselbach's arguments had been geared to defending Customs against Little Sister's section 52 challenge. He needed to persuade Justice Smith that although Customs laws infringed on freedom of expression, they nevertheless "constitute a reasonable limit and are saved by section 1 of the *Charter.*"

Senior Crown lawyer Hans Van Iperen sought to persuade Justice Smith about a different matter: that Customs legislation and practices, while not perfect, were good enough. He first took the time to refute several of Arvay's claims, point by point. For starters, Van Iperen echoed one of Kiselbach's arguments.

"Mr. Arvay would have it that it must be assumed that many of Customs' decisions at the first level are wrong," said Van Iperen. "However, in light of the *Glad Day* decision, that cannot be assumed." (The 1993 *Glad Day* decision in Toronto was clearly destined to haunt the queer community for some time to come.) As proof, Van Iperen listed the gay magazines judged to be obscene in the *Glad Day* case, including *Advocate Men, Hot Tricks,* and *Movie Star Confidential,* and noted that Customs had also deemed these publications to be inadmissible. Having established that Customs made some right calls, Van Iperen seemed strangely unconcerned about their innumerable wrong decisions.

He then briefly looked at various issues, from the ability of Customs officers to make competent and careful determinations, the alleged problems with backlogs and time lines, to the pre-screening process; in all instances, Van Iperen defended Customs' practices as reasonable, clear and consistent. The Crown's main goal was to demonstrate that the problems Little Sister's associated with Customs were neither intrinsic to the legislation nor especially serious.

"The purpose and effects of legislation are separate and distinct from the manner in which it is administered and operated," Van Iperen said. Since Customs legislation had a constitutionally valid purpose, then it couldn't be constitutionally damned if the effects of Customs officers' decisions were occasionally unfortunate.

"Even if it was established as fact that the detention of . . . [Jane Rule's] *Contract with the World* was unreasonable or done in bad faith, which is not admitted," said Van Iperen, "such a finding cannot be used . . . [for a] section 52 declaration. At most, it may lead to a section 24 remedy."

Section 24 of the *Charter* states that anyone whose *Charter* rights have been "infringed or denied may apply to a court of competent jurisdiction to obtain such remedy as the court considers appropriate and just in the circumstances." The government had always insisted that this avenue was available if Customs' internal appeal process proved unsatisfactory to Little Sister's or any aggrieved party. Little Sister's could take the government to court, sue them under common law, or seek damages under the *Crown Liability Act.*

If there are problems, Van Iperen said, "they do not stem from the scheme of the *[Customs] Act* but from the way in which those on whom the powers are conferred have chosen to exercise them." Van Iperen then argued that Customs met the principles of administrative law (procedural fairness, fettered discretion, adequate standards) and that Memorandum D9-1-1 "fairly reflected the principles set out in *Butler* as to what constitutes obscenity, as well as the other current jurisprudence on obscenity."

He closed by basically telling the judge that Little Sister's should chin up and have faith.

"There is no real reason to invalidate the legislation in the circumstances of this case," Van Iperen said. "The fact that it has not always been applied correctly cannot lead to the assumption that it cannot be properly applied in the future."

Discrimination—or Distinction?

Little Sister's claim that Customs violated the *Charter's* equality provisions by discriminating against gay and lesbian material—and against Jim Deva and Bruce Smyth personally—was handled by the Crown's Neena Sharma.

Sharma quickly drew a line: only Jim Deva, the homosexual man, had the ability to make this claim; the bookstore itself could not. (Bruce Smyth was not considered because he had not testified.) "This can only be in his individual, personal capacity," said Sharma, "and not in any capacity related to Little Sister's." Canadian courts, she said, had upheld the idea that section 15 guarantees did not apply to corporations.

Sharma then moved on to consider Deva's claim. She pointed out there was an essential difference between discrimination, which is prohibited, and making a "distinction," which can be acceptable, "especially if there is a social reality that contributes to a distinctive effect." This was part of the Canadian tradition of adopting "a contextual rather than an abstract approach in interpreting the *Charter* . . . ," said Sharma. Sharma was making use—albeit distorted use—of a legal argument popular among Canadians seeking social justice. Women and people of colour have argued for a contextual approach to remedying historical injustices, for example, when resisting the conservative legal notion that equal treatment means *same* treatment. Later in the week, the provincial AG would also use a progressive means for a repressive end.

Evidently, the Crown had been unswayed by Deva's moving testimony about life as a gay bookseller. Sharma observed that "his discrimination claim is based on [what he called] homophobia [sic] attitudes endemic in society"; such attitudes couldn't be blamed on Customs. When Deva said he made a "paranoid assumption" about a delayed shipment, Sharma construed his comment to mean there was no real basis for his complaint. Deva had testified that he felt affronted by the idea he would need to submit materials for pre-screening because, said Sharma, "he assumed heterosexual material did not go through the same process . . . The facts prove many heterosexual publications do submit to such a process."

Sharma then turned her attention to other Little Sister's witnesses from the book trade, considering only their *personal* experience of Canada Customs. Jearld Moldenhauer, the founder of Glad Day Books, was dismissed outright. "Obviously he has strong emotional views about the issue of censorship," said Sharma, ". . . which has a lot to do with his background and education with the First Amendment" in the U.S. Anything Moldenhauer said about Customs' impact on him, she said, reflected his political views, and was not "due to his homosexuality." The difficulties that Little Sister's Janine Fuller faced with Customs stemmed from "dealing with the various [Customs] forms and procedures . . . [her] evidence has nothing whatsoever to do with homosexuality . . ." Other witnesses were dismissed in a similar manner.

Next, Sharma reviewed the evidence of Little Sister's experts on the question of discrimination. "Little weight can be placed" on Gary Kinsman's testimony, she said, describing his opinions as "quite abstract." Becki Ross' views on lesbian sexual representations were also rejected. "Professor Ross was obviously committed to her views," said Sharma, "but this distracted from her ability [to analyze] issues in the manner of a true neutral expert." Worse, said Sharma, "she had the demeanour of being an advocate." On the other hand, the Crown's psychologist, William Marshall, was lauded for his even-handed manner, which "indicated he was a neutral expert." Marshall's study of the attitudes and opinions of Customs officers proved, in the Crown's assessment, that the bureaucracy was relatively prejudice-free. The judge, Sharma suggested, could "place great weight on Marshall's evidence."

Sharma finally turned to Little Sister's all-important claim that, in her words, "there is a disproportionate effect on homosexuals from Customs legislation and [they] have been impermissibly targeted." The Crown's answer to both matters was a resounding "no."

Little Sister's, said Sharma, says the problem stems in part from Customs' "failure to appreciate the distinctive nature of homosexual material." She tackled this from two angles. Firstly, she said, if one agreed that gay porn was indeed distinct from other porn, this didn't "necessarily lead to either a wrong or unreasonable decision, given the limited jurisprudence." Therefore, she said, the judge should not make a "finding of fact that there is a disproportionate effect on homosexuals."

Then Sharma launched a frontal attack on the whole idea of distinctiveness, saying Little Sister's request for a "constitutional exemption" for gay and lesbian porn should not be granted because "homosexual material is not distinctive; [it] cannot be defined in a meaningful way; and the intended audience is irrelevant."

It didn't take the Crown long to render gay and lesbian realities almost completely invisible. Little Sister's experts, said Sharma, had failed to establish that gay materials were distinctive (they were not, after all, credible witnesses by Crown standards). At best, Kinsman and Ross had reliable opinions about how gay and lesbian S/M was distinct from heterosexual S/M depictions, but this certainly didn't make S/M a distinctively homosexual practice. The issue of definition was even murkier. For example, said Sharma, "Ms. Ross indicated that images in *Hustler* magazine showing sexual interaction between two women is not *real* lesbian material." Finally, even defining "homosexual materials as that catering to homosexuals" was an irrelevant matter: Canadian courts had often stated that "the intended audience . . . cannot be used to determine if something is obscene."

As for the matter of being targeted, Sharma simply repeated what the government had said all along. If Little Sister's was closely watched, it was because Customs monitored "certain importers or exporters because of a pattern of known violations," said Sharma. ". . . Little Sister's did continue to import or attempt to import books which they knew had been prohibited entry into Canada. There can be no inference of distinctive treatment [on the basis of homosexuality]: Little Sister's is treated like any other importer who has a history of non-compliance with Tariff Code 9956." The Crown's position was like a textbook vicious circle: Customs detains Little Sister's books because it always has, because it always should; ergo, no discrimination.

Crowning Conclusions

The Crown's conclusion, naturally, was that Customs legislation was constitutionally healthy. There was no need either to strike down the legislation in its entirety or to opt for any of Little Sister's alternative demands. But Sharma proposed a revealing section 24 option to Justice Smith, in case the court didn't accept what she called "this ideal state" of the status quo. After strongly defending the government's right to "prohibit the written word where it is obscene," Sharma suggested that, in the event the judge found such Customs prohibitions to be unconstitutional, he needn't strike down the whole legislation. Instead, "Tariff Code 9956 can be read down (or severed) so as not to apply to written text," said Sharma. Rather than throwing out the legislation, the tariff code could simply be reinterpreted (hence: "read down, severed") by Customs.

This was a watered-down version of what Little Sister's was seeking with its second section 52 remedy. Without any fanfare or explanation, the Crown seemed to be halfheartedly acknowledging that books, unlike magazines and other pictorial representations, were deserving of less invasive treatment at the hands of Canada Customs.

A Tough Provincial Act

Throughout the trial, Little Sister's supporters had felt little bitterness towards the federal Crown lawyers. There was a feeling that Sharma, Van Iperen and Kiselbach were, after all, just doing their job. But the same generosity of feeling was not extended to the two lawyers for the provincial Attorney General. Frank Falzon and Angela Westmacott had often weighed in with an impressive show of force against Little Sister's, and their closing arguments were true to form.

When the case first began in the 1980s, Brian Mulroney's Progressive Conservatives were governing federally and Bill Vander Zalm's Social Credit circus was spinning British Columbia. By 1994, both men and parties were well out of the picture. The Liberals' Jean Chrétien was installed as prime minister in late 1993, and a few people wondered if Customs might be encouraged to clean up its homophobic act. But with a New Democratic Party ruling in B.C. since 1992—ostensibly a leftist party with a strong anti-discrimination tradition—many people questioned why the province was in Courtroom 65 at all.

Colin Gablemann, the provincial Attorney General, had some sensitivity to public reaction. He attended a meeting at Vancouver's Gay and Lesbian Centre on December 15, a block away from Little Sister's, the same week the lawyers for his ministry were making their case in court. Gablemann assured his audience that "We are just there to make sure that whatever decision is made, it should not affect our ability to classify films and videos . . . We want the case to go the way Little Sister's wants it to go."

But although Gablemann's lawyers stated in court that the province took "no position" on Little Sister's case against Customs, they fiercely objected to any "generalizations" about problems with prior restraint schemes. Falzon launched into a daunting defence of prior restraint that went well beyond the scope of moving pictures and gave powerful fuel to the Crown's case. (The *Moving Picture Act* of 1913 had given the province authority to judge the "fitness for public exhibition" of film; its current incarnation, the *Motion Pictures Act* [1970], had only slight modifications, such as changing the position of "censor" to "film-classification director.")

Perhaps all too accurately, Falzon summarized a hardy Canadian tradition. "Prior restraint is an ingrained and well-accepted part of the fabric of Canadian law generally, and provincial legislative jurisdiction particularly," he said. "It is a way in which Canada carries out its international obligations relating to the control of obscenity. Under the *Charter,* Canadian courts do not give all expression transcendent value. The unregulated 'marketplace of ideas' is viewed with healthy skepticism. Limits on marginal expression are easier to justify under [the *Charter's*] section 1 . . .

"Canadian courts recognize that chilling effects accompany all limitations on expression, and are willing to tolerate them provided they are not 'undue' . . . The refusal to be categorical about prior restraint is part of what makes us 'not Americans.'" In fact, the province argued, prior restraint was actually "less intrusive than a criminal offence, because the purpose is not to punish but to protect those harmed by the message."

After this ode to prior restraint, Falzon and Westmacott made substantial arguments about widening *Butler's* harms-based analysis beyond the specific harm to women. Concern for women, they said, was only a portion of what they called the Supreme Court's "ultimate value," which was the prevention of harm in *all* human relationships. They quoted Mr. Justice Sopinka in *Butler*: ". . . the legislation seeks to enhance respect for all members of society and to promote non-violence and equality in their relations with each other."

Like the Crown, the AG rejected outright the idea that gay and lesbian pornography had any essential differences from heterosexual varieties. But Falzon's and Westmacott's attack was far more thorough—and devious. Homing in on the work of gay and lesbian activists, the province turned the quest for social and political equality into proof that gays and straights are all alike.

"The argument that lesbians and gay men do not differ in significant ways from heterosexuals," said Falzon, "has also been advanced in recent constitutional and administrative law cases involving claims for the extension of social benefits to same-sex couples . . . The claimants in virtually all these cases have argued that homosexual intimate relationships are not qualitatively different from heterosexual relationships."

The AG also made highly selective use of Kinsman's and Ross' evidence to establish that harm existed in gay and lesbian relationships. Kinsman, they stressed, had "admitted" power imbalances could occur in gay relations due to social inequalities, and had agreed that little research had been conducted on the issue of same-sex violence in Canada. Ross had defended the *Bad Attitude* short story found to be obscene in the *R. v. Scythes* case, and her "categorical denial of any violence or inequality in lesbian s/m relationships . . . raised concerns about her objectivity as an expert . . ."

The province's conclusion was simple: There was "evidence that all sexual relationships are subject to power differences and inequalities," and because *Butler* had "embraced a broad conception of harm which encompasses all human interpersonal relations . . . the only principled approach to regulating pornography is to apply the same standards without regard to the sexual orientation of the intended audience." It was hard to imagine how Attorney General Colin Gablemann could square this argument with his claim that the province wanted the trial to "go the way Little Sister's wants it to go."

Meanwhile, Back at the Gay 'n Lesbian Ranch

During the trial, filmmaker Aerlyn Weissman had interviewed many of Little Sister's witnesses for a documentary about the historic case. Weissman had earlier collaborated with Toronto's Lynne Fernie on two of English-speaking Canada's finest documentaries on lesbian life: *Forbidden Love* and *Fiction and Other Truths: A Film about Jane Rule*. Her interviews, often taped immediately after the witnesses had given evidence, captured the emotions and perceptions of their experience in Courtroom 65.

For many, testifying was a deeply distressing experience. Despite many years in the often hostile public eye, Pat Califia said that defending her own work before the state was worse than any previous conflict. Wearing a T-shirt that read "The Worst Part of Censorship is [blotted out text]," Califia recalled the period leading up the trial.

"I don't think I've had a more difficult writing assignment than having to construct testimony for this trial," said Califia, "and I still feel that I fell far short of what I would like to do to eloquently plead my case. It's very hard for me to sit and look at people who would very happily burn my books, and shut down any bar, any public space where my people might congregate, and to have the quality of my life be in their hands. And then they think we're the ones who are abusers and perpetrators of violence. It's deeply ironic."

Other witnesses had already weathered an inhospitable courtroom. Becki Ross remembered testifying for the defence in the 1992 *Bad Attitude* trial in Toronto. Both she and Gary Kinsman had been through the fire.

"I felt nervous here," said Ross, "but not as nervous as I would have felt had it been my first pornography trial . . . The *Bad Attitude* trial was hell. I felt almost entirely alone. There was no support in the courtroom and the trial got no publicity, not even in the alternative media . . ."

The atmosphere of the Little Sister's trial was, happily, completely different. "In the courtroom, I felt very supported and embraced, held by the people in the room," said Ross. But there were other stresses.

"[Testifying] is a very stripping process, both emotionally and politically," said Ross. "It's very trying and very testing because one feels, or at least I did, that you carry the responsibility and the burden of speaking for a community, something I never want or like to do. I don't want to represent anyone but myself, but the terms of the trial forced me to speak for lesbian subcultures. For example, I had to speak for the lesbian

S/M community and lesbian S/M sexual fantasy consumers and producers, communities to whom I'm connected, but [which] I'm not an integral member of. That felt strange."

Ross' reasons for testifying were partially rooted in her personal history, and in trying to find a way to understand her changing relationship to feminist ideologies. Like other feminist witnesses, she had originally been an anti-porn activist.

"Achieving sexual liberation," said Ross, "achieving the possibility that each person is able to realize a world where sexual liberation is . . . actionable, without shame, is worth struggling for. It's worth fighting the state for, worth fighting the police for, worth fighting the censors for, worth fighting puritan, totally moralistic anti-porn feminists [for]." Ross then brought in the larger Canadian political scene, which has lurched to the right in the last decade.

"And it's worth fighting the Reform Party," said Ross, referring to Canada's entry in the far-right sweepstakes, "which recently reaffirmed their commitment to 'traditional family values' that formally exclude lesbians and gay men, and exclude anything but heterosexual procreation and religiously sanctioned marriage."

Gary Kinsman had expected the worst. "My whole sense of testifying changed entirely when the cross-examination started from the B.C. Attorney General," said Kinsman. "Immediately, the hostility level went up. Immediately, it was like I was on trial. There was a certain level of antagonism there . . . and I had a great sense of relief when it ended. I was actually expecting it to go on and on and on."

Bart Testa, semiotician and film studies instructor, mused about the scant attention he had been paid by the government lawyers.

"It's a little bit odd being a humanities scholar in a trial," said Testa, "because you're presenting material from a perspective that isn't usually brought into a courtroom. I didn't feel besieged . . . I felt under a good deal of stress to communicate as clearly and directly as possible." Testa commented on the apparent inability of the state to deal with pornography *anywhere*, never mind in a court of law.

"The state is like *Tyrannosaurus rex*: they only see something that moves," said Testa. "This [trial] is from *Jurassic Park*. Most pornography is inert, it's pretty much been the same for a really long time . . . Then there's pornography that never gets anywhere near the country, that censors or the people who block it claim is absolutely evil . . .

"Gay and lesbian pornography is not seen as completely evil, but s/m material and the whole concern with anal sexuality—[they] seem to be the leading edge. It's almost like these pornographers' materials are the avant garde of something that will pollute the entire population."

Bruce Ryder had testified for the Toronto Women's Bookstore. An Osgoode Hall law professor and expert in the history of Canada Customs, Ryder recounted some tales from Customs' shaky past.

"One of the biggest problems with a system of administrative censorship like Canada Customs," said Ryder, "is that decisions are being made on the whim of individual officials with no real accountability. A good example of that was in the late 1940s, when Customs banned Norman Mailer's anti-war novel called *The Naked and the Dead*. A journalist was interviewing the minister of National Revenue, a Dr. J. J. McCann, and the journalist said, 'Dr. McCann, have you read *The Naked and the Dead*? Why did you ban it?'

"And Dr. McCann said, 'Well, I haven't read the entire book, but I marked the passages, or I read the passages that were marked for me by my officials, and I have to say it was the filthiest, most disgusting piece of trash that I've ever read.' Which is the answer he gave to just about everything he did in those years. Then Dr. McCann said, 'I wouldn't want my daughter to read it.'

"When the journalist wrote up his article in *Maclean's* magazine, he [noted] that Dr. McCann had no daughter. The final standard of what Canadians were permitted to read was determined by the moral sensibilities of a young lady who did not exist."

Elite Censorship and Every Other Kind, Too

After testifying, novelist Sarah Schulman expressed her concerns about the contradictions and privilege she saw in even "being on trial."

"This trial addresses what I call 'elite censorship,'" said Schulman. "Let's go through all the different ways people are censored: Number one, illiteracy is probably the major form of censorship. Number two, people who do know how to read and write, but whose self-esteem is maintained at such a low level that they don't feel justified in expressing their own ideas. That's probably the next largest way of keeping ideas down and keeping people from understanding the process of how to get their work out.

"Then, if people do understand all of that and can transcend all of those obstacles, then we have a very nepotistic publishing and funding system, where certain forms are not permitted, along with certain points of view and personality types. A lot of it is based on personal relationships. That becomes an enormous filter.

"If you get past all of that and your work can rise to a level of visibility to even be noticed by the state, which is a whole other step, *then* you can be subjected to state censorship. But even if your work is allowed to cross into Canada, for example . . . there are other kinds of censorship. For example, keeping it out of mainstream stores, keeping it from being reviewed in mainstream places, keeping it from being taken seriously, from being integrated into the intellectual life of the country. All of these processes keep these ideas out. As we saw in court, even this judge has had no access to these ideas or the world of these ideas.

"This obvious level of state censorship is, in some ways, the easiest for us to oppose because it doesn't require any kind of self-analysis about what our own filtering structures have been."

Schulman was acutely aware of how the rules of the courtroom could back gays and lesbians into distorted corners, even inducing a kind of dishonesty.

"The trial is very complex, because as soon as you start participating in it, you're already coopted by it," said Schulman. "We can't argue that *Butler* is inappropriate because *Butler* is a fact. [Instead] we have to argue that all of these books should not have *Butler* applied to them. So even if the intent of an author was to write violent pornography with bestiality or whatever, we have to deny their intent in order to make their books available. That's a really corrupting factor in all of this."

Jearld Moldenhauer also saw the corrupting influence of the state, which he reflected on in a letter about the trial.

"It seems the purpose behind the endless forms of harassment and atmosphere of terror created by Canada Customs is to turn each individual into a censor," Moldenhauer wrote. "And to internalize censorship and thereby become an agent of those forces of the state which oppose freedom of imagination, which seek to stifle the evolutionary process in human society and sustain the status quo."

Reserving Judgement
Back in Courtroom 65, the bookstore's owners and their co-plaintiff, the B.C. Civil Liberties Association, were relieved when the week's worth of

government arguments finally came to an end. The power imbalance had seemed at its most pronounced during this last stage: even with Arvay's deft performance, the ratio of five lawyers to one had been a telling reality.

By Tuesday, December 20, 1994, everything that could be said had been said. Justice Kenneth Smith turned to the lawyers and the few remaining courtroom watchers. "I would like to wish you all the compliments of the season," Justice Smith said. "Obviously, I will reserve judgement." The Little Sister's trial had run for over two and a half months: almost 200 hours of testimony, 40 witnesses, over 260 exhibits of evidence, and more than 1,000 pages of court transcripts—which Justice Smith would now study, in pursuit of his judgement.

Little Sister's, the B.C. Civil Liberties Association and their loyal supporters were grateful to be finally released from the confines of Courtroom 65, but the feeling of closure would have to wait. Smith's ruling would come down at an unknowable future date—constitutional judgements are seldom rendered quickly—and even then, there was the prospect of an appeal, regardless of the verdict.

But along with relief, and apprehension about the future, there was a lingering sense that this trial was too wonderful, too powerful, to really be over. Little Sister's supporters had watched and listened while some of the most remarkable hearts and minds of their communities had withstood the adversarial climate of the courtroom. The testimony of the bookstore's witnesses had been a gift: enchanting exchanges of history, stories, theory, beliefs—often gloriously expressed. Whatever the verdict, the courthouse's iridescent roof would always symbolize that extraordinary and brave time.

August 1995: It's another crazy afternoon in the bookstore when Little Sister's phone rings. On the line is John Westwood from the B.C. Civil Liberties, calling in the latest hot tip: Justice Smith will

JANINE be releasing his decision before the Labour Day long weekend. Bruce takes the call and phones me at home. We hurriedly change the bookstore's work schedule, bring in some extra staff—we'll be swamped with media work if this rumour is true—then sit by the phone and wait.

And try not to wait too hard. But the word has hit the street and people start dropping in and asking, "Hear anything?"

"No," I say repeatedly. "Nothing yet . . . soon we hope . . . maybe tomorrow . . ."

This isn't the first rumour we've heard during the long, nerve-wracking months of 1995. As usual, I call the hotlist of reporters who covered the case; they thank me, ready their camera crews and stand by their fax machines.

"Do you think it'll be a good outcome?" people keep asking. I pause, cross my fingers behind my back and say, "Oh, yeah, definitely." Faxes flood the store with information requests and rumour updates, and Jim and Bruce and the others all bump around like water beetles, trying not to look preoccupied. My nerves are pretty well shot by the time Friday afternoon rolls along. I phone our lawyer friend barbara findlay at work, but she's gone for the day. How blasé, I think. What does she know that I don't?

It turns out barbara hadn't bothered to tumble for *this* rumour, like she had for the one in June. She'd just laughed it off. And barbara, as usual, was right. As this book goes to press, we're still waiting to hear from Justice Smith.

In the year since the trial ended, Little Sister's has seen some changes. Customs has altered some of their confusing forms, and when they make a detention, they now specify the offending page number. We've had relatively few detentions, but the same can't be said for Glad Day in Toronto: Kim Mistysyn reports business as usual as far as Customs detentions go. Little Sister's shipments are still routinely opened and examined—the tell-tale orange Customs tape gives the story away—and our invoices are just as routinely photocopied. Customs seems to be creating a record of what we import. There's no questions the bookstore is being closely scrutinized. The "lookout" remains, as does the mindset behind it. It's like living in a two-way mirror, knowing you're being monitored and judged, and having no option but to wait. I even wonder whether Customs will exact some kind of revenge if the ruling goes against us.

In more cynical moments, I look back on the trial and see Joel Oliver, the acting director of Prohibited Importations, listening to testimony and frantically jotting down—what? Memos to himself about all the problems in his bureaucracy? How nice, I think. Customs got themselves a $250,000 internal review, paid for by Little Sister's, the BCCLA and our supporters—on top of whatever Canadian taxpayers footed for the two governments' legal bills. A quarter of a million dollars—that's what the trial has cost Little Sister's and the BCCLA so far—from concerned lesbians and gay men, from writers and publishers, from progressive people, all for the privilege of choosing the books we want to read.

But I don't stay cynical for long. Books, after all, are too important. And as my friend and co-worker Jim Deva said, "This trial came from our sense of self-preservation. We had no choice other than to fight."

Memorandum D9-1-1

Canada Customs Memorandum D9-1-1 was amended on September 29, 1994. The following statement was issued by Canada Customs on that date:

In Brief

As a result of evolving jurisprudence, the departmental policy concerning the administration of tariff code 9956 has been revised by deleting paragraphs 6(a), (8), 9(b), 9(c), 9(d) and 9(e) of Memorandum D9-1-1 issued June 12, 1991. New paragraphs have been added at sections 9(b), 9(c) and 9(d). Please see attached revised Memorandum D9-1-1.

The importation of material that depicts or describes anal penetration or anal intercourse in and of itself is not a ground for prohibition. However, such material will be prohibited if it includes other areas prohibited in Memorandum D9-1-1 such as violence, degradation or dehumanization.

Descriptions or depictions of violent, degrading or dehumanizing sexual acts, whether or not they involve anal penetration will continue to be prohibited. The key factor to be taken into account is whether the nature of the sexual act described or depicted is violent, degrading or dehumanizing.

The following is the full text of the revised Memorandum D9-1-1:

MEMORANDUM D9-1-1
Interpretative Policy and Procedures
for the Administration of Tariff Code 9956

This Memorandum outlines and explains the interpretation of tariff code 9956 of Schedule VII to the *Customs Tariff* and provides procedures to be followed in this regard.

Legislation

Tariff code 9956 reads:

> "Books, printed paper, drawings, paintings, prints, photographs or representations of any kind that
> (a) are deemed to be obscene under subsection 163(8) of the *Criminal Code*;
> (b) constitute hate propaganda within the meaning of subsection 320(8) of the *Criminal Code*;
> (c) are of a treasonable character within the meaning of section 46 of the *Criminal Code*; or
> (d) are of a seditious character within the meaning of sections 59 and 60 of the *Criminal Code*."

Guidelines and General Information

1. This tariff code covers books, printed paper, drawings, paintings, prints, photographs, movie film, phonograph records, videotapes, audiotapes and representations of any kind.

2. Goods which are of a treasonable character are, for example, goods which advocate the use of force or violence to overthrow the Government of Canada or a province or, which communicate or make available, without lawful authority, to an agent of a state other than Canadian military or scientific information that may be used by that state for a purpose prejudicial to the safety or defence of Canada.

3. Goods which are of a seditious character are, for example, goods which advocate the use, without the authority of law, of force as a means of accomplishing governmental change within Canada.

4. Goods which constitute hate propaganda under the *Criminal Code* are those which advocate or promote genocide or promote hatred against an identifiable group distinguished by colour, race, religion or ethnic origin. In particular, the following goods should be prohibited as hate propaganda:

(a) goods that advocate or promote the destruction, in whole or in part, of any identifiable group by advocating or promoting:
  (1) killing members of the group, or
  (2) deliberately inflicting on the group conditions of life calculated to bring about its physical destruction.
5. Goods which are deemed to be obscene under the *Criminal Code* are those of, a dominant characteristic of which, is the undue exploitation of sex, or of sex and any one or more of the following subjects, namely, crime, horror, cruelty and violence.
6. The following goods, in so far as they are deemed to be obscene or hate propaganda within the meanings of the terms as set forth above, are to be classified under tariff code 9956 and their importation into Canada prohibited:
  (a) goods which depict or describe sexual acts that appear to degrade or dehumanize any of the participants, including:
    (1) depictions or descriptions of sex with violence, submission, coercion, ridicule, degradation, exploitation or humiliation of any human being, whether sexually explicit or not, and which appear to condone or otherwise endorse such behaviour for the purposes of sexual stimulation or pleasure;
    (2) depictions or descriptions of sexual assault (previously, rape). Any goods that depict or describe a sexual activity between male/female, male/male or female/female which appears to be without his/her consent and which appears to be achieved chiefly by force or deception;
    (3) depictions or descriptions of bondage, involuntary servitude and the state of human beings subjected to external control, in a sexual context;
    (4) depictions or descriptions which appear to be associating sexual pleasure of gratification with pain and suffering, and with the mutilation of or letting of blood from any part of the human body, involving violence, coercion and lack of basic dignity and respect for a human being;
    (5) depictions or descriptions of sexual gratification gained through causing physical pain or humiliation, or the getting of sexual pleasure from dominating, mistreating or hurting a human being. This includes depictions and descriptions of physical force which appear to be used so as to injure, damage or destroy;

of extreme roughness of action; of unjust or callous use of force or power; of spanking, beating or violent shoving in a sexual context;

(6) depictions or descriptions of mutilation or removal of any part of the human body or of the taking of human life, real or implied, for the purposes of sexual arousal; and

(7) depictions or descriptions of menstrual blood, fecal matter, urine or the inducement of feces through enemas as part of sexual arousal.

(b) goods depicting or describing sexual acts involving children or juveniles, and depictions or descriptions of children or juveniles in total or partial undress, alone or in the presence of other persons, and in which the context is even slightly sexually suggestive. Children and juveniles are persons actually or apparently under the age of 18;

(c) goods depicting or describing sexual acts between members of the same family, other than between husband and wife. This includes depictions or descriptions of any sexual activity among members of a family, whether or not they are genetically related (incest), except a husband and wife, which generally appear to condone or otherwise endorse this behaviour for the purposes of sexual stimulation or pleasure;

(d) goods depicting or describing sexual acts between human beings and animals (bestiality). This includes depictions or descriptions of bestiality, whether there is actual copulation with an animal or the animal is merely present and copulation is implied;

(e) goods depicting or describing sexual acts between live persons and dead persons or dead animals (necrophilia); and

(f) goods with some or all of the following characteristics may be subject to prohibition under tariff code 9956 as hate propaganda:

(1) goods that blame an identifiable group for serious economic or social problems;

(2) goods alleging that an identifiable group is manipulating media, trade and finance, government or world politics to the detriment of society as a whole; and

(3) goods alleging that an identifiable group is racially inferior and/or weakens other segments of society to the detriment of society as a whole; and

(4) goods alleging that an identifiable group seriously threatens society as a whole.

7. It should be noted that goods which may constitute hate propaganda, based on the above criteria, should be detained and forwarded to Headquarters for review.

8. It should be emphasized that a book, film, video cassette, etc., is to be assessed in its entirety. It is to be considered as a whole and its overall nature and dominant characteristic must be assessed. A section containing subjects outlined in this Memorandum must be assessed as an integral part of the entire work and in the context of its theme. However, goods which in their essence are made up of many individual elements are not to be treated as a whole and may be prohibited on the basis of any one of their elements which fall within the prohibitory provisions of tariff code 9956. Similarly, a magazine or newspaper is to be considered on a segment-by-segment basis.

9. Goods not classified under tariff code 9956 include the following:

(a) for the purpose of sections 22(3) and 464 of the *Criminal Code,* goods which counsel, procure or incite persons to commit criminal offenses are not to be classified under tariff code 9956, unless they are determined to be obscene or constitute hate propaganda or are of a seditious or treasonable character;

(b) goods which communicate in a rational and unsensational manner information about a sexual activity that is not unlawful are not to be prohibited;

(c) sex aids and toys are not to be deemed obscene and, therefore, are not to be classified under tariff code 9956; goods are not to be prohibited solely on the basis of advertisements which simply promote the sale of various sex toys or sex aids. However, explicit textual descriptions or visual depictions in the advertisements deemed to be obscene will be prohibited;

(d) in assessing goods under tariff code 9956, full recognition should be given to freedom of expression. In particular, with respect to goods which may constitute hate propaganda, classification under tariff code 9956 will not be made if there is a possibility that the goods may:

(1) communicate statements that are established to be true;

(2) predominantly express, in good faith, an opinion upon a religious subject;

(3) be relevant to any subject of public interest, the discussion of which is for the public benefit and, on reasonable grounds, believed to be true; or

(4) be intended, in good faith, to point out, for the purpose of removal, matters producing or tending to produce feelings of hatred towards an identifiable group in Canada.

Advance Reviews

10. For the importer or publisher who encounters difficulties in determining whether or not his goods are in compliance with the above-noted guidelines, the Prohibited Importations Unit in Ottawa reviews advance samples of goods, prior to commercial importation, suspected of falling within the provisions of tariff code 9956 and provides the importer or publisher with an opinion regarding its admissibility into Canada. The Unit also provides advice and guidelines and practices concerning the administration of this tariff code. These services are designed to encourage and promote voluntary compliance with legislation in this area. Importers or publishers who wish to obtain additional information about these procedures may contact the Manager, Prohibited Importations Unit, Tariff Programs, in Ottawa at 613 954-7048.

11. For the purposes of the prohibitory provisions of tariff code 9956, goods which are made (manufactured, printed, purchased, etc.) in Canada and exported are considered to constitute an importation on their return to Canada.

12. The decision to detain and classify goods under tariff code 9956 is to be communicated to the prospective importer or owner by means of a Notice of Detention/Determination, form K 27. The prospective importer or owner is also to be advised in writing of his/her statutory right to request a re-determination and to appeal to the courts the tariff classification of the goods under sections 60, 63, 67 and 71 of the *Customs Act.*

13. A request for re-determination or re-appraisal by a Tariff and Values Administrator (TVA) (who is a designated officer) must be made on form B 2 and filed within 90 days of the date of the written notice of classification (Part B of the tariff code 9956 form K 27) to the prospective consignee. If the prospective consignee is not satisfied with the TVA's decision, he/she may request a further re-determination or re-appraisal by the Deputy Minister of National Revenue, by filing a second form B 2 within 90 days of the date of the TVA's decision. It should

be noted that under paragraphs 60(1)(*b*) and 63(1)(*b*), the 90 day time period may be extended to two years where advisable. In these instances, the goods would have to be stored in a secure environment for the two year period. Given the nature of the goods and the administrative problems in ensuring their security, only under exceptional circumstances will the importer be given the right to file a request within the two year time period.

14. Requests should be filed at the respective Customs office or regional office where the goods were reported.

15. The decision of the Deputy Minister classifying goods under tariff code 9956 may be appealed to the court pursuant to section 67 (as modified by section 71) of the *Customs Act.*

16. When an importer attempts to import into Canada goods identical to those previously imported and prohibited at the Deputy Minister level, a decision pursuant to subsection 64(*a*) of the *Customs Act* may be rendered, thereby allowing the Importer to appeal directly to the court.

17. When importation of goods into Canada is prohibited, the importer is to be asked how they are to be disposed of (either exported or abandoned to the Crown).

18. Abandoned goods are to be handled as follows: a general receipt, form K 21, will be completed; the original copy will be signed and given to the importer which will include: the name and address of the importer and a statement to the effect that the goods described thereunder are classified under the prohibitory provisions of tariff code 9956 and are herewith abandoned to the Crown.

19. Goods may be exported by means other than through the mails (since mailing obscene matter constitutes an offence), providing this is done under Customs supervision and at the importer's expense.

20. The importer must notify Customs of arrangements for export of goods. If exportation is:
    (*a*) to be handled personally, the importer must present form E 15 completed in accordance with Memorandum D6-2-3, Identification of Goods Exported or Destroyed, Form E 15, and be escorted by Customs to the airline baggage check-in or departure area, or
    (*b*) by commercial conveyance (i.e., a Canada Customs bonded carrier), the exporting carrier must physically retrieve the goods and present completed form E 15 and the manifest or waybill.

21. Should the importer fail to effect release, or fail to abandon or to export

his/her goods within the prescribed period, the goods are to be deemed to be unclaimed and are to be handled in accordance with Memorandum D4-1-6, Disposal of Abandoned and Forfeited Goods.

22. Further particulars may be obtained by contacting the Manager of Tariff Programs and Appraisal at any regional Customs office.

References
Issuing Office—
    Tariff Programs
Legislative References—
    Customs Tariff, section 114 and Schedule VII, tariff code 9956
    Customs Act, sections 60, 63, 64(a), 67 and 71
    Criminal Code, sections 22(3), 46, 59, 60, 163(8), 320(8) and 464
Headquarters File—
    4545-1
Superseded Memoranda "D"—
    D9-1-1, June 12, 1991
Other References—
    D4-1-6, D6-2-3

Services provided by the department are available in both official languages.

This memorandum is issued under the authority of the Deputy Minister of National Revenue.

The *Constitution Act, 1982—* Relevant Sections

Part I of the Constitution Act *is entitled the* Canadian Charter of Rights and Freedoms. *The* Charter *includes the following sections relevant to the Little Sister's trial:*

Canadian Charter of Rights and Freedoms

Guarantee of Rights and Freedoms
Section 1.
The *Canadian Charter of Rights and Freedoms* guarantees the rights and freedoms set out in it subject only to such reasonable limits prescribed by law as can be demonstrably justified in a free and democratic society.

Fundamental Freedoms
Section 2.
Everyone has the following fundamental freedoms: (*a*) freedom of conscience and religion; (*b*) freedom of thought, belief, opinion and expression, including freedom of the press and other media of communication; (*c*) freedom of peaceful assembly; and (*d*) freedom of association.

Equality Rights
Section 15.
(1) Every individual is equal before and under the law and has the right to

the equal protection and equal benefit of the law without discrimination and, in particular, without discrimination based on race, national or ethnic origin, colour, religion, sex, age or mental or physical disability.

(2) Subsection (1) does not preclude any law, program or activity that has as its object the amelioration of conditions of disadvantaged individuals or groups including those that are disadvantaged because of race, national or ethnic origin, colour, religion, sex, age or mental or physical disability.

Enforcement
Section 24.

(1) Anyone whose rights or freedoms, as guaranteed by this Charter, have been infringed or denied may apply to a court of competent jurisdiction to obtain such remedy as the court considers appropriate and just in the circumstances.

(2) Where, in proceedings under subsection (1), a court concludes that evidence was obtained in a manner that infringed or denied any rights or freedoms guaranteed by this Charter, the evidence shall be excluded if it is established that, having regard to all the circumstances, the admission of it in the proceedings would bring the administration of justice into disrepute.

Part VII of the Constitution Act *is entitled* General, *and includes the following section, which entrenches the supremacy of the* Charter *over all government legislation and action:*

Section 52.

(1) The *Constitution* of Canada is the supreme law of Canada, and any law that is inconsistent with the provisions of the *Constitution* is, to the extent of the inconsistency, of no force or effect.

Little Sister's Statement of Claim

In the Supreme Court of British Columbia

Little Sisters Book and Art Emporium
and the British Columbia Civil Liberties Association
and James Eaton Deva and Guy Allen Bruce Smyth

PLAINTIFFS

AND:

The Minister of Justice and Attorney General of Canada,
and Minister of National Revenue

DEFENDANTS

AMENDED
STATEMENT OF CLAIM
(original filed on June 7, 1990; amended September 23, 1992
and filed October 7, 1992)

1. The Plaintiff, Little Sisters Book and Art Emporium ("Little Sisters") is a corporation duly incorporated pursuant to the laws of British Columbia

and has its registered office at 208 - 1242 Robson Street, Vancouver, British Columbia.

2. The Plaintiff, British Columbia Civil Liberties Association, is a Society duly incorporated as such pursuant to the *Societies Act* with its registered office at 518-119 W. Pender St., Vancouver, British Columbia, V6B 1S5, the objects of which include the promotion, defence, sustainment and extension of civil liberties and human rights. The Association has demonstrated a longstanding, genuine and continuing concern for the rights of disadvantaged groups or individuals in Canada and has likewise opposed censorship of allegedly obscene books and magazines.

3. The Plaintiffs, James Eaton Deva and Guy Allen Bruce Smyth, both of the City of Vancouver, in the Province of British Columbia, are the directors and controlling shareholders of Little Sisters. James Eaton Deva and Guy Allen Bruce Smyth are homosexual.

4. The Defendant, the Minister of Justice and Attorney General of Canada is named pursuant to the provisions of the *Department of Justice Act,* R.S.C. 1985, C. J-2.

5. The Defendant, the Minister of National Revenue is responsible for the administration of the *Customs Tariff,* S.C. 1987, c. 41 (3rd Supplement) and the *Customs Act,* S.C. 1986, c.1 (2nd Supplement).

6. The principal business of Little Sisters is the sale of books and magazines most of which are written by and for homosexual men and women. Little Sisters also operates a mail order business selling books to customers all across Canada.

7. Most of the books and magazines sold by Little Sisters are published in the United States and imported into Canada by Little Sisters.

8. From about 1985 and from time to time to the present, hundreds of books and magazines that Little Sisters has purchased and sought to import into Canada have been seized, detained, prohibited and/or destroyed by customs officials pursuant to the *Customs Tariff* and the *Customs Act* on the grounds that the books and magazines were "obscene." In most of these books and in some of the magazines there are no photographs but only written text.

9. The *Customs Tariff* S.C. 1987, c. 41 (3rd Supplement), s.114 provides:

> "The importation into Canada of any goods enumerated in Schedule VII is prohibited."

Code 9956 of Schedule VII reads in part as follows:

> "Books, printed paper, drawings, paintings, prints, photographs or representations of any kind that
> (a) are deemed to be obscene under subsection 159(8) of the Criminal Code . . .;

Section 159(8) [now 163(8)] of the Criminal Code provides:

> For the purposes of this Act, any publication a dominant characteristic of which is the undue exploitation of sex, or of sex and any one or more of the following subjects, namely, crime, horror, cruelty and violence, shall be deemed to be obscene.

10. Section 58(1) of the *Customs Act,* S.C. 1986, c. 1 authorizes a Customs officer to determine the tariff classification of imported goods and by virtue of section 71 of the *Customs Act,* S.C. 1986, c.1 (2nd Supplement) as amended the onus is placed on the person whose material has been seized or detained to seek a redetermination from a designated officer and if unsuccessful request a further determination from the Deputy Minister of National Revenue For Customs and Excise and, if unsuccessful, to appeal to the courts.

11. This system of prior restraint created by *Customs Tariff,* S.C. 1987, c. 41 (3rd Supplement) s. 114, Schedule VII, Code 9956 (a) and the *Customs Act* S.C. 1986 c.1 (2nd Supplement), s. 58 and s. 71 as amended has the purpose and/or effect of preventing, deterring and/or unduly delaying the importation of, and/or of causing the destruction of, material which is not "obscene" even as defined by Parliament in s. 163(8) of the Criminal Code. The Plaintiffs say that this system of prior restraint of any "books, printed paper, drawings, paintings, prints, photographs or representations of any kind" is an infringement of freedom of thought, belief, opinion and expression as guaranteed in s. 2(b) of the *Canadian Charter of Rights and Freedoms* and is not a reasonable limit prescribed by law in a free and democratic society.

12. The Plaintiffs say further that at all material times the provisions of the *Customs Tariff,* S.C. 1987, c. 41 (3rd Supplement) s. 114, Schedule VII, Code 9956 (a) and the *Customs Act* S.C. 1986 c.1 (2nd Supplement), s.

58 and s. 71 have been construed and applied to the books and maga-zines of the Plaintiff Little Sisters in a manner that discriminates on the basis of the sexual orientation of the authors and/or readers (including the Plaintiffs Deva and Smyth) of those books and magazines contrary to their right to equality before and under the law as guaranteed by sec-tion 15 of the *Canadian Charter of Rights and Freedoms,* and contrary to section 2 (b) of the *Canadian Charter of Rights and Freedoms,* and that such infringement is not a reasonable limit prescribed by law in a free and democratic society.

WHEREFORE the Plaintiffs claim:

(a) a declaration pursuant to s. 52 of the *Constitution Act 1982* that the *Customs Tariff,* S.C. 1987, c. 41 (3rd Supplement) s. 114, Schedule VII, Code 9956 (a) and the *Customs Act,* S.C. 1986 c.1 (2nd Supplement), s. 58 and s. 71 as amended are of no force or effect;

(b) alternatively, a declaration pursuant to s. 52 of the *Constitution Act 1982* that the *Customs Tariff,* S.C. 1987, c. 41 (3rd Supplement) s. 114, Schedule VII, Code 9956 (a) and the *Customs Act,* S.C. 1986 (2nd Supp), s. 58 and s. 71, as amended, *are* of no force and effect to the extent that they are construed and applied to detain, seize or prohibit the importation of books and printed paper into Canada on the ground that the written text is obscene within the meaning of s. 163(8) of the Criminal Code;

(b1) in addition, or in the alternative, a declaration pursuant to s. 52 of the *Constitution Act, 1982,* that the *Customs Tariff,* S.C. 1987, c. 41 (3rd Supplement) s. 114, Schedule VII, Code 9956 (a) and the *Customs Act,* S.C. 1986 (2nd Supp), s. 58 and s. 71, as amended, are of no force or effect to the extent that they are construed or applied to detain, seize or prohibit the importation of books, printed paper, drawings, paintings, prints, photographs or representations of any kind that are alleged to be obscene but produced for a homosexual audience.

(c) in addition, or in the alternative, a declaration pursuant to s. 24 of the *Canadian Charter of Rights and Freedoms* that the *Customs Tariff,* S.C. 1987, c. 41 (3rd Supplement) s. 114, Schedule VII, Code 9956 (a) and the *Customs Act,* S.C. 1986 c.1 (2nd Supplement), s. 58 and s. 71 as amended have at all material times been construed and applied in a manner that is contrary to s. 2(b) and/or s. 15 of the *Canadian Charter of Rights and Freedoms* and not justified pursuant to s.1 of the said *Charter*;

(d) costs;

(e) such other relief as this Honourable Court may deem appropriate and just in the circumstances.

PLACE OF TRIAL: Vancouver, B.C.

DATED at the City of Victoria, in the Province of British Columbia, this 7th day of June, 1990.

JOSEPH J. ARVAY, Q.C.
Counsel for the Plaintiffs

Little Sister's Witnesses

This is a complete list of the Little Sister's witnesses who testified at the 1994 trial. The testimony of some witnesses is not recounted in Restricted Entry, *and a brief description of their evidence is provided here.*

DON BENN   A resident of Victoria, B.C., Benn testified as an individual whose private mail—the magazine *Libido*—was seized by Canada Customs.

PIERRE BERTON   A widely published Canadian author and broadcaster, known chiefly for his award-winning popular histories.

PERSIMMON BLACKBRIDGE   A Vancouver artist and member of the Kiss & Tell artists' collective.

PAT CALIFIA   An American lesbian author and s/m activist; many of Califia's books have been seized by Canada Customs.

JUDY CAPES   The deputy director of the Vancouver Public Library. Capes testified that although the library carried several of the same books detained by Canada Customs en route to Little Sister's, such as Jean Genet's *Querelle*, the library had never experienced any problems with Customs.

JIM DEVA   A co-owner of Little Sister's.

CELIA DUTHIE   The owner of Duthie Books in Vancouver, the largest independent bookstore chain in western Canada.

SANDRA HAAR   A writer, artist and past employee at the Toronto Women's Bookstore.

LOUISE HAGER   A co-owner of Women In Print bookstore in Vancouver, and the former owner of Hager Books.

ROBIN HAND   The publisher of *Lezzie Smut,* a Vancouver-based lesbian sex 'zine.

MICHAEL FOSTER   The owner of Crosstown Traffic Comics store in Ottawa.

JANINE FULLER   The manager of Little Sister's.

GARY KINSMAN   An assistant professor of sociology at Laurentian University, Sudbury, Ontario. Kinsman is a gay and socialist activist, and the author of *The Regulation of Desire.*

DENNIS MAHONEY   A past employee of Inland Book Company in East Haven, Connecticut; his duties included handling shipments through Canada Customs and its appeals process.

KIM MISTYSYN   The manager of Glad Day Books in Toronto.

JEARLD MOLDENHAUER   The original owner of Glad Day Books in Toronto, and the present owner of Glad Day Books in Boston.

NINO RICCI   An award-winning Canadian author of several novels, including *Lives of the Saints.* Ricci is a past president of PEN Canada.

BECKI ROSS   At present, an assistant professor of sociology and women's studies at the University of British Columbia. In 1992, Ross taught the first lesbian history course in Canada at the University of Toronto.

JANE RULE An award-winning Canadian author of fiction and essays. Some of Rule's novels have been detained by Canada Customs.

BRUCE RYDER An associate professor of law at Osgoode Hall Law School, York University, Toronto. Ryder provided legal assistance to the Toronto Women's Bookstore when the lesbian sex magazine *Quim* was prohibited.

ANN SCALES A professor of law at the University of New Mexico School of Law.

SARAH SCHULMAN An award-winning American author and lesbian activist. Schulman's novel *Girls, Visions and Everything* was detained by Canada Customs.

ROB SKELLY A customs broker for Duthie Books. Skelly testified about brokering the shipment of previously banned books from Alyson Publications, described in chapter 2.

BART TESTA A senior tutor in the cinema studies program and semiotics program at the University of Toronto.

CAROLE S. VANCE An associate research scientist at the Columbia School of Public Health, New York. Vance is the editor of *Pleasure and Danger: Exploring Female Sexuality.*

SCOTT WATSON The director and curator of the Fine Arts Gallery at the University of British Columbia, Vancouver. Watson testified about the artistic merit of the work of Tom of Finland and of *Hothead Paisan.*

THOMAS WAUGH A professor of film and associate dean, Faculty of Fine Arts, Concordia University, Montréal. Waugh testified about the historical development of gay male sexual imagery.

LORRAINE WEIR A professor in the Department of English at the University of British Columbia, Vancouver.

Evidence Submitted in Writing

The following experts submitted their evidence in written form:

CHRIS BEARCHELL   A longtime Toronto lesbian and gay rights activist and journalist; she is a founding member of the Coalition for Lesbian and Gay Rights in Ontario. Bearchell offered an opinion on the value and significance of pornography to the gay and lesbian community.

BILL COLEMAN   A Vancouver psychologist. Coleman was originally scheduled to testify but was unable to do so due to scheduling difficulties. Coleman's evidence was admitted in published form; it concerned the relationship between gay men's sexual practices and pornographic depictions of gay s/m.

WILLIAM FISHER   A psychologist and professor in the Psychology Department of the University of Western Ontario, London. Fisher offered an opinion on the relationship between exposure to pornography and harm to individuals and to society. He also discussed the "exceedingly limited research [on the] effects of homosexual literary pornography on homosexual consumers . . ."

JOANN LOULAN   An American author (*Lesbian Sex*), therapist and licensed "Marriage Family Child Counsellor" in the state of California. Loulan offered an opinion on the relationship between healthy sexuality and access to sexual images, which "provide external ways to see what our minds create."

JAY SCOTT   A leading film and book critic, and columnist with the Toronto *Globe and Mail*. Scott died of AIDS in 1993. Scott offered critiques of *The Leading Edge: An Anthology of Lesbian Sexual Fiction,* edited by Lady Winston, and *Urban Aboriginals: A Celebration of Leathersexuality,* by Geoff Mains.

□

Notes on Sources

The primary source for *Restricted Entry* is the "Proceedings at Trial" (official trial transcripts) for the Little Sister's case, October 11, 1994 to December 20, 1994. The transcripts were made available to the authors through Arvay/ Finlay, the legal firm representing Little Sister's.

The cost of producing written transcripts is approximately $5.00 a page; a page usually represents a few minutes' worth of court time. Although a witness' testimony is part of the public record, official transcripts are evidently beyond the reach of all but the wealthiest researchers, clients and publishers. Arvay/Finlay was able to order copies of the transcripts because the prohibitive costs of the original transcription were graciously borne by the Crown; our thanks to senior Crown lawyer Hans Van Iperen for making this material accessible to Little Sister's.

All court testimony cited in *Restricted Entry* is therefore verbatim. However, court transcripts are not without flaws—misleading punctuation, phonetic misspellings and misconstrued statements from witnesses speaking unclearly and too quickly, or using unfamiliar references. To cite a humorous example: "Now all these guys are supposedly bottomless in the slang or the argyle." We understood, from the context of the testimony—gay male s/m—that the guys were supposedly "bottoms," a phrase in the s/m subculture's *argot*. When we encountered such an obvious error, the transcript was cross-referenced with the extensive notes of Stuart Blackley and Little Sister's lawyer Irene Faulkner, both of whom attended almost every day of the trial.

The trial transcripts are a source of biographical information about the witnesses (including their credentials, published works, awards, etc.). As well, the transcripts are a source of verbatim quotes from trial exhibits discussed during testimony, including letters between various parties, and excerpts from books, magazines, psychological studies, government reports, memoranda, historical documents and so forth. Specific books discussed in the testimony are listed in the section "Books Cited in Testimony." General research materials are listed in the "Bibliography."

Other sources are detailed below.

Chapter 1: Shaking the Foundations

Information about Little Sister's early history and the bombings are derived from Stuart Blackley's interview with Jim Deva in the spring of 1992, and from Blackley's interviews with Jim Deva, Bruce Smyth, Barbara Thomas and John Lucke in the summer of 1995. The quote from David Goble is taken from his letter to the Hon. Pat Carney, MP on December 10, 1986; the letter comes from Little Sister's archives, as do the bookstore's first press release ("Canada Customs Declares War on Little Sister's") and documentation about the 1986 seizures.

The history of Glad Day Books comes from Jearld Moldenhauer's affidavit to Arvay/Finlay and from his testimony on October 13. Judge Bruce Hawkin's decision in *The Joy of Gay Sex* case is quoted from "Canadian Judge Lifts Customs' Ban" by Peter Frieberg (*The Advocate*, May 12, 1987).

Information about the 1987–88 legal action against Customs' banning of *The Advocate* comes from the files of the B.C. Civil Liberties Association (including a press release entitled "Government Gives Up in Little Sister's Censorship Case" [April 24, 1988]). Information about the September 1993 motion for delay and the statement by Joseph Arvay comes from Blackley's court notes from October 4, 1993.

Chapter 2: O SCanada

The opening list of detained or prohibited books and magazines is taken from various court exhibits and trial transcripts, and from Little Sister's archives.

Trial transcripts are dated as follows: Dennis Mahoney, October 12; Jearld

Moldenhauer, Michael Foster and Kim Mistysyn, October 13; Sandra Haar and Louise Hager, October 14; Celia Duthie, October 18.

Jim Deva's comments about testifying were made during an interview with Stuart Blackley in the summer of 1995. The statement by Crown lawyer Mary Humphries is taken from Blackley's court notes from September 10, 1992; Humphries repeated this same statement on October 4, 1993. In September 1995, Louise Hager, co-owner of Women In Print, reported in a phone interview with Janine Fuller that the bookstore's advance shipment had still not been returned. A copy of the September 1, 1994 letter from Laurel Miller (sales manager of Golden-Lee Distributors) to Kim Mistysyn (Glad Day Books) is in Little Sister's archives. Information about *American Psycho, Sex* and *The Satanic Verses* is from the testimony of Customs officials and from various magazine and newspaper articles, including "X-Rated" by Jeffrey Toobin (*New Yorker,* October 3, 1994) and "Breaking the Ties That Bind" by Mark Leiren-Young (*Georgia Straight,* October 7–14, 1994). PEN Canada's declaration against censorship was reported in a September 15, 1993 editorial in the *Globe and Mail*; a copy of the declaration is in Little Sister's archives.

Chapter 3: Strange Bedfellows

The *Butler* decision is officially known as: *R. v. Butler* [1992] 1 S.C.R. 452, 11 C.R. (4th) 137, 2 W.W.R. 577, 70 C.C.C. (3rd) 129, 89 D.L.R. (4th) 449.

The *Glad Day* case is known as: *Glad Day Bookshop Inc. v. Deputy Minister of National Revenue for Customs and Excise* (July 14, 1992; unreported), (Ont. Ct.—Gen. Div.) Hayes J.

The *Bad Attitude* case is known as: *R. v. Scythes* (January 16, 1993; unreported), (Ont. Ct.—Prov. Div.) Paris J.

A number of magazine and journal articles are cited: "LEAF and Pornography: Litigating on Equality and Sexual Representations" by Karen Busby (*Canadian Review of the Law and Society,* Vol. 9, No. 1, Spring 1994); "Canada: Antipornography Breakthrough in the Law" by Michele Landsberg (*Ms.,* Vol. 2, No. 6, May/June 1992); "False Promises: Feminist Antipornography Legislation in the U.S." by Lisa Duggan, Nan Hunter and Carole S. Vance, in *Women Against Censorship,* edited by Varda Burstyn (Vancouver: Douglas & McIntyre, 1985).

Helena Orton's statement is taken from LEAF's press release entitled "LEAF applauds Supreme Court decision in Butler case" (February 27, 1992). The quote from Robin Morgan is reprinted in her book *Going Too Far* (1977). Information about the *Glad Day* and *Bad Attitude* trials comes from various articles, including "Obscenity Chill: Artists in a Post-*Butler* Era" by Clare Barclay and Elaine Carol (*Fuse,* Winter 1992–93) and "X-Rated" by Jeffrey Toobin (*New Yorker,* October 3, 1994). Joe Arvay's letter to the B.C. Civil Liberties Association is dated August 10, 1992.

Carole Vance's trial transcript is dated October 26.

Chapter 4: Name Your Pleasure
Trial transcripts are dated as follows: Persimmon Blackbridge, October 14; Ann Scales, October 19; Pat Califia, October 20; Robin Hand, October 26.

LEAF's untitled letter to the minister of National Revenue, critiquing Canada Customs, is dated September 12, 1994. A draft position on Customs entitled "Submission to the Minister of National Revenue by West Coast LEAF Association" is dated June 13, 1994; an even earlier draft entitled "Draft for discussion purposes only—LEAF case proposal form" is dated September 27, 1993; the section "Things to stay away from" is from this draft. These papers were made available to Little Sister's by West Coast LEAF.

Information about the proposal made by Little Sister's and the B.C. Civil Liberties Association (BCCLA) to the federal government is taken from a letter sent by Joe Arvay to Mary Humphries (Department of Justice) dated January 10, 1994. Phil Bryden's resolution to the board of the BCCLA appears on a memorandum from Bryden dated April 11, 1994.

Chapter 5: Churning Out the Sex Tracts
Trial transcripts are dated as follows: Sarah Schulman, October 17; Nino Ricci, October 18; Bart Testa, October 20; Pierre Berton, October 21; Lorraine Weir, October 24–25; Jane Rule, October 24.

Information about Pierre Berton and the Writing Thru Race conference is taken from several sources, including Berton's *My Times: Living with History 1947 to 1995* (New York: Doubleday, 1995) and "Captain Canada at 75" by Val Ross (*Globe and Mail,* October 7, 1995). Information on the Langer trial is from "Art and Soul" by Lorraine Johnson (*This Magazine,* Vol. 29, No. 2, August 1994); "The Battle over Censorship" by Brian Bergman (*Maclean's,* October 24, 1994); and "What Does the Criminal Code Mean by Artistic Merit?" [excerpts from the ruling by Mr. Justice David McComb] (*Globe and Mail,* April 24, 1995).

The Langer case is officially known as: *R. v. Langer,* Paintings, Drawings and Photographic Slides of Paintings, [1995] O.J. No. 1045, Court File No. U219/94.

Chapter 6: Lies, Damn Lies and Statistics
Trial transcripts are dated as follows: Gary Kinsman, October 20; Becki Ross, October 24; Carol Vance, October 26; William Marshall, November 14–15.

Chapter 7: Strange Customs
Trial transcripts are dated as follows: John Shearer, November 3–4; Linda Murphy, November 4, November 7–9; Frank Lorito, November 16; Corinne Bird, November 18.

Information about Canada Customs' structure and procedures is taken from the testimony of various Customs witnesses. Anne Griepenburg of Inland Books provided information about Inland's experience with Customs' pre-screening process. Lawrence Boyle's letters to Customs about *Empire of the Senseless* are included in the trial transcripts, as are the letters from Bruce Ryder and Brenda Cossman to Customs and the minister of National Revenue.

Chapter 8: Watching the Detectives
Trial transcripts are dated as follows: James Maitland, November 22; Noreen Wolff, November 22–24; Robert Matthews, November 24.

Information about the Toronto-based Project P unit also comes from "Obscenity Chill: Artists in a Post-*Butler* Era" by Clare Barclay and Elaine Carol (*Fuse*, Winter 1992–93).

Chapter 9: Final Arguments and a Very Long Wait
Final arguments by Little Sister's, the federal government (the Crown) and the Attorney General of British Columbia were submitted to Mr. Justice Kenneth Smith in written form; these written submissions are the major source for this chapter. Arguments were also delivered orally from December 7 to December 20.

The Oakes test is from a ruling officially known as: *R. v. Oakes* [1986] 1 S.C.R. 103, [1986] S.C.J. No. 7.

The *Dagenais* ruling is known as: *Dagenais v. Canadian Broadcasting Corp.* [1994] 3 S.C.R. 835, [1994] S.C.J. No. 104, File No. 23403.

The statement by Attorney General Colin Gabelmann is taken from "Little Sister's Wraps Up in Court" by Imtiaz Popat (*Angles*, December 1994). The closing comments from witnesses are taken from filmmaker Aerlyn Weissman's videotaped interviews with Bruce Ryder, Bart Testa, Sarah Schulman, Pat

Califia, Gary Kinsman and Becki Ross; the interviews were conducted in October 1994. Jearld Moldenhauer's letter was sent to Stuart Blackley in October 1995.

□

Books Cited in Testimony

The following books (and comic book) were the subject of testimony cited in Restricted Entry. The editions listed below are not necessarily the first editions.

Afterglow: More Stories of Lesbian Desire ed. by Karen Barber (Boston: Alyson Publications, 1993)

Against Sadomasochism: A Radical Feminist Analysis ed. by Robin R. Linden et al. (San Francisco: Frog-in-the-Well, 1981)

American Psycho by Bret Easton Ellis (New York: Random House, 1991)

Bizarre Dreams ed. by Stanislaus Tal and Caro Soles (New York: Masquerade Books, 1994)

Boiled Angel by Mike Diana (self-published, 1992; P.O. Box 5254, Largo, Florida 34649-5254)

Brothers and Sisters: Lesbians and Gay Men Write about Their Lives Together ed. by John Preston and Joan Nestle (New York: Harper Collins, 1994)

Bushfires: Stories of Lesbian Desire ed. by Karen Barber (Boston: Alyson Publications, 1991)

Coming to Power: Writings and Graphics on Lesbian S/M by Samois (Boston: Alyson Publications, 1982)

Contract with the World by Jane Rule (Tallahassee: Naiad, 1980)

Doc and Fluff: A Dystopian Novel of a Girl and Her Bike by Pat Califia
  (Boston: Alyson Publications, 1986)

Drawing the Line by Kiss & Tell (Vancouver: Press Gang Publishers, 1991)

Empire of the Senseless by Kathy Acker (New York: Grove, 1989)

Entertainment for a Master by John Preston (Boston: Alyson Publications,
  1986)

Flesh and the Word: An Anthology of Erotic Writings ed. by John Preston
  (New York: Penguin, 1993)

Gay Ideas: Outing and Other Controversies by Richard D. Mohr (Boston:
  Beacon Press, 1992)

Girls, Visions and Everything by Sarah Schulman (New York: Penguin, 1986)

Herotica by Susie Bright (San Francisco: Down There Press, 1988)

Hometowns: Gay Men Write about Where They Belong ed. by John Preston
  (New York: Penguin, 1992)

Hot Living: Erotic Stories About Safer Sex ed. by John Preston (Boston: Alyson
  Publications, 1985)

I Once Had a Master by John Preston (Boston: Alyson Publications, 1984)

In Search of a Master by John Preston (New York: Carol Publishers Group,
  1989)

The Joy of Gay Sex by Charles Silverstein (New York: Crown Publications,
  1977)

The Lesbian S/M Safety Manual ed. by Pat Califia (Boston: Alyson Publications, 1988)

Macho Sluts by Pat Califia (Boston: Alyson Publications, 1988)

Melting Point ed. by Pat Califia (Boston: Alyson Publications, 1990)

Moby Dick, or, The Whale by Herman Melville, ed. by Tony Tanner (New
  York: Oxford University Press, 1988)

My Biggest O ed. by Jack Hart (Boston: Alyson Publications, 1993)

101 Uses for a Severed Penis by Dan Murphy (Burnaby: Serious, 1994)

Public Sex: The Culture of Radical Sexuality by Pat Califia (Pittsburgh: Cleis
  Press, 1994)

The Satanic Verses by Salman Rushdie (Dover: Consortium, 1992)

Sex by Madonna (New York: Time/Warner, 1992)

The Story of O by Pauline Reage (New York: Ballantine, 1990)

Urban Aboriginals: A Celebration of Leathersexuality by Geoff Mains (San
  Francisco: Gay Sunshine Press, 1991)

The Young in One Another's Arms by Jane Rule (Tallahassee: Naiad, 1984)

□

Bibliography

The following books and magazine/periodical articles were used for general research purposes.

"Anthropology Rediscovers Sexuality: A Theoretical Comment" by Carole S. Vance (*Social Science & Medicine,* Vol. 33, No. 8, 1991)

"Art and Soul" by Lorraine Johnson (*This Magazine,* Vol. 29, No. 2, August 1994)

"Avoiding Constitutional Depression: Bad Attitudes and the Fate of *Butler*" by Ann Scales (*Canadian Journal of Women and the Law,* Vol. 7, No. 2, 1994)

"The Battle Over Censorship" by Brian Bergman (*Maclean's,* October 24, 1994)

"Book Bind" by Robert Hough (*Globe and Mail,* February 12, 1994)

"Breaking the Ties That Bind" by Mark Leiren-Young (*Georgia Straight,* October 7–14, 1994)

"Business as Usual" by Nancy Pollak (*Ms.,* Vol. 5, No. 6, May/June 1995)

"Canada: Antipornography Breakthrough in the Law" by Michele Landsberg (*Ms.,* Vol. 2, No. 6, May/June 1992)

"Censorship and Receiving" by Lucinda Johnston (*Fuse,* May/June 1993)

"Cut That Out!" by Chris Bearchell (*This Magazine,* Vol. 26, No. 6, January/February 1993)

The Everyday World As Problematic: A Feminist Sociology by Dorothy E. Smith (Toronto: University of Toronto Press, 1987)

"Feminist Fashion or Morality in Drag? The Sexual Subtext of the *Butler Decision*" by Brenda Cossman; a paper prepared for the Entertainment, Media and Communications Law conference, Vancouver, B.C., 1994.

"Gay s/m in Pornography and Reality" by Alex van Naerssen et al. (*Journal of Homosexuality*, No. 13, 1987)

Girls Lean Back Everywhere: The Law of Obscenity and the Assault on Genius by Edward de Grazia (New York: Random House, 1993)

"A Guide to the Social Science Evidence on the Effects of Pornography; Part 2: Working Document" by Augustine Brannigan (Ottawa: Department of Justice, Research Section, 1990)

"Hard to Imagine: Gay Erotic Cinema in the Postwar Era" by Thomas Waugh (*CineAction*, Fall 1987)

A Hot-Eyed Moderate by Jane Rule (Toronto: Lester & Orpen Dennys, 1986)

The House That Jill Built by Becki Ross (Toronto: University of Toronto Press, 1995)

How Do I Look? Queer Film and Video ed. by Bad Object-Choices (Seattle: Bay Press, 1991)

"Keeping Pornography in Perspective" by Jonathan L. Freedman (*Contemporary Psychology*, No. 33, 1988)

"LEAF and Pornography: Litigating on Equality and Sexual Representations" by Karen Busby (*Canadian Review of the Law and Society*, Vol. 9, No. 1, Spring 1994)

"Little Sister's v. Big Brother" by Chris Dafoe (*Globe and Mail*, October 8, 1994)

"Little Sister's Wraps Up in Court" by Imtiaz Popat (*Angles*, December 1994).

Male Intergenerational Intimacy: Historical, Socio-Psychological and Legal Perspectives ed. by Theo Sandfort, Edward Brongersma and Alex van Naerssen (New York: Harrington Park Press, 1991)

"Men's Pornography: Gay vs. Straight" by Thomas Waugh (*Jump Cut*, No. 30, 1985)

"Must We Censor Pornography? Civil Liberties and Feminist Jurisprudence" by Thelma McCormack, in *Freedom of Expression and the Charter* ed. by David Schneiderman (Toronto: Thomson Professional Publishing, 1991)

My American History: Lesbian and Gay Life During the Reagan/Bush Years by Sarah Schulman (New York: Routledge, 1994)

My Times: Living with History 1947 to 1995 by Pierre Berton (New York: Doubleday, 1995)

"Negotiating Sex and Gender in the Attorney General's Commission on Pornography" by Carole S. Vance, in *Uncertain Terms: Negotiating Gender in American Culture* ed. by F. Ginsberg and A. Tsing (Boston: Beacon Press, 1990)

"Obscenity Chill: Artists in a Post-*Butler* Era" by Clare Barclay and Elaine Carol (*Fuse,* Winter 1992–93)

"A Personal View of the History of the Lesbian S/M Community and Movement in San Francisco" by Pat Califia, in *Coming to Power* ed. by SAMOIS (Boston: Alyson Press, 1987)

Pleasure and Danger: Exploring Female Sexuality ed. by Carole S. Vance (London: Harper Collins, 1992)

"The Pleasure of Looking: The Attorney General's Commission on Pornography vs. Visual Images" by Carole S. Vance, in *The Critical Image* ed. by C. Squires (Seattle: Bay Press, 1990)

"Porn Again" by Varda Burstyn (*Fuse,* Vol. 10, No. 6, Spring 1987)

"Regulating Queerness: A New Age of Light, Soap and Water" by Becki Ross; a lecture delivered in the President's Lecture Series on Lesbian and Gay Studies, University of British Columbia, Vancouver, B.C., October 7, 1993.

The Regulation of Desire: Sexuality in Canada by Gary Kinsman (Montréal: Black Rose Books, 1987)

"The Rhetoric of Degradation" by Christopher Eamon (*Fuse,* Winter 1992–93)

"Saving Canada from 'Betty Page' " by Lucinda Johnston (*Canadian Bookseller,* February 1993)

"Sex and the Law" by Paul Kaihla (*Maclean's,* October 24, 1994)

"Strange Customs" by Don Gillmor (*Saturday Night,* March 1993)

"Strictly Confidential" by David Demchuk (*What,* No. 27, September 1991)

"What Does the Criminal Code Mean by Artistic Merit?" [excerpts from Mr. Justice David McComb's ruling in the Eli Langer case] (*Globe and Mail,* April 24, 1995)

Women Against Censorship ed. by Varda Burstyn (Vancouver: Douglas & McIntyre, 1985)

"X-Rated" by Jeffrey Toobin (*New Yorker,* October 3, 1994)

JANINE FULLER is a bookseller and manager at Little Sister's in Vancouver, where she has lived since 1989. Originally from Toronto, Fuller has an eclectic history in the arts as a performer, actor and writer. Her performance piece "My Dinner with Charles" is published in the Women's Press anthology *Dykeversions*. She has played feature roles in several video dramas, including *Night Visions*, *Playing with Fire* and *Shirley to God*.

STUART BLACKLEY writes from Vancouver. He was an original member of the *Rites* editorial collective in Toronto, and has frequently written for the gay and lesbian press. His fiction, poetry and essays have appeared in journals in Canada and the U.S. Two of his recent plays, *The Fruit Machine* and *The Reverse Transcriptease* (co-authored by Kevin Gregg), were produced in Vancouver; the latter will be published in 1996 in the anthology *Plague of the Gorgeous, and Other Tales*. Stuart Blackley is currently working on a play about Oscar Wilde's tour of Canada, entitled *Happy Trials*.

NANCY POLLAK is a Vancouver editor and writer. She is a former editor of *Kinesis*, the feminist newsmagazine, and the author of *Critical Choices, Turbulent Times: A Community Workbook on Social Programs*.

□ THE LITTLE SISTER'S DEFENCE FUND □

Little Sister's legal challenge to Canada Customs is a long, expensive process that relies on the support of many different individuals and communities. Please consider making a donation to the Little Sister's Defence Fund:

Little Sister's Defence Fund
1221 Thurlow Street
Vancouver, British Columbia
Canada V6E 1X4

A portion of the royalties from this book are being donated to the fund.

PRESS GANG PUBLISHERS has been producing vital and provocative books since 1975.

A free catalogue is available from Press Gang Publishers, #101 - 225 E. 17th Avenue, Vancouver, B.C. V5V 1A6 Canada